BEYOND TERRITORY AND SCARCITY

EXPLORING CONFLICTS OVER
NATURAL RESOURCE MANAGEMENT

edited by

Quentin Gausset, Michael A. Whyte and Torben Birch-Thomsen

NORDISKA AFRIKAINSTITUTET 2005

Indexing terms

Resources management
Environmental degradation
Natural resources
Conflicts
Boundaries
Living conditions
Burkina Faso
Cameroon
Democratic Republic of
the Congo
Ghana
Lesotho
Niger
Nigeria
Senegal
Sudan

Cover photo: Andreas de Neergaard/SLUSE
Language checking: Robert Parkin
© the authors and Nordiska Afrikainstitutet, 2005
ISBN 91-7106-540-7
Printed in Sweden by Elanders Gotab, Stockholm 2005

Foreword

Neo-Malthusian theories have been extremely influential in inspiring interpretations of conflicts on natural resource management. Most environmental programmes in the South still limit themselves to those resources that are fixed within delimited territories. Management becomes a matter of sharing finite resources among an increasing number of people. However, recent research in anthropology and geography suggests that territory as a bounded unit defining scarcity plays a contingent role in environmental management. People and key resources flow across boundaries. Local actors do not just undergo environmental changes passively; they are active agents able to mobilize natural and political resources far from the sites of conflict or management. Scarcity is moreover a relative concept. The same territory, landscape or resource can be perceived very differently by different people, and what has been interpreted as conflict over scarce resources often appears to be conflict of perspectives, over the definition of resource, and over the resource management rules.

A group of researchers at the Institute of Anthropology and the Institute of Geography, University of Copenhagen, organised an international seminar in Copenhagen on the 7–9th of November 2002 in order to explore further issues related to conflicts over natural resources, and to strengthen existing experience and expertise within the field of natural resource management. National and international researchers were invited to present case studies of conflicts over natural resource management where social, cultural and political dimensions were given full weight, and social actors and their strategies were foregrounded. At the seminar 11 papers were presented and nine are published in this volume. The editors have added an introduction to the volume, which is indebted to three days of stimulating exchanges that took place during the seminar.

The seminar was directed towards further developing interdisciplinary approaches to the study and analysis of environmental degradation and conflicts over resources. This is a theme that is central for the Danish University Consortium on Environment and Development (DUCED) and, in particular, for its focal program on Sustainable Land Use and Natural Resource Management (SLUSE) in which both the organizing institutes participate. Funding for DUCED-SLUSE was from the Danish International Development Agency (Danida). Within the funding period (1998–2006) the DUCED-SLUSE universities (University of Copenhagen, the Royal Veterinary & Agricultural University and Roskilde University) have worked to strengthen educational and research capacity internally, as well as in collaboration with partner-country universities in Malaysia, Thailand, South Africa, Swaziland and Botswana.

The organizing of the seminar and publication of this volume was funded by the North–South Research Area of the University of Copenhagen, by the two organizing Institutes of Anthropology and Geography, and by the DUCED-SLUSE, all of whom I thank warmly for their support.

Torben Birch-Thomsen
Associate Professor, Institute of Geography and Coordinator of DUCED-SLUSE collaboration at University of Copenhagen

Table of Contents

Map of Case Studies

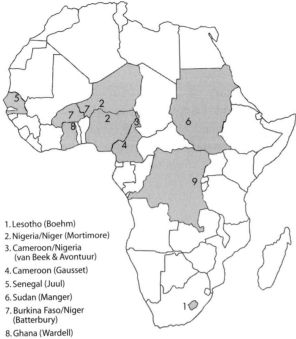

1. Lesotho (Boehm)
2. Nigeria/Niger (Mortimore)
3. Cameroon/Nigeria
   (van Beek & Avontuur)
4. Cameroon (Gausset)
5. Senegal (Juul)
6. Sudan (Manger)
7. Burkina Faso/Niger
   (Batterbury)
8. Ghana (Wardell)
9. The Democratic Republic of the Congo
   (Fairhead)

Introduction

Quentin Gausset and Michael A. Whyte

Sound and sustainable environmental management is one of the greatest challenges that humanity will face in this century. It is evident that some natural resources are currently being exploited beyond the rate at which they can be renewed, thus threatening the ability of future generations to live from these resources. We need to find new ways to exploit resources 'sustainably' so as not to undermine the chances of survival for future generations (WCED 1987). Although the specific phrasing of this idea can be discussed at length (Redclift and Woodgate 1997), few people would challenge the statement that unlimited population and consumption growth are impossible in a finite world (Gowdy 1998; Meadows et al. 1992, Trainer 1998). Beyond a certain threshold, more people must necessarily mean a reduction in resources per capita. Disagreement starts with the analysis of particular terms. Where is the threshold, what are the limits, and have we reached them yet? When is consumption too much? What levels are sustainable? What is the scale at which we should measure sustainability – local, regional, national, global? How should limits to population or consumption be distributed in the world? Are conflicts over natural resources symptomatic of their scarcity?

These questions reflect real issues in an Africa that is characterised by social, historical and geographic diversity, as well as by real dilemmas for policy and planning at different levels. The answers will themselves always be partial, contingent and context-dependent, part of a continuing process of discovery and collaboration. It is therefore important to avoid seeing Africa as 'the symbol of worldwide demographic, environmental, and societal stress' (Kaplan 1994: 46) and reducing the cause of African social, economic and political problems to a presumed scarcity of resources.

This well-known framework for discussing future policy, which focuses on the scarcity of resources, springs from the Malthusian idea that, all things being equal, population increase must outpace available resources, leading to 'misery and vice'. In this framework, future security relies on limiting population growth. A second and equally well-known framework, often called neo-Malthusian, focuses more specifically on the environmental consequences of population growth. Here the imbalance between population and resources is believed to lead to environmental degradation, which in its turn, reinforces the imbalance in a downward spiral.

These two positions predict – indeed, guarantee – outcomes for which no politician would like to be held responsible: social misery and the increasing degradation of the environment. Malthus was, of course, not only the founder of academic demography but also an active political voice in the policy discourses of his time. His ideas have inspired policy-making by politicians and bureaucrats alike for two centuries, and they have also been extremely influential in the green movement and the mass media, as well as, most certainly, among the general population. The strength of the Malthusian and neo-Malthusian approaches has been their capacity to reduce complex problems to very simple equations. But this has also been their weakness.

Our goal in this volume is not to reject Malthusian and neo-Malthusian insights entirely. Population growth *does* have an impact at many levels, from the strategies of actors to the social, cultural and environmental consequences of those strategies. It is important to understand the consequences of growth, and setting territorial limits is one useful way to identify and model these consequences. But it is only *one* way. All the essays presented in this volume seek to move 'beyond territory and scarcity' in order to emphasise the social, cultural and political construction of the territories through which competition occurs and livelihoods operate. This perspective allows us to introduce new actors and requires that we follow action through new spatial and historical scales. This collection of essays seeks to make room for greater complexity and to enrich both our theoretical understanding and our capacity to develop appropriate policies.

Territory and Scarcity

The Malthusian Approach

Malthus is the founding father of demography and also the 'dismal philosopher' whose ideas about the role of social policy in relation to poverty have enflamed some and inspired others for over two hundred years. Malthus's approach is to look at territory and scarcity as the limit for population growth. As population is assumed to grow at rates which outstrip any growth of resources, the scarcity that results must inevitably be disastrous for the many, causing famines, misery and wars, and leading to population decline. At its most elemental, the Malthusian argument can be depicted as a series of curves that are continually limited by an overall value representing the growth of productive resources (Figure 1). In stepwise fashion local populations increase 'geometrically', only to be checked by the constraints provided by the lineal growth of production. In policy terms, it may be possible to introduce the preventive checks of restraint (and contraception), but ultimately this is a system based on scarcity.

Figure 1. The Malthusian saw-tooth pattern of population growth and decline over time, around a carrying capacity defined by increasing productivity (straight line)

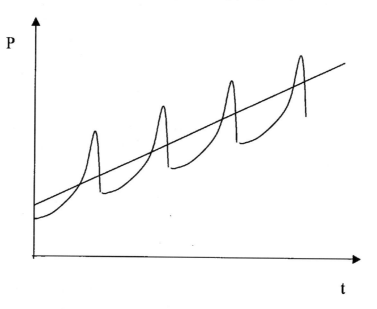

This is an argument which is essentially individualizing. The sum of private decisions to procreate leads to collective tragedy. The private exercise of restraint in order to live within one's means is the key to controlling population and thus to placing a greater share of wealth in the hands of the poor. Policy is directed towards ensuring that the cost-benefit calculations which individuals must make reflect the full cost of profligacy. Liberalism and market mechanisms, when unchecked by sentiment, lead individuals to frame the costs calculations which, in the end, are both moral and expedient. Writing of 'Mr Pitt's Poor Bill' (an eighteenth-century attempt at welfare legislation), Malthus notes that the proposed law has the defect of 'tending to increase population without increasing the means for its support…'.

> Were I to propose a palliative…it should be…the total abolition of all parish laws. This would at any rate give liberty and freedom of action to the peasantry of England. […] They would then be able to settle without interruption, wherever there was a prospect of a greater plenty of work and a higher price for labour (Malthus 1970 [1798]: 101).

The argument is also essentially territorial. The poor may indeed be encouraged to be mobile, but only within a system of bounded units. The units may change from the parish to counties, regions and nations, but the dynamics of scarcity demand borders. Without the limit of territoriality, the policy impact of 'liberty and freedom of action' would soon destabilize a society based on a system of private property (Malthus 1970 [1830]: 245).

Finally, Malthus's argument, and indeed that of his followers, is essentially a moral one. For him, it is the 'lower classes' which suffer most, though they bring about their own suffering. His famous positive checks, misery and vice, are brought about by feckless and irresponsible behaviour by the poor, resulting in situations of absolute want, when mortality increases drastically and differentially (Malthus 1970 [1798]: 102–3). As the positive checks work like the invisible hand of the market, Malthus advocates a policy of laissez-faire, although it is also hoped that this may lead to the development of moral restraint and preventive checks on the birth rate: celibacy and, today at any rate, contraception. Moral education, combined with a system which rewards restraint and punishes profligacy, is in the end the only truly charitable social policy. Basically, the poor and unfortunate are victims of their own moral failings.

The Neo-Malthusian Approach

Where Malthus's focus is on the consequences of reproduction outstripping production for *people*, neo-Malthusians look most intensively at the consequences of the same factors with respect to the *environment*, and only indirectly at the consequences for people. In a situation of scarcity created by an imbalance between people and resources, the people are seen as over-exploiting the resources in an unsustainable way. This leads to a degradation of the resource base (soil degradation, fishing beyond the natural rate of reproduction, etc.), which leads to greater scarcity, greater over-exploitation and greater degradation (Brown and Kane 1995; Brown et al. 1998; Meadows et al. 1992; WCED 1987). Over time, population will tend to fall because the environment which sustains production is increasingly degraded through the actions of the population itself (Figure 2). In stepwise fashion again, localized populations increase 'geometrically', only to be checked by the constraints provided by the level of production. However, while Malthus was optimistic in that he believed that production (and population) would continue to increase, many neo-Malthusian are deeply pessimistic, predicting that resources (and population) *must* decline. In policy terms, it may be possible to introduce the preventive checks of good husbandry and better technology, but ultimately this is a system grounded in the fragility of the resource base itself. The concept of environment is basic here, as is the idea of an ecology into which human activities are placed.

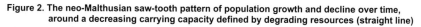

Figure 2. The neo-Malthusian saw-tooth pattern of population growth and decline over time, around a decreasing carrying capacity defined by degrading resources (straight line)

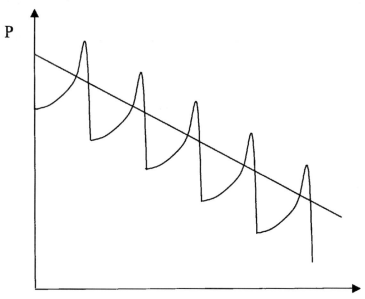

As with Malthus, the neo-Malthusian approach focuses on the collective outcome deriving from choices made by individuals. It is in trying to maximize their own private benefit that actors are led to overexploit resources. When the resources are communally owned, the mechanism is believed to be even more pronounced. Whenever a person cannot be excluded from the benefits that others provide, each individual is supposed to be motivated not to contribute to the joint effort, but to free-ride on the efforts of others (Hardin 1968; Ostrom 1990). As with Malthus, the collective outcome of individual action shapes the system.

The neo-Malthusian approach is also resolutely territorial, even more so than the Malthusian perspective, because of its particular focus on a situated ecology or environment. Scarcity is defined within tightly drawn borders. Even the migration of 'environmental refugees' is not seen as a solution to the imbalance of the population; on the contrary, it is a mechanism which makes the problem worse by spreading the over-exploitation and degradation of resources elsewhere, through spill-over and snowball effects (Jacobson 1988).

While Malthus saw nature as a threat (or limit) to culture, the neo-Malthusians reverse the relationship and see culture as a threat to nature (and therefore, indirectly, as a threat to itself). The environment needs to be protected from reckless human exploitation. Many neo-Malthusians adopt an ecocentric perspective, or even at times a Gaea-centric perspective, concerned with human 'stewardship' of the earth. Some promote an 'eco-doomster' scenario: unless we radically change our selfish way of life and capitalist approach to natural resource management, we are on the path to chaos, disasters, and possibly the collapse of civilization (Dobkowski and Walliman 1998; Lewis 1998; Meadows et al. 1992;

Rimmerman 1998; Roth 1998). According to this scenario, conflict (along with famines or migration) is no longer a simple matter of negative feedback, returning the population to a state of equilibrium. Instead it is seen as a permanent and inevitable consequence of environmental scarcity and degradation (Homer-Dixon 1994; 1998; 1999; Kaplan 1994). It becomes a matter of deviation amplification, something which makes things worse, instead of 'solving' problems.

Although it is also an individualistic model, the neo-Malthusian approach at times nourishes a suspicion of the market, which becomes part of the problem rather than part of the solution. People are seen as 'cheating' the market mechanisms and the 'positive checks' defined by Malthus by over-exploiting the resource base, instead of letting it strike back and re-establish a balance. In doing so, they are threatening the livelihood of future generations. Since the outcome of individual behaviour is collective and has global implications (on a much larger scale than for Malthus), solutions too must be collective and global. The state must intervene, or the collective resources must be privatized, in order to ensure that its 'stewards' act in a responsible manner. As in Malthusian models, there is no need to conceptualize society, even though bounded units (political or 'natural') are necessary, indeed basic.

This conventional neo-Malthusian perspective has become a 'received wisdom' (Leach and Mearns 1996; see also below), but it remains extremely influential in international development agencies (IFAD 1994: 10; World Bank 1996: 22–5, see Woodhouse et al. 2000: 12).

The Boserupian Elaboration

The work of Esther Boserup in the 1960's marked a critical elaboration of the Malthusian position. Her general argument (1965) is well-known: although population growth leads to pressure on resources, this pressure may in its turn lead to innovation, in particular agricultural intensification. Intensification allows more labour to be invested in production, though generally with diminishing efficiency. The Malthusian dilemma of population increasing faster than resources is 'solved' by arguing that a concentration of rising population leads to an intensification of production and thus to survival for greater numbers of people within a limited territory. Production no longer represents a limit, population growth no longer a 'bomb'. But there is a cost: labour productivity declines, and people must work longer hours. More recently other researchers have developed Boserup's insights, if not her theoretical position by demonstrating that more people does not necessarily mean more environmental degradation, but may on the contrary lead to more and better forests or to soil conservation (Tiffen et al. 1994; Fairhead and Leach 1996a, 1996b, 1998; Leach and Mearns 1996; Mortimore and Tiffen 1995).

Robert Netting (1993) represents another elaboration of the idea of intensification. Inspired both by Chayanov's peasant mode of production and by detailed empirical studies of peasant society around the world, Netting builds on this approach in his focus on the creative autonomy of peasant agriculture. He stresses the knowledge and skills which smallholders employ in their increasingly intensive systems of production. One key to understanding such systems is to recognize their flexibility: they balance subsistence production and cash sales, and they also have the capacity to withdraw from the market, as well as the 'discipline' to avoid becoming tied to market production at the expense of subsistence. Smallholder systems emphasize individual agency, but it is an agency which accepts the constraining context of family reproduction (see Chayanov 1986 [1925]) and which has a positive collective outcome.

While (neo)-Malthusian approaches only see 'dismal' consequences in scarcity, Boserup and Netting examine population growth and intensification as an opportunity. Scarcity may have positive consequences by triggering higher productivity and environmental conservation in a sustainable manner. The Boserup/Netting approach remains, however, essentially territorial. Scarcity and constraints within a defined territory are explicit conditions of existence. Territory and scarcity remain central to all causal explanation, and models remain grounded in the restricted dynamic of the territory–population growth equation. Yet, because they focus on production, Boserup and Netting provide an opening to events and relationships beyond the limits of the particular territory.

Beyond Territory and Scarcity

Policy-making relies heavily on theories which are reductionist and oversimplifying, this being nowhere more true than in the field of resource management. A Malthusian approach reduces all resource management to population control. The neo-Malthusian alternative succeeds in avoiding some of the reductionism of the Malthusian perspective by focusing on ecological equilibrium and its relationship with population growth. However, this approach in fact merely replaces one reductionism by another, only slightly less narrow one. While population growth is no longer regarded as the key causal factor, the framework of analysis remains the relationship between population and consumption on the one hand, and production and territory on the other. Both approaches conceptualize people as a threat to other people and to nature, and advocate curbing individual greed through either impersonal market mechanisms or state interventionism. Both reduce the huge complexity of human livelihood strategies to sheer egoism. Both reduce complex cultural, social, historical and political aspects of environmental management to a question of numbers (of people, resources, carrying capacity), and to a dichotomy between nature and culture. Malthusian and neo-Malthusian approaches therefore mislead policy-makers in over-simplifying problems and alternatives.

The Boserupian approach is less reductionist. Boserup and Netting do recognize local creativity and flexibility; Netting in particular has provided many persuasive studies of the complexity of local resource management. There is a clear movement away from dismal philosophy towards a better balance between natural and cultural determinism, a more optimistic view of human nature and more flexible policies. However, there remains a certain Malthusian inheritance in the tendency to reduce natural resource management to a question of what happens within a bounded territory. The analytical focus on constraint and scarcity may at times make it difficult to see smallholders in larger contexts, as agents in their own right and not simply as carriers of indigenous knowledge. While concentrating on local creativity, researchers may overlook those forms of creativity and experimentation which take them outside the territorial framework to which peasants have been assigned.

There is a need to examine causes of intensification or conflict other than scarcity and at consequences of scarcity which lead neither to intensification nor to conflict. When and where, for example, are scarcity and conflict and intensification causally connected, and when and where are they not (Stone 2001: 168)? But above all, we need to look beyond territory and scarcity in order to free ourselves of the perspective into which previous approaches have been locked and to broaden our understanding of natural resource management.

In this collection, we critically address four general issues which are part of our Malthusian inheritance: we explore alternatives to the strong natural determinism which reduces natural resource management to questions of territory and scarcity; we present material and methodologies which allow us to discover something more than 'rational choice' in the agency of individuals and to explore the different contexts in which social and cultural values intervene; we examine the ways in which different conceptions of territory are relevant for the ways in which people manage, or attempt to manage, natural resources; and finally, all authors seek to place their studies within the developing discussion of policy and politics in natural resource management.

We shall address these issues from the perspectives of anthropology, geography and development studies. The studies themselves are all drawn from sub-Saharan Africa, some reporting on recently completed field studies, while others draw and reflect on many years of regional experience. Although all the chapters address natural resource management critically, they do so from a range of positions or points of view. The most localized level is the single-community study. Christian Boehm studies the environmental strategies developed by retrenched miners in Lesotho. Michael Mortimore discusses the development and adaptation of farmers' strategies in Kano and Maridi (Nigeria and Niger). Boehm and Mortimer focus on conflicts and patterns of management that are inscribed within local communities, although also clearly articulated with the changing impact of state policy, and even, in Lesotho, issues of world trade.

The next three papers make the jump from intra- to intercommunity resource management and the ways in which interethnic conflicts are projected on to territories, political structures and systems of production. Walter van Beek and Sonja Avontuur analyse how farming strategies in the Kapsiki (Cameroon) have evolved over time and examine the impact on them of inter-ethnic warfare and colonial peace. Quentin Gausset analyses agro-pastoral conflicts between nomadic Fulbe and settled autochthonous groups in Amadawa (Cameroon). Kristine Juul focuses on the strategies developed by various groups of pastoralists to cope with droughts in Senegal and analyses the conflicts that have arisen both among these different groups and with first-comer groups. These authors all draw attention to the scope for individual agency within a social, cultural and historical matrix which shapes action, aspirations and conflicts.

Finally, four authors have chosen to focus on issues that emphasize the asymmetric interactions between communities and entities such as states, international organizations/NGOs or other global actors. Leif Manger deconstructs the New Institutional Economics with a case study from the Sudan, which shows how state land reforms have continued to create problems in practice. Simon Batterbury analyses donor assistance as a resource which is part of the environment that determines management strategies, and examines how two communities from Burkina Faso and Niger have opportunistically responded to the development or withdrawal of foreign aid. D. Andrew Wardell studies the history of forest policy in Ghana and Burkina Faso, and the different aspects, both natural and socio-political, which have influenced them. Finally, James Fairhead analyses the responsibility of Belgian colonization and the current investments of multinational corporations for having created and maintained violent structures of exploitation of both people and natural resources in the eastern Congo.

Natural Determinism, Cultural Relativism

Environmental management is, of course, all about dealing with the interface between complex physical or natural systems and social systems. However, one of the qualities that policy-makers appreciate about the (neo-)Malthusian model (population growth within a bounded territory creating scarcity) is that it allows them to define environmental management in physical or natural terms. This tends to favour management solutions which are both technical and context-free, as well as to downplay the social and political context in which problems are inscribed (Bryant and Bailey 1997: 28; Peluso and Watts 2001: 14) and which creates local resistance to them (Hoben 1996).

The lure of a technical solution to environmental problems can be compelling, not least if 'the environment' is seen as a set of natural 'facts' that can be independently determined. The biological concept of climax vegetation may imply that any deviation from this ideal state is a sign of degradation, a condition requiring action to bring the system back into equilibrium – a classic neo-Malthusian approach. Recently, in discussions of the topic of 'range ecology,' research has suggested that a disequilibrium model, depending closely, for example, on irregular rain patterns, is often more appropriate than a climax progression. The lesson is that great caution must be exercised by policy-makers in initiating any actions to restore an 'equilibrium' or to re-establish 'natural' climax vegetation (Behnke et al. 1993; Beinart 1996; Scoones 1994; 1996). The point, of course, is that 'nature' is not always what we believe it to be. The African landscape has a history that has been shaped by long-lasting interactions with the people who have lived in it (Beinart and McGregor 2003, Cline-Cole 1996; Fairhead and Leach 1996a, 1996b; Hirsch 1995; Kreike 2003, Leach and Mearns 1996; Neumann 1998).

Nonetheless environmental resources are contextually limited and do constitute constraints that influence environmental exploitation. In the present volume, for example, D. Andrew Wardell shows the significance of onchocercosis for the depopulation of large areas close to the river Volta. The demarcation of forest reserves in the region, contrary to widespread opinion, has not led to population displacement. It is only with the eradication of flies and the recent demographic pressure that these areas have become interesting again and the object of environmental conflicts. Walter van Beek, Sonja Avontuur and Michael Mortimore identify resource management issues in Cameroon and Nigeria/Niger, which demand a knowledge of natural as well as social and cultural contexts. These authors develop an intermediate position that rejects both an oversimplified natural determinism and the parallel pitfall of one-sided cultural determinism. The point, of course, is that the physical environment does constrain land use, and some conflicts do appear to have some foundation in the consequences of such constraints. But such natural conditions do not by themselves explain all aspects of conflicts or management.

The concept of scarcity is a case in point. Scarcity can be absolute (without a minimum of food and water, one dies), but the term also describes a perceived condition, often the consequence of social or political machinations (Smith, R.W. 1998: 201–3). Scarcity is, of course, a constraint in all policy discussion, but as a real-life problem for people in Africa, it is more than an analytical implication: it is also central to peoples' agency, as expressed (for example) in personal biographies: 'When I was young we had tea with milk before school; today there is no milk for village children', 'When the war was here, there was nothing to eat and people died; today we are a bit all right'. These scarcities are, of course, real and material, but they are socially and culturally constructed out of experience and hope, experience-rich and relative, formulated in categories that are meaningful culturally and in terms of action. In this volume, Walter van Beek, Sonja Avontuur and Quentin Gausset argue that in northern Cameroon, scarcity is embedded in a social, political and historical context. The definition of the territory depends closely on perceived opportunities, which are dependent in their turn not only on physical constraints, but also on the existence of war or peace, on the power relationship between different stakeholders (neighbouring ethnic groups, gender), and on the existing technology available. The perception of scarcity depends not just on the density of population and availability of resources, but also on the livelihood strategies that have been developed and on those things that are maximised (quality, quantity, time, labour, security, etc.). On the basis of case studies from Nigeria and Niger, Michael Mortimore argues that scarcity is defined not so much by the limits inherent in supposedly scarce resources, but rather by the limits set by livelihoods which are cannot be adapted to satisfy new needs. In this perspective, the definition of scarcity depends more on society, economic structures and cultural understanding than on natural limits. More generally, D. Andrew Wardell argues that the perception of scarcity and the solutions designed to address it are strongly influenced by the state and by western scientists and are hotly contested locally. Scientific forestry in Ghana is a good example of a programme which makes use of neo-Malthusian management strategies and discourses, with natural systems becoming scarcer and having to be protected from the inroads of cultural practice, population growth and economic necessity. This chapter shows, however, that forest conservation owes more to political and global economic processes (and to epidemics such as onchocercosis) than to the threat that people are believed to represent to forests.

Agency and Social Resilience

One of the important contributions of Malthusian and neo-Malthusian models is that they make individual agency central, although the agency itself is often postulated rather than observed. The range of 'choices' facing individual actors can be derived from an analysis of environmental conditions and consequences rather than from grounded studies of individual strategies. Actors' actions are thus often reduced to mere reactions to environmental constraints. Management consists in introducing a 'better' (more direct) appreciation of the costs which decisions entail. In the social sciences, the actor-agency approach has developed into a mature set of concepts and theories reflecting and exploring the complexity of social behaviour. In Malthus-inspired environmental policy discourses, complexity is generally reduced significantly in the hope of achieving a clarity that will ease decision-making. The result can be reductionist; real agents acting from social positions in broader cultural contexts become postulated individuals – economic men and women. In the course of the exercise, much valuable data on actual behaviour, strategies and motives is lost. A classic case in point here is the debate over the tragedy of the commons. Far from being open access systems where individuals can 'free-ride' on the efforts of others, many common property regimes (CPR) are based on complex rules and degrees of access to the property or resource held in common (Berkes and Farvar 1989; Cousins 2000; Feeny et al. 1990; Leach and Mearns 1996; Little and Brokensha 1987; McCabe 1990; Swift 1996; Gausset, Juul and Manger, this volume). Only by ignoring specific, grounded complexity and the social embeddedness of individuals is it possible to argue that tragedy is inevitable. Replacing a CPR system that works well and secures a relatively equitable redistribution of resources by a private system that excludes potential users, thus exacerbating social tensions and inequities, can do more harm than good.

In the present volume, Leif Manger criticizes the use of game theory (another body of work which rests on decontextualised and constructed actors) to explain social action. Drawing on ethnographic and political data from the Sudan, he argues that an empirical complexity cannot be reduced to the strategies of atomized and homogenous social actors. The rules of the game are never fully independent of explicit human manipulation, sanctions are not the same for all actors, and the different strategies that real actors employ are rooted in a complex social and historical context. Along the same lines, Kristine Juul describes the interplay between the different logics of common property and of the privatisation of resources among pastoralists of the Ferlo. She shows that herders, who are usually fierce defenders of common grazing rights, tend to accept user restrictions where their own wells are concerned. One individual can play by different rules according to the context, and the result is a somewhat unstable institutional equilibrium, which can itself change and evolve according to changing circumstances. There is scope here for a form of environmental management that can engage Ferlo herders in their different social contexts.

Several authors in this volume emphasize the crucial importance of the social capacity to respond to, adapt to and recover from shocks, be they demographic, political, economic or due to natural hazards. Kristine Juul argues that climatic shocks (in this case, droughts), far from always being detrimental to pastoralists' survival and forcing them to over-exploit their resources in a downward spiral, can also trigger important social changes, including a redefinition of the norms and rules pertaining to the management of resources. Michael Mortimore discusses how farmers in Nigeria and Niger have coped with declining rainfall and population growth, as well as how knowledge, flexibility, adaptability and values have been instrumental in maintaining or increasing per capita output of cereals at levels above nutritional requirements. Simon Batterbury analyses how local communities are reacting to the sudden withdrawal of donor support for environmental conservation. Christian Boehm shows how Sotho rural society has had to adapt to the huge change brought about by a mine closure in South Africa and how this has impacted on land use in Lesotho. In all these cases, crises, whether caused by demographic, climatic or political-economic shocks, have triggered social, technological and strategic innovations, which have produced astonishing examples of social change and resilience. This shows that vulnerability is not necessarily an obstacle to adaptability – on the contrary, it can trigger it. It also shows that policy-makers should allow for flexibility in recovering from shocks, and facilitate (or at least refrain from preventing) the strategies and creative solutions that are developed to cope with them.

Regional Linkages and Scales

Territory is an essential component of policy analysis, and indeed of governance. But it too is socially and culturally constructed, a point which is central to most contributions to this volume. The authors draw on fieldwork-based, grounded research to explore multiple, at times overlapping 'territories' and to problematize Malthusian and neo-Malthusian assumptions about the causal role of any particular 'ground'. As anthropologists and geographers, they come from disciplines where 'territory' has long been an organizing framework for enquiry and explanation. In recent years, the two fields have begun to look more critically at the general issue of space, thus appreciating and investigating the importance of crossing boundaries, real and conceptual (Appadurai 1997; Gupta and Ferguson 1997; Reenberg 2001). The territory becomes a series of spaces in and between which goods and people and ideas move. These kinds of territory can be extensive, and as in diaspora studies, the relevant space may be discontinuous. Territory is still bounded, but there is not necessarily a border or customs post. We now also recognize that much that is of interest to us does not pass through customs posts or the crossing points established by formal studies of farming systems, communities or regions. Our aim in this volume, both empirically and conceptually, is to test the conceptual as well as the physical and political boundaries with which we have been working.

Any sound policy on natural resource management needs to go beyond looking narrowly at bounded territories in order to analyze the complex interlinkages that exist at higher geographical levels. Almost all the chapters in this volume demonstrate that regional migrations are an integral part of local livelihood strategies. Several articles also show that local systems of natural resource management would be meaningless without understanding the regional or global contexts in which they are inscribed. Simon Batterbury focuses on the impact that foreign donors' money, or its withdrawal, has on local environmental management in Niger and Burkina Faso. Christian Boehm analyses how the changes in apartheid policy and in global mineral prices have influenced migratory patterns, as well as demonstrating the impact that this is having on local field management in Lesotho. Leif Manger shows how failed land reform, corruption and the privatisation of common resources for large-scale agricultural schemes in Sudan have had dramatic impacts on local ways of accessing and managing resources. James Fairhead argues that the global interest in strategic resources in eastern Congo is one of the main causes of the maintenance of exploitative patterns dating back to pre-colonial and colonial times, as well as of the continuation of conflicts marked by extreme violence. All these chapters show that the narrow focus of the (neo)-Malthusian model on population and production within a localized territory neglects important regional and global linkages, in which the state plays a crucial role.

Conflict and Political Ecology

Conflicts over natural resource management can often not be explained by scarcity or population growth (Hussein 1998; Wenche and Ellingsen 1998). Of course, conflicts may arise over resources, and of course increasing scarcity may make conflicts more serious. But saying that conflicts are directly caused by a scarcity of resources is an assumption that is poorly documented, and even contradicted by the evidence. Even Homer-Dixon (1999), in arguing for the existence of a causal relationship between scarcity and conflict, recognises the importance of political aspects in shaping both. The relationship between scarcity and conflict is often postulated rather than demonstrated (Hartmann 2001; Peluso and Watts 2001: 20–2). At this level of abstraction, the opposite could just as easily be postulated: scarcity may reduce conflicts by producing greater levels of solidarity, sacrifice and collaboration, as people realise the value of individual self-restraint for the collective good, a well known response to scarcities created by national war efforts, for example.

A narrow (neo-)Malthusian perspective misleads policy-makers into perceiving conflicts over natural resources as the result of population pressure, territorial limitations and environmental degradation. It may, of course, be convenient for policy-makers to turn a blind-eye to the political, historical and social causes of conflicts and to assign blame to nature or to the victims themselves. However, this is no substitute for the in-depth understanding required to prevent or solve conflicts. Obviously, conflicts do have something to do with the environment. But rather than being always caused by scarcity, conflicts often arise over the control, management and distribution of resources (Peluso and Watts 2001). As such, environmental conflicts are also political and social, and should be understood by using a political ecological approach (Bryant and Bailey 1997; Forsyth 2002).

An increasing number of studies argue that it is 'political scarcity' (the deprivation of the resources of one group by another) rather than 'natural scarcity' (created by an unbalance between population and territory) which leads to conflicts over natural resource management. Resource deprivation of one group for the benefit of another creates frustration and resentment that can lead to violent conflict (Bobrow-Strain 2001; Cobb 1998; Moralles 1998; Peluso and Watts 2001; Smith, R.W. 1998). Even in Rwanda, the most densely populated country in Africa, scarcity is arguably not the result of insuperable environmental barriers, but of a policy that restricted agricultural production and oriented it towards export products rather than staples (Smith, D.N. 1998: 241). Although conflicts might be framed in terms of access to natural resources, and be made more acute by environmental degradation, we should not forget that their cause is often socio-political. Provisions that prevent people from accessing a resource might appear at first sight to be a matter of environmental exclusion, but it is first and foremost a political exclusion of the powerless by those holding power. Even nation states play a dangerous game when they deprive local users of their means to control resources and create insecurity by deregulating markets and systems of tenure and management (Borrow-Strain 2001; Neumann 2001; Peluso and Harwell 2001; Sundar 2001). In the words of Smith: 'Power sharing, protection of basic rights, and equality of treatment could go a long way in overcoming the difficulties otherwise exacerbated by deteriorating resources and expansion of population' (Smith, R.W. 1998: 203). We do not need to study exotic societies to understand that conflicts over natural resources are political in nature. Conflicts within developed societies, including the scientific community, between the ecocentric and anthropocentric approaches to natural resource management provide ample examples that these are not conflicts about nature, but about how nature is defined and by whom, and about who has the right to manage it (Boal 2001; Einarsson 1993; McCarthy 2001).

The fact that conflicts over natural resource management might owe little to scarcity is nowhere more obvious than in situations of relative abundance, where it is precisely the availability of valuable resources that fuels the conflict (Fairhead 2001; Richards 2001; Watts 2001). In this volume, for example, James Fairhead argues that the wealth of mineral resources found in the Kivu is one of the main forces driving a war that has claimed more than a million victims in the past decade. Quentin Gausset argues that the past and present abundance of resources in Adamawa has never prevented the existence of agro-pastoral conflicts, just as it has never prevented tenure conflict among agriculturalists or among pastoralists. Christian Boehm analyses how food shortages and high unemployment in rural Lesotho coexist with a high rate of fields being left uncultivated.

Almost all the contributions to this volume demonstrate that the exploitation of resources is the result of complex political strategies that are played out and contested at different levels. Kristine Juul describes the political strategies developed by first-comer and latecomer herders of the Ferlo (Senegal) in trying to secure themselves the best access to resources. She analyses how formal rules are bent from within and pushed to their limits in order to accommodate new situations, and how this leads to the slow adaptation of new rules. Quentin Gausset, Walter van Beek and Sonja Avontuur describe the political nature of agro-pastoral conflicts in northern Cameroon, which cannot be understood without reference to the historical and political context of the region (Fulbe conquest of the empire of Sokoto, local resistance, the slave trade, etc.). African states, far from being neutral actors always dampening down environmental conflicts, often appear to have vested interests of their own and to be playing a crucial role in creating or worsening these conflicts. In the Sudan, the abolition of native administration and tribal homelands, coupled with the privatisation of large tracks of land, which has mainly benefited well-connected individuals in a context of widespread corruption, has made it difficult to maintain former land-use arrangements. This situation has led to a few people becoming rich but to most people (especially poor herders) becoming worse off and being forced to work as labourers for the rich. The agendas of the state or of the international community seldom reflect local practices and strategies. As D. Andrew Wardell shows for forest conservation in Ghana, studying state environmental policies in their historical context reveals their highly political nature, as well as the political and cultural biases of the supposedly 'objective' western scientists. James Fairhead demonstrates how, for decades, the global need for strategic resources has choked all hopes of democracy, equity and independence in eastern Congo. Along the same lines, Christian Boehm analyses the wide-ranging social and environmental consequences of mineral world prices and the closure of mines in South Africa. Even the best intentions of donor support can be instrumental in disturbing existing local power balances, as Simon Batterbury shows in Niger and Burkina Faso. In all these cases, politics is at the core of environmental management. Either political decisions are the cause of environmental conflicts, or else a closer analysis of conflicts about resources reveals that they are political or social in nature.

Conclusion: Science, Policy and the Environment

Studies of African environments are seldom neutral. Beinart and McGregor have drawn our attention to the considerable historical lineage of environmental research for policy purposes. They note that generations of scientific argument are not simply about nature; researchers are also making 'implicit and explicit claims about who best understands African environments, and who should have the right to control them. [...] Such arguments have become centrally important as bases for intervention, conservation and regulation' (Beinart and McGregor 2003: 2).

The chapters in this volume stress the need to go beyond territory and scarcity in analysing environmental problems and designing solutions for them. Our message to planners and policy-makers is not just to beware models based on Malthusian equilibria between resources and population. Policy-makers must also recognize that they must give more weight to the social construction of the environment and its management, to the collective and cultural aspects of agency. They must frame environmental management on regional scales, and to understand rural-urban and regional networks as an integral part of local livelihoods. Finally, policy-makers must also reassert the importance of politics and conflict management: they can no longer give up and give away their political responsibility to scientific specialists who are unaccountable to the local people who will bear the cost of environmental management. Policy-making must seek to avoid reductionist models even when such models appear convenient, allowing them to make easy predictions, define simple problems and devise 'straightforward' solutions. We stress, and demonstrate here, the need to understand the complexity of a case before addressing it. Environmental management, today more than ever before, must take more completely into account the complexity of local histories and of cultural, political and socio-economic contexts.

Acknowledgements

The chapters published in this volume were presented at a seminar organised jointly by the Institute of Anthropology and the Institute of Geography at the University of Copenhagen, on 9–11 November 2002. The seminar was funded by the North–South Research Program of the University of Copenhagen, by the Danish University Consortium on Land Use and Natural Resource Management (SLUSE, funded by DANIDA), and by the two organising institutes, whom we would like to thank warmly for their support.

Bibliography

Appadurai, A. 1997. *Modernity at Large: Cultural Dimensions of Globalization.* Delhi: Oxford University Press.

Behnke, R. et al. 1993. *Range Ecology at Disequilibrium.* London: ODI.

Beinart, W. 1996. "Soil Erosion, Animals and Pasture over the Longer Term: Environmental Destruction in Southern Africa" in M. Leach and R. Mearns (eds) 1996, pp. 54–72.

Beinart, W. and J. McGregor. 2003. "Introduction" in W. Beinart and J. McGregor (eds), *Social History and African Environments*, pp. 27–42. Oxford: James Currey.

Berkes, F. and M.T. Farvar. 1989. "Introduction and Overview" in Berkes, F. (ed.), *Common Property Resources: Ecology and Community-based Sustainable Development*, pp. 1–17. London: Belhaven Press.

Boal, I.A. 2001. "Damaging Crops: Sabotage, Social Memory, and the New Genetic Enclosures" in Peluso N.L. and M. Watts (eds) 2001. *Violent Environments*, pp. 146–54. Ithaca: Cornell University Press.

Bobrow-Strain, A. 2001. Between a Ranch and a Hard Place: Violence, Scarcity, and Meaning in Chiapas, Mexico. In N.L. Peluso and M. Watts (eds) 2001, pp. 155–85.

Boserup, E. 1965. *The Conditions of Agricultural Growth: The Economics of Agrarian Change under Population Pressure.* London: Allen and Unwin.

Brown, L.R., Gardner, G., and Halweil, B. 1998. *Beyond Malthus: Sixteen Dimensions of the Population Problem.* Worldwatch Paper, 143. Washington, DC: Worldwatch Institute.

Brown, L.R. and Kane, H. 1995. *Full House: Reassessing the Earth's Population Carrying Capacity.* London: Earthscan Publications.

Bryant, R. and Bailey, S. 1997. *Third World Political Ecology.* London: Routledge.

Chayanov, A.V. 1986. *The Theory of Peasant Economy.* Manchester: Manchester University Press.

Cline-Cole, R. 1996. "Dryland Forestry: Manufacturing Forests and Farming Trees in Nigeria" in M. Leach and R. Mearns (eds) 1996, pp. 123–39.

Cobb, J.B. 1998. "The Threat to the Underclass" in M.N. Dobkowski and I. Walliman (eds) 1998, pp. 25–42.

Cousins, B. 2000. "Tenure and Common Property Resources in Africa" in Toulmin, C. and J. Quan (eds.), *Evolving Land Rights, Policy and Tenure in Africa*, pp. 151–79. London: IIED.

Dobkowski, M.N. and I. Walliman (eds), *The Coming of Age of Scarcity: Preventing Mass Death and Genocide in the Twenty-first Century.* Syracuse: Syracuse University Press.

Dobkowski, M.N. and Wallimann, I. 1998. "The Coming of Age of Scarcity: An Introduction" in M.N. Dobkowski and I. Walliman (eds), *The Coming of Age of Scarcity: Preventing Mass Death and Genocide in the Twenty-first Century*, pp. 1–20. Syracuse: Syracuse University Press.

Einarsson, P. 1993. "All Animals are Equal but some are Cetaceans: Conservation and Culture Conflict" in K. Milton (ed.), *Environmentalism: The View from Anthropology*, pp. 73–84. ASA Monographs, 32. London: Routledge.

Fairhead, J. 2001. "International Dimensions of Conflict over Natural and Environmental Resources" in N.L. Peluso and M. Watts (eds) 2001.

Fairhead, J. and M. Leach. 1996a. *Misreading the African landscape: Society and Ecology in a Forest-Savanna Mosaic*. Cambridge: Cambridge University Press.

___ 1996b. "Rethinking the Forest-Savanna Mosaic: Colonial Science and its Relics in West Africa" in M. Leach and R. Mearns (eds) 1996, pp. 105–21.

___ 1998. *Reframing Deforestation: Global Analyses and Local Realities: Studies in West Africa*. London: Routledge.

Feeny, D. et al. 1990. "The Tragedy of the Commons: Twenty-Two Years Later" in *Human Ecology* 18 (1): 1–19.

Forsyth, T. 2002. *Critical Political Ecology: The Politics of Environmental Science*. New York: Routledge.

Gowdy, J.M. 1998. "Biophysical Limits to Industrialization" in M.N. Dobkowski and I. Walliman (eds) 1998, pp. 65–82.

Gupta, A. and G. Ferguson, G. 1997. "Discipline and Practice: 'The Field' as Site, Method, and Location in Anthropology" in A. Gupta and G. Ferguson (eds), *Anthropological Locations: Boundaries and Grounds of a Field Science*, pp. 1–46. Berkeley: University of California Press.

Hardin, G. 1968. "The Tragedy of the Commons" in *Science* 162: 1243–8.

Hartmann, B. 2001. "Will the Circle be Unbroken? A Critique of the Project on Environment, Population and Security" in N.L. Peluso and M. Watts (eds) 2001, pp. 39–62.

Hirsch, E. 1995. "Landscape: Between Place and Space". In E. Hirsch and M. O'Hanlon (eds), *The Anthropology of Landscape: Perspectives on Place and Space*, pp. 1–30. Oxford: Clarendon Press.

Hoben, A. 1996. The Cultural Construction of Environmental Policy: Paradigms and Politics in Ethiopia. In M. Leach. and R. Mearns, eds., *The Lie of the Land: Challenging Received Wisdom on the African Environment*, pp. 186–208. London: James Currey.

Homer-Dixon, T.F. 1994. Environmental Scarcities and Violent Conflict: Evidence from Cases. *International Security* 19 (1): 5–40.

___ 1998. Environmental Scarcity and Violent Conflict: The Case of South Africa. *Journal of Peace Research*, 35 (3): 279-98.

___ 1999. *Environment, Scarcity and Violence*. Princeton: Princeton University Press.

Hussein, K. 1998. *Conflicts between Farmers and Herders in the semi-arid Sahel and East Africa*. Norwich: University of East Anglia (Overseas Development Group and School of Development Studies).

IFAD. 1994. *A Dialog on Capitol Hill: Workshop on Land Degradation and Poverty in Sub-Saharan Africa: Challenges and opportunities*. Rome: International Fund for Agricultural Development.

Jacobson, J.L. 1988. *Environmental Refugees: A Yardstick of Habitability*. Worldwatch Paper 86. Washington, D.C.: Worldwatch Institute.

Kaplan, R.D. 1994. The Coming Anarchy. *Atlantic Monthly* (Feb.): 44–76.

Kreike, E. 2003. Hidden Fruits: A Social Ecology of Fruit Trees in Namibia and Angola, 1880s–1990s. In W. Beinart and J. McGregor, eds., *Social History and African Environments*, pp. 27–42. Oxford: James Currey.

Leach. M. and R. Mearns (eds) 1996. *The Lie of the Land: Challenging Received Wisdom on the African Environment*. London: James Currey.

Leach, M. & Mearns, R. 1996. "Environmental Change and Policy: Challenging Received Wisdom in Africa" in M. Leach and R. Mearns (eds) 1996, pp. 1–33.

Lewis, C.H. 1998. "The Paradox of Global Development and the Necessary Collapse of Modern Industrial Civilization" in M.N. Dobkowski and I. Walliman (eds) 1998, pp. 43–60.

Little, P.D. and D.W. Brokensha. 1987. "Local Institutions, Tenure and Resource Management in East Africa" in D. Anderson, D. and R. Grove (eds), *Conservation in Africa: People, Policies and Practice*, pp. 193–209. Cambridge: Cambridge University Press.

Malthus, T.R. 1970 (1798; 1830). *An Essay on the Principles of Population* and *A Summary View of the Principle of Population*. Harmondsworth: Penguin.

McCabe J.T. 1990. "Turkana Pastoralism: A Case Against the Tragedy of the Commons" in *Human Ecology* 18 (1): 81–103.

McCarthy, J. 2001. "States of Nature and Environmental Enclosures in the American West" in N.L. Peluso and M. Watts (eds) 2001, pp. 117–45.

Meadows, D.H. et al. 1992. *Beyond the Limits: Global Collapse or a Sustainable Future*. London: Earthscan.

Morales, W.Q. 1998. "Intrastate Conflict and Sustainable Development: Lessons from Bosnia, Somalia and Haiti" in M.N. Dobkowski and I. Walliman (eds) 1998, pp. 245–68.

Mortimore, M. and M. Tiffen. 1995. "Population and Environment in Time Perspective: The Machakos Story." in T. Binns (ed.), *People and Environment in Africa*, pp. 69–91. Chichester: John Wiley.

Netting, R.McC. 1993. *Smallholders, Householders: Farm Families and the Ecology of Intensive, Sustainable Agriculture*. Stanford: Stanford University Press.

Neumann, R.P. 1998. *Imposing Wilderness: Struggles over Livelihood and Nature Preservation in Africa*. Berkeley: University of California Press.

____ 2001. "Disciplining Peasants in Tanzania: From State Violence to Self-Surveillance in Wildlife Conservation" in N.L. Peluso and M. Watts (eds) 1998, pp. 305–27.

Ostrom, E. 1990. *Governing the Commons: The Evolution of Institutions for Collective Action*. Cambridge: Cambridge University Press.

Peluso, N.L. and M. Watts. 2001. "Violent Environments" in N.L. Peluso and M. Watts (eds), *Violent Environments*, pp. 39–62. Ithaca: Cornell University Press.

Peluso, N.L. and Harwell, E. 2001. "Territory, Custom and the Cultural Politics of Ethnic War in West Kalimantan, Indonesia" in N.L. Peluso and M. Watts (eds), pp. 83–116.

Redclift, M. and Woodgate, G. 1997. "Sustainability and Social Construction" in M. Redclift and G. Woodgate (eds), *The International Handbook of Environmental Sociology*, pp. 55–70. Cheltenham: Edward Elgar.

Reenberg, A. 2001. "Agricultural Land Use Pattern Dynamics in the Sudan-Sahel: Towards an Event-driven Framework" in *Land Use Policy*: 18: 309–19.

Richards, P. 2001. "Are 'Forest' Wars in Africa Resource Conflicts? The Case of Sierra Leone" in N.L. Peluso and M. Watts (eds) 2001, pp. 65–82.

Rimmerman, C.A. 1998. "Critical Reflections on the Doomsday, Apocalyptic Vision" in M.N. Dobkowski and I. Walliman (eds) 1998, pp. 283–95.

Roth, J.K. 1998. "Foreword. Despair is no Solution" in M.N. Dobkowski and I. Walliman (eds) 1998, pp. ix–xiii.

Scoones, I. (ed.) 1994. *Living with Uncertainty: New Directions in Pastoral Development in Africa*. London: Intermediate Technology Publications.

____ 1996. "Range Management Science and Policy: Politics, Polemics and Pasture in Southern Africa" in M. Leach and R. Mearns (eds) *1996*, pp. 34–53.

Smith, D.N. 1998. "Postcolonial Genocide. Scarcity, Ethnicity and Mass Death in Rwanda" in M.N. Dobkowski and I. Walliman (eds) 1998, pp. 220–44.

Smith, R.W. 1998. "Scarcity and Genocide". in M.N. Dobkowski and I. Walliman (eds) 1998, pp. 199–219.

Stone, G.D. 2001. "Theory of the Square Chicken: Advances in Agricultural Intensification Theory" in *Asia Pacific Viewpoint* 42 (2/3): 163–80.

Sundar, N. 2001. "Beyond the Bounds? Violence at the Margins of New Legal Geographies" in N.L. Peluso and M. Watts (eds) 2001, pp. 328–53.

Swift, J. 1996. "Desertification: Narratives, Winners and Losers" in M. Leach, M. and R. Mearns (eds) 1996, pp. 73–90.

Tiffen, M. et al. 1994. *More People, Less Erosion: Environmental Recovery in Kenya*. Chichester: Wiley.

Trainer, T. 1998. "Our Unsustainable Society" in M.N. Dobkowski and I. Walliman (eds) 1998, pp. 83–100.

Watts, M. 2001. "Petro-Violence: Community, Extraction, and Political Ecology of a Mythic Commodity" in N.L. Peluso and M. Watts (eds) 2001, pp. 189–212.

Wenche, H. and Ellingsen, T. 1998. "Beyond Environmental Scarcity: The Causal Pathways to Conflict" in *Journal of Peace Research*, 35 (3): 299–317.

Woodhouse, P. et al. 2000. "Africa's 'Wetlands in Drylands': From Commons to Enclosures?" in P. Woodhouse et al. (eds), *African Enclosures? The Social Dynamics of Wetlands in Drylands?*, pp. 1–28. Oxford: James Currey.

World Bank 1996. *Towards Environmentally Sustainable Development in Sub-Saharan Africa: A World Bank Agenda*. Washington, DC: World Bank.

World Commission on Environmental Development (WCED) 1987. *Our Common Future*. Oxford: Oxford University Press.

Land and Labour:
Agrarian Change in Post-Retrenchment Lesotho

Christian Boehm

Introduction

Lesotho, located completely within the borders of South Africa, has for more than a hundred years been what, with some justification, could be termed a labour reserve for the South African gold-mining industry. During this period, its population grew from approximately 128,000 in 1875 to 950,000 in 1966 (Gay 1999) and more than 2.1 million in 2000 (Sechaba 2000). Such a significant population growth within the limited territory of the country has led to a relatively high population density. Today, virtually every square metre is or has been agriculturally utilised, whether as rangeland, fields or sites for human habitation. Seen from this perspective, Lesotho is a classic case illustrating the neo-Malthusian argument that population growth within a limited territory ultimately forces its inhabitants to over-utilise the natural resource base, resulting in agricultural decline and environmental degradation.

At first glance, neo-Malthusians appear to be right. Although the nature and extent of degradation is debatable, parts of Lesotho could be characterised as heavily degraded, overgrazed and depleted, the valleys being scarred by deep erosion gullies. It is this view that has informed generations of agriculturalists and environmentalists in their efforts to reverse the negative trend of degradation and enhance agricultural production. However, high population figures and a limited territory are not the only variables that are important in the equation leading to low agricultural outputs (Boserup 1990). As I demonstrate below, Basotho do not live simply from their fields, but mainly on wage labour opportunities both within and beyond the borders of their country. Fields are still important as an additional livelihood strategy and security in retirement, but on a larger scale, compared to other assets (e.g. labour) they constitute only a relatively minor component of Basotho's overall livelihoods and in contributing to their survival, resilience and persistence. Today Basotho live in a highly diversified cash economy where the majority of economic actors deploy a host of different strategies to eke out a living on their 'overcrowded' and 'degraded' territory, namely migratory wage labour, occasional jobs, selling fruit and vegetables and hawking, as well as the more occasional and dubious activities such as dagga trading and prostitution, which are combined in different ways and with different economic outcomes. As Turner has put it in a recent study: 'Livelihoods in Lesotho are subtle, complex and dynamic. Identifying points for effective intervention by policy and programmes is hard. That is why so few development efforts in Lesotho over the 35 years since independence have been successful' (Turner 2001: 57).

However, talking to Basotho themselves, one often hears statements such as 'We farm' (*rea lema*). At first glance, one is tempted to interpret such expressions as dominant discourses of how Basotho choose to represent themselves to outsiders, especially if we remind ourselves of the fact that most outsiders coming to rural Lesotho are in fact interested in farming. *Rea lema* is a cultural narrative rather than a realistic representation of Basotho livelihood practices. This becomes clearer when we consider that the proportion of households in Lesotho that were able to live by means of their agricultural production in 1999 was estimated to be below 3% (Sechaba 2000). Nationally, the proportion of landless households had risen above 40%, and it has become usual that, unless subsidised by the Government, approximately 40% of all fields are not ploughed at all.[1] It is here that the explanatory and predictive capacity of neo-Malthusianism has some serious limitations. For how can large tracts of land lie fallow while the population continues to grow[2] and while periodic food shortages are the norm?

Based on case material from a rural community in the Lowlands of Lesotho,[3] the present article will set out to explore the deeper meaning of *rea lema* and to re-examine some important aspects concerning the contemporary conditions of Sesotho farming within the context of two dimensions: first, the chronic crisis of agriculture and food security in Lesotho; and secondly, recent changes on the labour market, and in particular the significant reduction in the number of men employed in the South African mines, resulting in high unemployment figures. While I believe that neo-Malthusianism has some explanatory value, my main argument is three-fold. First, following scholars such as Berry (1993), I argue that any understanding of agrarian change must be based on research focusing on the multilevel social processes and institutions that make farming possible and that are themselves made possible through farming. This entails producing a grounded ethnography of the social relationships involved in the different stages of a given farming practice. Secondly, as with James Fairhead's study of the DRC (this volume), I argue that Lesotho is an excellent, if not an extreme example showing the critical importance of wider economic relationships on both social structures and processes in a wider sense of these terms, and natural resource management and farming in a more specific sense; this is my main criticism of neo-Malthu-

1. Previous researchers during the 1970s (Murray 1981, Turner 1978) reported that approximately 25% of all fields lie fallow.

2. Although precise figures are not available at present, overall population growth is currently assumed to be significantly reduced, if not stagnant, due to the HIV/AIDS pandemic. Due to internal migration, however, the urban and peri-urban areas of Lesotho continue to experience rapid population growth.

3. The material for this article was collected during eight months of anthropological fieldwork in a Lowland community in the vicinity of the capital, Maseru. Fieldwork was generously supported by a grant from the 'Sustainable Land Use' University Consortium (SLUSE) in Denmark.

sianism thinking. Thirdly, I believe that natural resources in general and land in particular must be thought in terms of what can be done with it, which in turn is a function of a complex and dynamic variety of factors. In this sense, land is not just territory, but a resource on both the productive and social and reproductive levels. What is crucial, as I shall argue in this chapter, is not land as such, but the capacity to cultivate it.

From Deagrarianisation to Deindustrialisation: The Historical Context

With these objectives and propositions concerning the social embeddedness of agricultural practice in mind, I now provide some historical background to agrarian change in Lesotho throughout the past century. Much has been written on this topic in the context of Lesotho, especially on the reasons for the chronic and acute crisis faced by farming in this small southern African country over a long period.[1] For the purposes of the present article, I shall briefly recapture some important historiographical points concerning the importance of wider economic relations and the nature of the relationship between the system of oscillating labour migration and domestic agriculture.

Colin Murray (1981) has vividly described how, during the second half of the nineteenth century, the Basotho were a prosperous and self-sufficient people, who were quick to grab the economic opportunities for grain export offered by the newly opened diamond mines in Kimberly in the north-west of the Orange Free State. In 1873, Basotho exported some 100,000 bags of grain as well as other agricultural products such as wool and mohair (Ferguson 1990). Subsequent historical developments are the result of a complex combination of factors, leading to the gradual decline of agriculture within what was called Basutoland during the time of the British colonial administration. In addition, almost the entire Basotho male labour force became engaged in the South African mining industry. By the 1930s, the 'transition' from 'granary to labour reserve' (Murray 1981: 1) was largely complete.

There are several main reasons for this radical reorganisation of the relationship between Basotho and their powerful neighbour, South Africa, during this period: first, the imposition of protectionist measures by South African governments, coupled with cheap grain imports from overseas, especially Australia and the USA; secondly, the introduction of the hut tax by the British colonial admin-

---

1. E.g. Wallman 1969; Turner 1978; Eckert 1980; Murray 1981; Showers 1982; Robertson 1987; Prah 1989; Ferguson 1990; Christensen 1994; Franklin 1995; Sechaba Consultants 1991, 1994, 2000; Phororo 1999; and others.

istration;[1] thirdly, armed conflicts and the associated weapons purchases; fourthly, a number of livestock epizootics such as the rinderpest; and lastly, a series of droughts and plagues of locust, which resulted in periodic food shortages and starvation. The number of Basotho men working in the South African mines during this 'transitional' period rose from 15,000 in 1875 to 78,604 in 1936 (Foulo 1996).

By 1935, the Pim Report, which was commissioned by the British colonial authorities in Basutoland, reported on the devastating effects of recent socio-economic developments in relation to the state of the natural environment in general and domestic agriculture in particular. Inspired by the 'Dust Bowl' debate in the USA, this report, together with subsequent ecological surveys, formed the foundation for a number of colonial measures to combat surface and gully erosion on the one hand and to improve the conditions for domestic agricultural production on the other in the decades to come. The main elements of the colonial programmes were building terraces and contour ploughing, gully control, the distribution of phosphate fertilisers, fruit-tree distribution and livestock improvement programmes (Showers 1982). It was during this period that today's landscape began to take shape. Ever since the implementation of the recommendations put forward by the Pim Report, generations of agricultural experts have come to Lesotho. Until independence in 1966, they were paid by the colonial administration, and afterwards by international development aid agencies. At best, their collective efforts have merely managed to slow down the further decline of agriculture in Lesotho.[2]

From this brief historical account, it becomes clear that the crisis in agriculture in Lesotho is by no means a recent phenomenon; rather, it has been an established fact of rural life in Lesotho for at least seventy years. Nonetheless the relationship between migrant labour and domestic agriculture remains complicated. While the first generations of Basotho miners went down the mines for limited periods, simply to earn money for taxes, guns and livestock purchases, the need to migrate soon became determined by food shortages back home in their villages in Basutoland. The decline of agriculture has many causes, such as soil erosion, population pressure, maize mono-cropping, pests and, of course, the loss of large tracts of land to the west of the Caledon River following the first (1858) and second (1865) Basotho–Boer Wars, as well as the declaration of Basutoland as a British Protectorate in 1868 (Gill 1993). But it is also clear that the system of labour mi-

---

1. The hut tax was the condition imposed on the Basotho rulers by the British Government in return for the establishment of the Protectorate of Basutoland and protection against the Boers. Ten shillings had to be paid by each homestead, and it is said that Chiefs rigorously enforced the collection (Sechaba 1991).

2. A discussion of the successes and failures of environmental protection measures goes beyond the scope of this article. The further decline of agriculture is linked to other factors than exclusively the environment. I thus do not intend to blame any agricultural expert for the crisis in agriculture in Lesotho.

gration as such has substantially contributed to the disintegration of the 'granary' and the decline of agricultural production. Mining took some of the population pressure away from the land and led to a substantial part of the male population disappearing for long periods, but it also meant that fields were left to be worked by the old, the young and the remaining 'gold widows' on behalf of absent husbands, sons and fathers. Farming thus came to count merely as supplementary income, both subordinated to and, because of the cash-intensive nature of agriculture in Lesotho, highly dependent on migrant labour. Basotho made substantial gains from migrant labour and put comparably little energy into agriculture. In a cash economy, cash always has a priority. The irony is that, while wages are relatively low, meaning that farming continues to be necessary for survival, farming outputs are so low that wages are necessary.

Recent Labour Market Changes: The Contemporary Context

In this section, I argue that Lesotho has entered a new 'transitional' phase, consisting in part of 'de-industrialisation', the proletarianisation of women and the diversification of livelihood strategies. The South African labour market has undergone radical changes in terms of employment opportunities for both men and women. Two major aspects of changes are crucial here.

First, there has been a severe retrenchment of Basotho men employed in the South African mining industry, a decline from up to 130,000 in the 1970s and 1980s to around 50,000 at present.[1] There are a number of reasons for this, such as the falling gold price on the international market, the restructuring of the South African mining industry due to falling ore grades and profitability, and political pressures on the South African government to employ national rather than foreign labour after the collapse of apartheid.[2]

Secondly, the worldwide trend of Asian investors relocating the production of textile garments (Warren and Borque 1991; Dyer 2001) has reached Lesotho, among other things as a result of Lesotho and the USA signing the African Growth and Opportunities Act (AGOA) in 2000. Lesotho has been successful in attracting industries from the Far East because of plentiful availability of a relatively well educated and 'docile' labour force, favourable legislation and a developed infrastructure across the border in South Africa. Employment figures in the industry were around 40,000 in 2002, the majority being young women. The future seems promising for the industry, with labour being cheap and the local currency being weak, thus making exports to the USA very profitable.[3]

---

1. Personal interview with Chris Hector, Regional Manager for Lesotho and the Eastern Free State at TEBA (The Employment Bureau of Africa), 13.02.2002.
2. See also T. Foulo, *Emerging Trends in the Migration of Basotho Miners*, Central Bank of Lesotho, 1996; Central Bank of Lesotho, *Annual Report for 2000*, March 2001; Westermann, G., *Survey on Migrant Workers Retrenchment*, Irish Consulate, Lesotho, 1999.

These labour market changes are summarised in Figure 1, below. It must be stressed that all employment figures are subject to uncertainty, as sources differ and nobody really knows precisely how many people are working in the South African mines.[1] The graph below is thus based on figures from a variety of sources, such as TEBA (The Employment Bureau of Africa), the Lesotho National Bank and other studies carried out on this topic.

Figure 1. Lesotho labour market developments

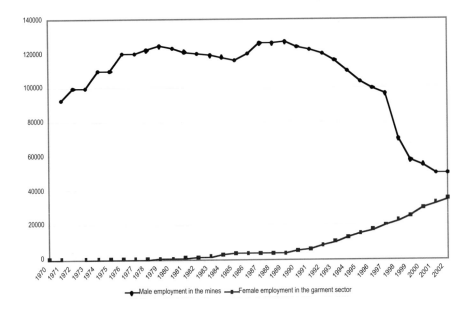

What the loss of mining as a labour opportunity has meant for the micro economy of households and communities within Lesotho must be examined under two different aspects. First, a miner usually supports not only his own family (with a mean household size of approximately five persons per household), but also other kin members who have no direct access to cash. Secondly, the population of Lesotho has doubled since the 1970s, when employment of Basotho men in the South African mines was at its highest. While 49.7% of all households in Lesotho had at least one household member working in the mines in 1979, this figure had declined to 11.9 by 2002.

---

3. Literature is sparse on this very recent phenomenon. See also Dyer 2001 and Salm, A. et al., *Lesotho Garment Industry Subsector Study for the Government of Lesotho*, 2002.

1. There are several recruitment agencies, subcontractors as well as direct recruitment operations, working simultaneously.

The principal ethnographers of the Basotho[1] have described a situation where up to 80% of mean rural household incomes were derived from men's earnings from migrant labour. What used to be the absolute economic backbone of Basotho villages and rural economies has become the privilege of a few. The loss of the opportunity to work in the mines has only partly been compensated for by newly created jobs for young women in the garment sector.

Fields without Money, Money without Fields: The Case of Molapo's Farming Strategy

In order to investigate the impact of these changes in the labour market for contemporary Sesotho farming conditions, I now leave the macro perspective to consider case material from a Lowland[2] village in the vicinity of the capital Maseru. However, the scope of this paper does not permit a detailed investigation of all the technical elements involved in farming strategies. The focus will thus rest on what *rea lema* means in practice and on the social relationships that constitute, and are constituted by, a system of production.

Ha Sechaba is a village of 815 inhabitants, including the 13.1% (16.2% of males and 10.2% of females) who are away on migrant work in other parts of Lesotho or in the Republic of South Africa. However, Ha Sechaba is well endowed with fields, with only 25% of all households having no fields at all and 42.4% of all households having two or more fields.[3] In terms of retrenchment, Ha Sechaba carries its share of the burden in that the number of households with direct access to mining income (i.e. at least one household member employed in the mines) has been reduced to 14%, while the 1991 figure for the Lowland region was 49.7% (Central Bank of Lesotho 1991). Being in commuting distance from the Industrial Areas, 12.8%[4] of all households in Ha Sechaba have direct access to wages earned in the Asian textile factories. Hence, as can be seen from these few income status indicators, the lives of Ha Sechaba's rural dwellers are intimately tied up with, and correspond well to, the larger processes described above.

---

1. Such as Ashton, E.H. 1967; Turner, S. 1978; Gay, J. 1980; Ferguson, J. 1990; Murray 1981; Spiegel 1980.

2. Lesotho is commonly divided geographically and socio-economically into three (Urban, Lowlands/Foothills, Mountains), four (Maseru, Lowlands, Foothills and Highlands) or five (Maseru, Lowlands, Foothills, Highlands and Senqu River Valley) regions. The Lowlands are the main agricultural as well as the main labour supplying area. It is therefore appropriate to study retrenchment and agrarian change in a Lowland setting.

3. By comparison, the national figure for landless households in 1999 was 41% and for the Lowland region 40% (Sechaba Consultants 2000).

4. The total number of women employed in the garment sector (20 in January 2002) fluctuates significantly because employment periods are short and staff turnover in the factories very high.

In Ha Sechaba we find the household of Molapo,[1] who lives together with his mother, his two children and one of his brother's children in his deceased father's house along the dirt road that ends in the village. He is in his early thirties and has no field of his own as yet. Having worked as a miner for ten years at Western Holdings, a South African gold mine, he returned home to live in Ha Sechaba and 'try life as a farmer', as he expressed it. His wife, he claimed, had left him when he was made redundant.

Table 1: Schematic Overview of Molapo's farming strategy

	Field 1	Field 2	Field 3	Field 4
Field Owner	Molapo's deceased father is the formal owner mentioned on Form C, the official field document proving ownership. His mother will have the field until her death and formal inheritance by one of her three sons. 'Whom she likes most, he will have it', according to Molapo.	Mohlomi brings in half of a big field. Mohlomi owns two fields in total. His other field remains unploughed. The chief had threatened to take away his fields because they have been lying fallow for some years. He was thus forced to 'keep the field busy', as he put it.	'Me Matankiso's deceased husband is the formal owner. He has two fields but cannot plough alone following the death of her husband.	'Me Matlanyane's deceased husband formerly owns the field. She has agreed to leave it to Molapo for a ten-year period in exchange for Molapo repairing and maintaining her house.
Ploughing	Moses, a distant relative, does the ploughing. 50% of the ploughing costs (120 Rand per ha.) were supposed to be subsidised by the government, but apparently was never paid. Ploughing was done in time.	One of Mohlomi's friends from a neighbouring village agrees to plough the whole field with a tractor and keeps one half of the field as payment for him. The ploughing was done late.	'Me Matankiso owns a few cattle and manages the ploughing with the help of relatives, who are rewarded in kind (home brew). Ploughing was done late.	Moses, a distant relative does the ploughing. 50% of the ploughing costs are subsidised by the government. Ploughing was done late.
Fertiliser, Seed and Pesticides	Molapo covers the costs of fertilisers, seeds and pesticide, with substantial help from his two brothers, who are both working in the RSA.	Molapo covers the costs of fertilisers, seeds and pesticide with substantial help from his two brothers, who are both working in the RSA.	Molapo purchases some more fertiliser and mixes it with cow dung from 'Me Matankiso's cattle. Seeds and pesticide are also bought by Molapo.	Molapo covers the costs of fertilisers, seed and pesticide with substantial help from his two brothers, who are both working in the RSA.
Labour	For hoeing, a number of poor women are hired for 7 Rand per day. Moeketsi, the owner of a cart and cattle, assists with both hoeing and harvesting.	Molapo and Mohlomi both work the field together, assisted by members of their family.	Molapo and 'Me Matankiso harvest the field together, with the help of a few relatives. 'Me also does a little weeding on the field.	Molapo does most of the work himself. For hoeing, a number of poor women are hired for 7 Rand per day
Sharing and Payment Arrangements	Moeketsi will receive a small share (10 kg) of the harvest in exchange for his labour and be allowed to graze his cattle on Molapo's mother's field. Molapo keeps the rest for himself.	Molapo and Mohlomi claim to share the harvest fifty / fifty.* This is a formal sharecropping arrangement with a social dimension. 'I help them by ploughing with them', as Molapo expressed it.	Molapo and 'Me Matankiso claim to share the harvest fifty–fifty.	Molapo keeps the entire harvest. In exchange for the field, Molapo pays a friend from Maseru in kind for repairing 'Me Matlanyane's house. 'The field is the payment for the labour I organise', as Molapo put it.

* How to share is, not surprisingly, a frequent source of conflict between sharecropping partners. A fifty–fifty arrangement is the ideal, based on one partner bringing in the field, the other taking care of the ploughing, and both partners paying for the necessary fertilizer and seeds. However, being relatively abundant, the value of fields appears to suffer from inflation in relation to the other inputs. Most partnerships where one partner brings in the field while the other takes care of the rest will share seventy–thirty rather than fifty–fifty.

1. All names are pseudonyms. Molapo was one of the first persons I came to know more closely during my stay in Ha Sechaba. Although he is fairly young, he often participated in meetings and court cases at Moreneng (Chief's place), which is where I stayed myself. Many conversations with him started there. In addition to that, Molapo is a proud farmer who would willingly walk for hours to show to me all his agricultural endeavours.

In order to show how redundant miners may react to global changes and manoeuvre through the vagaries of coping in an uncertain environment, I shall present here in some detail Molapo's agricultural strategy for the last main summer season, which started with the spring rains back in October 2001 and came to an end around May/June 2002. In the table above, I show how Molapo collected together his main farming implements (rows) for the four fields (columns) on which he worked during the season. More importantly, I wish to explore and draw attention to the multiplicity of social arrangements that are required to manipulate the essentials of farming.

When I revisited Molapo in January 2003, he reported the following harvest figures:

— Field 1 had yielded eight 80 kg bags, all of which belonged to Molapo.
— Field 2 had yielded six 80 kg bags, three of which went to Mohlomi.
— Field 3 had yielded seven 80 kg bags, three of which went to 'Me Matankiso.
— Field 4 had yielded thirteen 80 kg bags, all of which belonged to Molapo.

According to Molapo, although the output on Fields 1, 2 and 3 was not satisfactory, he assured me that the general picture was that of an average agricultural season.[1] I shall comment below on what Molapo did with the harvest. What is crucial to note concerning his farming strategy at this stage is that he mobilises a fairly complex set of social relationships and makes a series of agreements with other community members in order to obtain the main implements he needs to carry out a season's farming, namely land, traction power, labour and implements such as fertilisers, seeds and pesticides.

Few people in Ha Sechaba control all the means of agricultural production and can farm alone. For the types of arrangement made, the different sorts of asset must complement one another. Newly established households with access to some cash need access to land, while widows (39% of all households are headed by widow(er)s, 90% of whom are female) holding their deceased husbands' fields but with hardly any cash sources need some financial input in order to be able to harvest at least part of their land. This forces people to join together and makes individual trajectories and farming strategies intersect within the framework of specific strategies for particular fields. In the construction of these highly flexible and constantly changing farming units, kinship naturally plays an important role,

---

1. His argument stands in stark contrast to the ongoing claims of various United Nations organisations and the Government of Lesotho, that Lesotho is facing serious food shortages as the result of a failed harvest. It appears that, while some parts of southern Africa were facing serious famine, this fate was projected to the entire region within the global media. As a visible sign of the international effort, the Government had distributed fertilisers and seeds to large parts of rural Lesotho, with the result that a much larger proportion of fields than usual had been ploughed during the 2002/2003 season. The situation may be different in other parts of Lesotho, which I did not visited at the time.

even though a number of informants insisted that agreements have become more business-like and cash-based.

Institutions of productive relationships facilitating the pooling of different resources that are needed on particular fields and at specific times exist in many parts of sub-Saharan Africa and are generally termed 'sharecropping'. In the context of Lesotho (*lihalefote* or *seahlolo*), this has already been studied in detail by Turner (1978), Spiegel (1979) and Robertson (1987). Here, therefore, I shall merely recapitulate some of the main points that are deemed important for an understanding of the impact of retrenchment and unemployment on the conditions of contemporary Sesotho farming.

In brief, sharecropping means that two or more households join together in order to form a farming unit with the purpose of obtaining the implements mentioned above that are necessary in order to plough, plant and harvest a particular field for a particular season. Robertson (1987) makes a distinction between *seahlolo*, the traditional Sotho type of communitarianism, redistribution and 'social welfare', and *lihalefote* (derived from Afrikaans 'half – half'), the more business-like and entrepreneurial contract aimed at individual advantage, which has its roots in the co-operation between Basotho and Boers during the latter's settlement in what is today the Eastern Orange Free State. In practice, however, I found that the two concepts are mixed and that both aspects can be found within the same relationship. It is important, though, to emphasise that certain types of sharecropping have a strong social element of income diffusion, while others do not. The farming units are highly flexible and frequently change from season to season. Other partners work together for long periods, and many successful partnerships are terminated by the death of one partner. Because households typically have different kinds of farming implements available during different stages of their life-cycle, sharecropping often involves more than one generation.

It is important to stress that not all forms of co-operation across different stages of the life-cycle are sharecropping. Co-operation with household members, as is the case on Molapo's Field 1, is not sharecropping. The type of arrangement on Field 4 is not sharecropping either, because the field has been provided as payment in exchange for repairing the house of an old widow. Furthermore, it is crucial to note that sharecropping is often represented as a necessity rather than an ideal. The ideal, which is also part of the discourse of *rea lema*, is to plough alone, to be a strong and independent individual as well as – and this is the crucial point – to be able to help others. Thus, sharecropping is part of a strong moral discourse of mutual obligation and help.

Sharing Poverty: Sharecropping and Rising Unemployment

As sharecropping is a phenomenon of differentiation, and because differentiation is bound to increase in a situation of retrenchment and rising unemployment, sharecropping has become a lot more common lasting recent decades. While the researchers of sharecropping and rural development during the 1970s, mentioned above, reported figures of approximately 25%, in Ha Sechaba, 51% of all households sharecropped during the last season. This figure must be seen against two factors. First, in a survey situation, many social arrangements are never called sharecropping, but casually described as: 'We just work together.' Secondly, many households with fields want to sharecrop, but cannot find partners willing to enter into a contract with them – hence the large number of fallow fields. On the other hand, households with access to cash but no fields have few problems finding a partner, which has led to an inflation of the relative value of fields in relation to other agricultural inputs. From the above, it can be concluded that an efficient sharecropping system that optimises the means of production and works the land that is available to the community can only function well if there are fairly precise proportions of different types of household which need to integrate as a unit.

In the case of Molapo, his ability to work four fields is determined by the inter-household flow of cash coming from his two brothers, who are working in the Free State mines. Molapo is not among the better off community members, and he is not even regarded as a skilled farmer in the technical sense. But for the majority of community members with access to land but no cash, he is an attractive partner because he has indirect access to a wage income. Furthermore, what determines his relative success as a farmer during this season, besides his entrepreneurial qualities and personal skills, is his ability to optimise both social and material resources and to make things happen on the ground at the right time. Of course, he has not established the network on which he draws for the sake of this particular farming season. Most of the relationships that become important here are a part of social life in a much more general sense. Some of them are kin-based, while others were established by Molapo's father and inherited from him. Farming is thus an arena where social relations and values are put to work, and in doing so, maintained and extended. As Molapo's strategy emerges in a wider social life, he should not be seen solely as an economic individual who is surveying his fields and his potential partners. The social situation was there already before he applied it to his agricultural goals.

Because ploughing, hoeing and harvesting in a high altitude environment with erratic rainfalls, frequent hailstorms, early frosts and recurring droughts must be timed in a precise and flexible manner, the amount of social capital and social skills that Molapo must deploy and manipulate at specific times during the farming season is considerable. The 2001/2002 agricultural season is a good example: the rains came in October, and ideally the maize ploughing should have been done by the end of October.[1] Yet by Christmas most fields had still not been ploughed, investigations of the various arrangements usually revealing that people where waiting for something or somebody: the brother had to come from the mine with the cash; the neighbour had to get his tractor repaired; somebody had just died; the eldest daughter had to come home from Maseru and contribute to the expenses; the government had promised subsidised seeds but failed to deliver them; many poor field-holders were waiting for a sharecropping partner willing to enter into an arrangement with someone with nothing but a field. Some of those who had a good agreement in place had to make secondary agreements in order to be able to enter a contract. Even in a relatively wet season such as 2001/02, practising successful and timed farming was very difficult because nobody could just go out and do it. Everybody had to wait and devote immense amounts of energy in making social arrangements. In the first week of April we woke up to the first frosts, which put a stop to the maize growth and turned the landscape from green to brown within a matter of days. What this meant was yet another poor harvest due to late ploughing or no ploughing at all.

In practice, we see a situation of shortage in respect of most of the necessary implements. First, there is a shortage of cash (for seeds, ploughing, fertiliser, etc.) due to unemployment and the lack of income-generating opportunities. Secondly, labour is scarce due to the almost culturally prescribed absence of men between 20 and 50 and the recent migration of young women. Thirdly, there is a relative shortage of land. While the dominant discourse in and on Lesotho, as informed by neo-Malthusian thinking, argues that Lesotho is suffering from land shortages, I suggest that this shortage of land is relative because of the large tracts of arable land that lie fallow. However, shortages can be real enough for those without direct access to land (25% in Ha Sechaba). In terms of the life-cycle, it could be argued that the dynamics that underpin the various developmental stages have changed and that this has considerable implications for agriculture. The necessary nodal points,[2] where different households meet at different stages in their lives with different resources to put into a farming arrangement, are struggling to become established and are becoming fewer and fewer, hence the apparent abundance of fallow fields.

In a way, the social embeddedness of fields used to be one of the strengths of agriculture in Lesotho because the various exchange arrangements worked as

---

1. It is said that October to mid-December is the ideal time to plough maize. If more than one field is worked, the ploughing is usually staggered in order to allow time for the labour-intensive weeding of each field. Thus Molapo timed ploughing on the four fields for the 2002/2003 season as follows: Field 1: October 6; Field 2: November 11; Field 3: November 20; Field 4: January 3.

2. Hastrup & Olwig (1997) define 'nodal points' as follows: '*Important cultural sites in research...are found in nodal points in the different networks of local and global relations that constitute the context of life...* (Ibid: 12). Nodal points are intersections of individual trajectories within a farming context, i.e. the social field that emerges when people farm together in one way or another.

channels for the diffusion of wealth and facilitated access to land even for landless households. In this sense, farming accentuates social values, cohesion and nearness, as well as mutual help and obligations. However, I also suggest that this strength is also a general weakness, in the sense that it becomes fragile in a situation where the balance between the different sorts of capital available in a rural community is distorted by changes in the macro environment.

To Plough or Not to Plough?

Every year, when the spring rains have softened the arid soil of Lowland Lesotho's fields, Basotho farmers must ask themselves: 'How will we be able to plough this season?' Two dimensions of Sesotho farming seem to be of great relevance when Basotho make up their minds about this: first, the high risk involved in the cash investments necessary for a farming season; and secondly, the importance of having a social support network in place, which can be optimised in order to provide the right implements at the right time.

Concerning the first issue, it is common to hear Basotho farmers say that they have put their 'hope' in a particular field, a specific crop or some chickens. Their use of the concept of 'hope' in this context expresses well what Sesotho farming is in fact, namely a kind of 'gambling'. In order to illustrate what Basotho farmers mean by 'hoping', and to emphasise the elements of risk and uncertainty in contemporary Sesotho farming, I shall briefly return to Molapo's budgetary calculations in relation to Field 1:

— Field 1 is said to have a size of 1.2 ha and to provide a harvest of between 800 kg and 2400 kg (10–30 80-kg bags), depending on climatic conditions and the amount of fertilisers applied.

— If sold to the government mill, the value was said to be between 800 and 2400 Rand at the beginning of 2002. This value increased considerably to between 1440 and 4320 Rand later during the year, when maize prices rose as a result of the alleged food crisis in southern Africa as a whole. If sold locally, the value is between 1600 and 4800 Rand (though the grinding must be paid for at between 120 and 360 Rand for the total harvest at the local mill).

— The costs involved in ploughing Field 1 in this particular season were as shown below:

Item	Cost
Seed	116 Rand
Fertiliser	560 Rand
Tractor	150 Rand
Labour	200 Rand
Total	1,026 Rand

— Thus, Molapo risks making only a marginal profit if he sells to the government mill. By selling locally, he can make a slightly better profit, depending on the outcome of the harvest.

— Purchasing 800 kg of ground maize meal in the supermarket (which is slightly cheaper than local prices) costs approximately 1,350 Rand, meaning that in the case of a bad harvest, Molapo could have purchased 800 kg for roughly the same amount that he paid for having Field 1 ploughed. Only in the case of a good or medium harvest can Molapo realistically 'hope' for a significant surplus in either cash or kind. Because prices in the supermarkets rose during the year, purchasing would have become more costly.

When harvested in June 2002, the total harvest of Field 1 was 640 kg., worth 1152 Rand in the capital Maseru and 1280 Rand in Ha Sechaba at the time of harvesting – a fairly disappointing outcome seen in relation to total inputs. However, the output of some of the other fields he worked was more satisfying and thus partly compensated him for this. In reply to my enquiries, he considered the total harvest to be average. After harvesting and paying his sharecroppers and partners, Molapo was left with a total of 28 bags, 13 of which he sold in Maseru for a total of 1900 Rand. He decided to sell the bulk of what was left in the village, apart from some bags he kept back for his own consumption. The exact price was difficult to determine, as many of his custumers were neighbours and relatives who could not always pay straightaway, but he usually charges two Rand per kg. The 1900 Rand were used for household expenses and farming inputs for the next season.

What it is crucial to emphasise here is the marginal nature of the potential rewards that can be obtained from farming under the current specific conditions of a third-world enclave. Lesotho is surrounded by the modern agricultural economy of South Africa, with which competition in inherently unequal. As the case of Molapo shows, farming may be a source of cash for a few farmers in Ha Sechaba. Yet the returns that can be expected are low, the risks involved in choosing this livelihood strategy high, and the financial inputs required considerable. Farmers in Ha Sechaba invest cash in what might be both cash cropping and/or subsistence production in the hope that the outcome will be a marginal economic improvement over buying maize meal directly in the supermarket. This is another reason why so many households in Ha Sechaba choose not to farm, but to seek work instead.

Needless to say, there are other considerations of a social, moral and cultural nature in Molapo's mind than pure cost-benefit 'bottom-line thinking' when it comes to planning for Field 1. However, the risk inherent in investing a large sum of money in the context of the uncertainties of the Lesotho climate should not be underestimated, especially when there are many other pressing needs, such as schooling and health expenses.

The second issue concerns the social network that must be in place in order for resources to be optimized. As we have seen above, farming in general, and sharecropping in particular, are of an extremely social nature. The tradition to co-operate is reflected in a wealth of vernacular terms for different forms of co-operation[1] in relation to agricultural activities. In this situation, the difference between being able to plough or not being able is not just a matter of access to wages, but also of the ability to mobilise a social network for a specific purpose. Farming puts social values into practice, but can at the same time also be a source of conflicts and disappointments. Stories about unreliable partners are many, and frequently agreements are never implemented in practice. The ability to find the right partners at the right time in a climate of competition for good partners is a key agricultural skill that is more precious than knowledge of soil types, surface erosion, seed types or fertiliser mixtures. Many farmers in Ha Sechaba are not as successful as Molapo because their social claims are not strong enough to provide them with what is needed to farm. Consequently their fields lie fallow, and they can only wait and try again the next season.[2]

By investigating what resources are crucial for household farming strategies at different stages on the life-cycle, it becomes clear that social resources of any kind are especially critical during stages of fission and decline. In a situation of retrenchment and unemployment, even younger households enter a state of, if not decline, then certainly stagnation because they do not control even a minimum of the financial resources necessary to get into farming.[3] Of course social skills have always been important, but I suggest that their significance for successful farming has increased, and that the continued crisis in agriculture results from too many people competing for a decreasing pool of economic and social resources, making social capital in the form of the right agreements at the right time critical for success. One might think that retrenched miners return 'home' to their farm and that the relative significance of agriculture would increase as a result of unemployment. The opposite seems to be the case, however. Farming has become a privilege of those homes with stable access to wages, whether directly or, as in Molapo's case, indirectly through strong inter-household links. As the proportion of households with access to wages declines, fewer people in Ha Sechaba are managing to collect the farming tools they require.

---

1. E.g. *thusana*, helping each other; *kopana*, joining together; *kopanetse*, working in a group; *kalmia*, borrowing.

2. Some people in Sechaba chose to plant winter wheat. But, as one elderly male informant stated, 'This is just to keep the hunger away'.

3. Two young men interviewed in the Maseru industrial area called *Stationeng* expressed it like this: 'We still live with our parents in Ha Mokhalinyane. Now we've come here for months but still no job. All jobs are for women only. We want to live by means of agriculture, but without money it is impossible. The job is necessary, but it's only to get life started. Fertilisers, seeds, a house, a wife – it all needs money.'

These considerations, the financial risk as well as the social capital required for farming, point towards how retrenched miners cope with a condition in which many of them are not as lucky as Molapo. For most retrenched or retired miners, investments of more than 1,000 Rand are impossible. Here Molapo's budget items can provide guidance. Retrenched miners stress the importance of becoming independent from a regular source of cash and that cattle are the best way to achieve this.[1] Cattle can do the ploughing and replace the tractor, at least in theory.[2] As they graze on common grazing grounds, cattle come free of charge apart from minor vaccination costs and the costs of employing a herding boy.[3] Cattle provide manure, which can partly replace artificial fertilisers. Cattle can also be sold if one needs cash, and cattle reproduce. Also, cattle can draw carts for harvesting, assist in hoeing, provide milk, etc. Those retrenched miners who invested in cattle before retrenchment are considered the lucky ones.[4] In practice, farmers who lack cash mix small amounts of fertiliser with larger amounts of cow dung. If they have cattle they plough with them, otherwise they can hire a span, which is significantly cheaper than hiring a tractor. Labour costs can simply be reduced by not hiring labour for hoeing, but instead hoeing oneself or, just as frequently, not at all. All these cash expenditure-reduction strategies have one significant disadvantage: they reduce the final output. 'Our fields are weak nowadays', farmers in Ha Sechaba would say. Soil degradation as a result of erosion, maize monocropping and the continued use of fertilisers[5] represent the reality of a situation that neither the rural dwellers of Lowland Lesotho nor a social analysis of the conditions of Sesotho farming can ignore.

The emerging multiplicity of livelihood strategies and the diversification of survival strategies may also answer the question of what those who cannot plough are going to eat. Most will 'muddle through', while the poorest ones might re-

1. This is one reason why cattle are so important to Basotho. See also Ferguson (1990) for a discussion of the 'bovine mystique'.

2. In practice, cattle are often extremely weak and/or sick after the winter and are hardly able to do this very demanding job.

3. Sons often do this job. If herding boys are hired, they nowadays often have to be paid in cash.

4. One might expect cattle numbers to be rising. However, at 1.58 (my data from 2002), the mean number of cattle per household in Sechaba is slightly lower than the national average for the Lowlands, at 1.83 (Sechaba Consultants Survey in 1999). Total livestock numbers have been stagnant for a while, meaning that cattle numbers per household are declining due to population growth. There are a number of reasons for this stagnation despite the attraction of cattle for retrenched miners: first, rampant stock theft, which affected nearly 10% of all households during 1999 (Sechaba 2000); secondly, unemployment itself, meaning that fewer people can invest in purchasing livestock; thirdly, in Ha Sechaba the grazing is limited and is also said to have been affected by a pest destroying the grass.

5. A concern over the causal relationship between soil degradation and fertiliser use is expressed by local farmers. Seen from the biophysical perspective, Lesotho's soil suffers from phosphorus deficiency, which is why fertilisers are necessary.

ceive food aid[1] or, if they are lucky, some assistance from either the chief or the social welfare department in Maseru. Again, we must stress that farming in Lesotho itself is fairly costly, while buying food is relatively cheap, meaning that the margin between growing food and buying it depends greatly on conditions in that season and is sometimes very small. Being able to farm does not mean that one can eat. Nor does not farming mean that you will starve. Nor does it mean that you are socially marginalized. Farming is one of several potential livelihood strategies, and a fairly risky one. As demonstrated above, Basotho can never count on their fields alone, which is why it may be more advantageous for them to keep other options open. The circumstance that wages are necessary for successful farming, which has developed during Basotho men's long involvement in the South African mining industry, explains why Basotho cannot return to their fields in a situation of unemployment and poverty. On the contrary, the disintegration of the migrant labour system appears to have further marginalized the significance of farming in Basotho livelihood strategies and deepened the overall crisis of agriculture in Lesotho.

Conclusion

Sesotho farming faces an apparent paradox. On the one hand, farming activities form and maintain social life in general and bridge factions in a society that is characterised by far-reaching, disintegrating tensions along the axes of men and women, young and old, royal and common, residents and newcomers. *Rea lema* plays an important role in questions of identity and ethnicity because farming is an integrated part of Sesotho custo; it is thus not only a social performance (Richards 1993) but also a cultural one. This function is actualised by the current economic depression resulting from mass unemployment among Basotho men. On the other hand, farming has long played a marginal economic role in Basotho livelihood strategies, a situation that seems to have been reinforced by recent labour market changes.

Rea lema signifies how life should be, not how it is. The ideal of agriculture as the 'social backbone' of Basotho rural communities and as the proper Sesotho road to economic independence stands in stark contrast to the marginal economic role that farming plays in reality. Only in theory can this be done without cash. The significance of social skills in putting together and managing a season's farming has, I believe, increased as a result of the labour market changes discussed above. The high level of uncertainty inherent in an existence without access to cash while living in a cash economy has made investments in the means of negotiation and exchange within social networks equally, if not more important than investments in productive implements. Risk and uncertainty mean that actors

---

1. During the winter months of 2002 (May–August), elderly people, orphans and people with disabilities received food aid.

need to keep options open in case the rains fail, job-hunting proves unsuccessful, a productive household member dies, livestock is stolen or any other vicissitude of daily life occurs that is so typical of southern Africa today. The flexibility required to keep options open is not achieved by a flexible agro-pastoral system itself, but rather by means of, first, risk alleviation by means of livelihood diversification, and secondly, building up social claims and social capital by means of participation in social networks based on exchange and mutual obligation. Exploring the 'social life of fields' equally reveals an all-encompassing social system of magnitude within a community that involves every single inhabitant in one way or another – including those abroad doing migrant labour – concerning the agricultural territory. In order to understand the crisis of agricultural production, this approach may give some clues. There is always a long story behind the decision to plough or not to plough.

It is clear by now that farming strategies, just like other aspects of everyday life in Lesotho, must be understood and interpreted within a larger framework that encompasses both local social institutions and wider economic relations. Put more bluntly, to understand a particular field in a rural community, global aspects such as gold prices, textile trade agreements or EU donor policies are just as important as local dimensions of social life. While the neo-Malthusian factor of territory remains a relevant and important variable in the equation, resulting in scarcity, other factors, such as wages, production in a wider sense, social institutions and processes, as well as changing patterns of consumption, move to the foreground in determining what can be done with territory.

References

Ashton, E.H. 1967. *The Basuto: A Social Study of Traditional and Modern Lesotho*. Oxford University Press.

Berry, S. 1993. *No Condition is Permanent: The Social Dynamics of Agrarian Change in Sub-Saharan Africa*. Wisconsin.

Boserup, E. 1990. *Economic and Demographic Relationships in Development*. Baltimore.

Central Bank of Lesotho 1991. *Migrant Workers Retrenchments: Implications for the Lesotho Economy*. Maseru.

Central Bank of Lesotho 2001. *Annual Report for 2000*. Maseru.

Christensen, M.L. 1994. *Gender and Household Differences in a Soil Conservation Project*. Unit of Development Studies, Uppsala University, Sweden.

Dyer, K. 2001. *Gender Relations in the Home and the Workplace: A Case Study of the Gender Implications of Lesotho's Current Economic Development Strategy for the Clothing Industry*. The Institute of Southern African Studies, National University of Lesotho at Roma. Lesotho.

Eckert, J. 1980. *Lesotho's Land Tenure: An Analysis and Annotated Bibliography*. Special Bibliography No. 1. Lesotho Agricultural Sector Analysis Project, Ministry of Agriculture and Colorado State University.

Ferguson, J. 1990. *The Anti-Politics Machine: Development, Depoliticization and Bureaucratic Power in Lesotho*. University of Minnesota Press.

Foulo, T. 1996. *Emerging Trends in the Migration of Basotho Miners*. Central Bank of Lesotho.

Franklin, A.S. 1995. *Land Law in Lesotho: The Politics of the 1979 Land Act.* Avebury.

Gay, John 1999. "The Human Environment" in Chakela, Q.K. (ed.), *State of the Environment in Lesotho.* Maseru.

Gay, Judy 1980. *Basotho Women's Options: A Study of Marital Careers in Rural Lesotho.* Ph.D. thesis, University of Cambridge.

Gill, S. 1993. *A Short History of Lesotho.* Morija Museum and Archives, Lesotho.

Hastrup, K. and Fog Olwig, K. 1997. "Introduction" in K. Hastrup and K. Fog Olwig (eds), *Siting Culture: The Shifting Anthropological Object.* London.

Murray, C. 1981. *Families Divided: The Impact of Migrant Labour in Lesotho.* African Studies Series. Cambridge.

Phororo, D.R. 1999." Agriculture and Poverty in Lesotho". unpublished manuscript.

Prah, K. 1989, "Land Degradation and Class Struggle in Rural Lesotho" in Hjort af Ornäs, A. and Salih, M.A. (eds), *Ecology and Politics: Environmental Stress and Security in Africa.* Scandinavian Institute of African Studies, Uppsala.

Richards, P. 1993. Cultivation: "Knowledge or Performance". In M. Hobart (ed.), *An Anthropological Critique of Development: The Growth of Ignorance.* London.

Robertson, A.F. 1987. "Lesotho: seahlolo and lihalefote", in A.E. Robertson *The Dynamics of Productive Relationships: African Share Contracts in Comparative Perspective.* Cambridge: Cambridge University Press.

Salm, A. et al. 2002. *Lesotho Garment Industry.* Subsector Study for the Government of Lesotho. Maseru.

Showers, B. K. 1982. *Assessment of the Land Use Potential at Ha Makhopo, Lesotho: A Holistic Approach to Agricultural Evaluation.* Ph.D. Thesis, Cornell University.

Sechaba Consultants 1991. *Poverty Mapping Exercise.* Lesotho.

Sechaba Consultants 1994. *Poverty Mapping Exercise.* Lesotho.

Sechaba Consultants 2000. *Poverty and Livelihoods in Lesotho 1999: More than a Mapping Exercise.* Lesotho.

Spiegel, A.D. 1979. *Migrant Labour Remittances, the Developmental Cycle and Rural Differentiation in a Lesotho Community.* M.A. Thesis, University of Cape Town.

Spiegel, A.D. 1980. "Rural Differentiation and the Diffusion of Migrant Labour Remittances in Lesotho" in Philip Mayer (ed.), *Black Villagers in an Industrial Society.* Oxford University Press.

Turner, S. 1978. *Sesotho Farming: The Conditions and Prosperity of Agriculture in the Lowlands and Foothills of Lesotho.* Ph.D. Dissertation, School of Oriental and African Studies (SOAS), London.

Turner, S. 2001. *Livelihoods in Lesotho.* CARE Lesotho.

Wallman, S. 1969. *Take Out Hunger: Two Case Studies of Rural Development in Basutholand.* London: The Athlone Press, London School of Economics Monographs on Social Anthropology No. 39, London.

Warren, K. and S. Borque 1991. "Women, Technology, and International Development Ideologies: Analyzing Feminist Voices" in di Leonardo, M. (ed.) *Gender at the Crossroads of Knowledge: Feminist Anthropology in the Post-modern Era.* Berkeley.

Westermann, G. 1999. *Survey on Migrant Workers' Retrenchment.* Irish Consulate, Lesotho.

Social Resilience in African Dryland Livelihoods: Deriving Lessons for Policy

Michael Mortimore[1]

Three narratives

There are three narratives linking rural poverty, natural resources and social change in Africa. The first reflects a pessimistic, or neo-Malthusian ideology; the second a cautious anti-Malthusian (or 'Boserupian') optimism; and the third is agnostic, denying the value of grand models.

1. *Failing Africa.* This narrative is driven by macro-scale data and analyses. In terms of food sufficiency, Africa imports increasing amounts of food. Since the 1970s, large quantities of foreign exchange have been used for this, and some countries have become 'food aid-dependent'(Clay and Stokke, 2000; Somerville, 1986). With a population doubling-time of 30 to 35 years and many agro-ecological constraints, the classic ingredients of a Malthusian diagnosis appear to be present. Recurring famines – at the time of writing, in southern Africa and Ethiopia – remind the world that food insecurity and starvation are nowhere near to being abolished. Environmental indicators appear to show degradation on a huge scale (Middleton and Thomas, 1997; Oldeman and Hakkeling, 1990; UNEP, 1992), as the result of productive activities, with the implication that population growth is unsustainable. Conflict and HIV/AIDS threaten to destroy the institutional and economic basis of agriculture and to decimate labour and skills.

   While some regions of the world are reported to be 'on target' towards the Millenium Development Goal (MDG) of reducing the proportion of their population who are living in 'dollar poverty' by a half by 2015, Africa is getting worse (White and Killick, 2001).

2. *Adapting Africa.* This narrative is driven primarily by empirical and local studies. It documents the rapid pace of change to which African communities must adapt, the force of external drivers, and the often unequal terms under which Africans must make the necessary adjustments. In response to these, there is evidence of resilience, enterprise and continuity. Several authors have advanced 'Boserupian' hypotheses of agricultural intensification driven by in-

---

1. Mary Tiffen and other colleagues in Africa and the UK made valuable contributions to the ideas expressed in this article, which is based on work mainly funded by the UK Department for International Development.

creasing rural population densities (Boserup, 1965; Tiffen and Mortimore, 1994). In this view, hybrid knowledge, including technological transfers from outside and indigenous knowledge, which often require additional inputs of labour, drives productivity on small farms. An influential case is that of Machakos District, Kenya, where rural population densities reflected a nearly six-fold increase in population from 1930 to 1990. New or adapted technologies, together with growing urban and export markets, migration to new lands, income diversification, education, investments in land (acquisition, conservation and productivity) and flexible social organisations and institutions, produced a nearly four-fold increase in agricultural productivity per head, and eleven-fold per hectare (Tiffen et al., 1994). The management of natural resources had meanwhile become more, not less, sustainable.

A number of other cases have been documented where smallholders have intensified primary production, integrated crops with livestock, and sustained output on a decadal time-scale while controlling or reducing degradation (Mazzucato et al., 2002; Turner et al., 1993). A model of the transition from extensive to intensive land use has been advanced (Mortimore, 1998).

3. *Complex Africa.* Social anthropologists, among others, have tended to resist model-based approaches. It can be argued, first, that they imply a degree of determinism that gives insufficient scope for observed adaptation or individuality. Secondly, the social determinants of behaviour should not be ignored in privileging economic drivers. Development interventions have often been criticised for focusing on economic or technical targets to the exclusion of structural and behavioural dimensions which may eventually frustrate the uptake of new technologies. Not only the meaning of 'development', but also its progression through time should be placed in its social context. Thirdly, a general model appears to deny the specifics of time and place, as well as the huge diversity of individual or community trajectories of change (Brookfield, 2001; Scoones, 2002).

It is a paradox that, notwithstanding the popularity of the *failing Africa* narrative, most especially with policy-makers, poor rural Africans in many areas continue to demonstrate a capacity to produce more food, to supply urban labour, to educate themselves, to endure oppression and deprivation, and to reconstruct broken economic or social systems. It is by trying to understand how poor people manage their livelihoods and their natural resources in conditions of great difficulty that science can learn to make itself more useful to them, rather than by promoting transformations based on imported models. I justify my focus on the drylands[1]

---

1. My own experience has been largely confined to drylands in West Africa and Kenya (Mortimore, 1998).

on the grounds that this is where nature's greatest constraints (low agro-ecological productivity and high rainfall variability) must be managed.[1]

I shall proceed by briefly reviewing some long-term data series which suggest that the *Failing Africa* narrative may be wide of the mark. I then want to pursue the nature of the resource – here termed *social resilience* – that has enabled rural Africans to sustain themselves against outsiders' expectations, asking how this links in with theories about society and the environment, and suggesting how a better understanding of it can contribute to policy.

Shocks

Besides living with natural resource endowments that offer, on average, low productivity potentials, rural dryland people have to manage the impact of unpredictable shocks from a wider range of sources of greater potential severity than inhabitants of the humid tropics and temperate marginal climate zones. These sources are summarised in Table 1. Risk is not exclusive to drylands, but when overlaid by extreme poverty and (as often) by geographical inaccessibility, it can be intensified by a reduced capacity for self-insurance through financial, accumulative, or social claim strategies. Damage to livelihoods may also be accentuated on account of the necessary compression of agricultural activity within a short growing season.

Table 1: Sources of risk

Climatic	Ecological	Economic	The state	Accident
Intra-seasonal drought	Grasshoppers, locusts, birds	Exchange rate over-valuation	Changes in taxation policy	Mortality, morbidity
Annual drought	Rodents, baboons	Input price, supply constraints	Changes in duties or subsidies	Divorce, disputes, courts
Storm, flood	Livestock disease	Fuel and general inflation	Non-consultative legislation	Fire
	Crop viruses	Market failures	Land appropriation	Civil disorder, police
Long-term rainfall decline	Erosion, degradation	Falling export demand	Withdrawal of services	Cash flow (for timely inputs)

The major source of risk in dryland environments is inter-year and intra-seasonal variability in rainfall, especially in a context of long-term decline as experienced in the Sahel from the 1960s to the 1980s, which exceeded in magnitude any changes predicted in climate change scenarios (Hulme et al., 2001). A decline in average rainfall meant an increasing frequency of negative departures from the mean, and of agricultural drought in a region such as eastern Niger and northern Nigeria (Hess et al., 1995; Mortimore, 2000). Uncertainty surrounds the recov-

---

1. The drylands are defined as the arid, semi-arid and dry sub-humid zones (UNEP, 1992). However, some authorities believe that drylands possess compensating advantages in a seasonal rhythm that allows cultivated soils a rest period, reduces the risk of leaching and acidification, and permits the keeping of livestock throughout the year by preventing trypanosomiasis.

ery of Sahelian rainfall during the 1990s. It should be noted that Sahelian patterns have not been observed in eastern or southern Africa.

Negative long-term trends, whether ecological or economic, increase poor peoples' vulnerability to shocks. Much has been done, both conceptually and methodologically, to define and map vulnerability (Bohle et al., 1991; Downing et al., 1989). Such work quite properly focuses attention on deprivation and on the constraints acting on livelihood development. Much work has also been done on adaptive livelihood strategies, often called 'coping strategies' (Corbett, 1988; Davies, 1996).[1] However, the point where vulnerability and adaptive capacity meet is ill-defined and poorly understood, though its strategic importance is obvious.

Adaptation in progress

It is perhaps unfashionable to challenge a consensual pessimism about African economic performance, agricultural productivity and natural resource management, which is supported by reports of interviews with farmers or herdsmen, macro-economic analysis, theoretical interpretations of economic history, specific country cases, and a host of anecdotes popularised in the press (Wiggins, 2000). But analysis of longer term trends, which is possible now that many data series are forty years old or more, adds complexity to these simplistic characterisations. In some cases, recently documented, a very different picture of change emerges (Gichuki et al., 2000). Aggregated data for large areas (districts, departments, provinces, states) raise questions about the processes of adaptation which must be addressed at the local level. I shall confine this discussion to the Kano-Maradi region of Nigeria and Niger, beginning with adaptation at a micro-scale in the Kano Close-Settled Zone, and proceeding to selected data series at higher scales.[2]

The Kano Close-Settled Zone, Nigeria

The city of Kano, with a population of about 1.5 million, sits at the centre of a densely populated and closely farmed region where 6–8 million rural people raise crops and livestock. This historic *Kano Close-Settled Zone* (KCSZ) forms the cen-

---

1. I prefer not to use this term since, as normally used, it is taken as a typological basis for particular strategies whose function may change through time or vary among individuals and households. For different persons or times, mat-making (for example) may be accumulative in intent or driven by despair.

2. Studies of long-term change were carried out by Drylands Research in collaboration with scientists in four countries (in whose co-ordination I have been privileged to work with Mary Tiffen and John Nelson) (Faye et al., 2001; Mortimore et al., 2001). The extensive findings of this project, including detailed analyses of the policy environment and of village- and farm-level adaptations, are reported in *Drylands Research Working Papers* (www.drylandsresearch.org./uk). Micro-scale studies were carried out in Nigeria in collaboration with J Afolabi Falola, Bill Adams and Frances Harris.

tre of a much larger region that Kano City dominates commercially, culturally and formerly politically, extending over central northern Nigeria and southern Niger (including Maradi Department). With an average annual rainfall ranging from 800 mm in the extreme south to 450 mm in the north, and being substantially covered by medium-textured, sandy desert-edge soils, the KCSZ has been suffering a decline in average rainfall and increased frequency of agricultural drought since the 1960s. Long-term demographic growth has raised on-farm population densities to over 220 persons/km^2 in some local government areas, and more than 80% of the surface soils have been under annual cultivation since 1957 or earlier (Mustapha and Meagher, 2000). Kano Hausa farmers are famous throughout Nigeria for their intensive and market-oriented agriculture and commercial abilities.

Government policy promoted groundnut and cotton production for export until the 1960s, but fell into a vacuum when rosette disease, drought and poor prices undermined exports after 1975. Cotton was diverted to domestic mills, and groundnuts (as production slowly recovered with new varieties) to a domestic market for nuts and oil, whose rapid growth was fuelled by the dispersal of oil revenues through the economy. A spontaneous switch to growing cereals for urban markets responded to improving real prices. A coherent agricultural policy was introduced in 1986, which imposed restrictions on food imports and, at least for a while, maintained subsidies on fertilisers (Mustapha and Meagher, 2000).[1] Meanwhile, livestock holdings, meat and milk production and marketing increased in the long term.

Such was the regional context in which smallholder families in the KCSZ adapted their livelihoods to two underlying challenges: a need to maintain or enhance the productivity of the natural resource base, and a need to find alternative income streams to those provided by agriculture in order to meet the reproductive and developmental needs of a growing population. The first of these needs provoked a response that is best characterised in terms of a rubric of *intensification*, the second in terms of *diversification*.

In relation to the first, dryland farmers attempted to optimise their use of the scarce factors: first erratic rainfall, secondly a diminishing supply of farmland per capita, thirdly capital including livestock, and lastly (even under conditions of population growth) family labour. Given their poverty, labour is the input over whose supply farmers appear to exercise the greatest degree of control, but in reality this is constrained by rising opportunity costs, increasing off-farm income diversification, migration and fission in the extended family. Nevertheless, farmers attempt to allocate labour optimally in a best fit between spasmodic and unpredictable rainfall events and the developmental cycles of chosen crop varieties

---

1. The re-orientation of Nigeria's structural adjustment policy towards a liberalisation of import controls and reduction of farm subsidies may have been influential in partially reducing momentum in the 1990s.

(Figure 1). 'It is not just the *stock* of labour which matters but the *flow*, as the timing of inputs can significantly alter yields' (Iliya and Swindell, 1997).

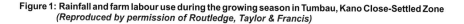

Figure 1: Rainfall and farm labour use during the growing season in Tumbau, Kano Close-Settled Zone
(Reproduced by permission of Routledge, Taylor & Francis)

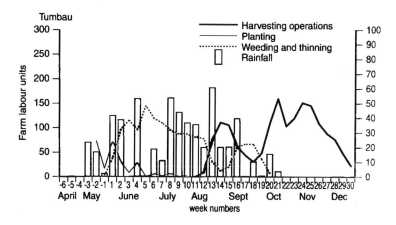

To maximise yields, dense intercropping, careful sequencing of operations from manuring and planting through multiple weedings to harvesting, carting and storage – given the urgency imposed by a short growing season – can come up against a shortage of labour, even where the ratio of labour to land is high. All except the poorest own some animals, yet there are virtually no rangelands remaining in the densely farmed landscape. Animals provide not only invested capital but also manure, draft energy, saleable products and breeding potential. In order to maximise these benefits, substantial amounts of labour must be allocated to animal management (more, proportionately, than in extensive systems, where common rangeland is available; see Figure 2). There are trade-offs between animal and crop management; for labour is needed for many operations. Some of these operations assume the character of micro-investments to maintain or increase the productivity of every hectare (Table 2). Consequently, labour use per hectare reaches much higher levels in an intensive than in an extensive system. The question arises whether farm intensification, which is analysed in greater detail elsewhere (Harris, 1996; Harris, 1998), has gone as far as it can go in the KCSZ, and whether only worsening poverty, resource degradation and a flight from the land can ensue. It is apt to point out that similar sentiments were expressed 37 years ago (Trevallion, 1965).

Figure 2: Farm and livestock labour inputs in Tumbau, Kano Close-Settled Zone

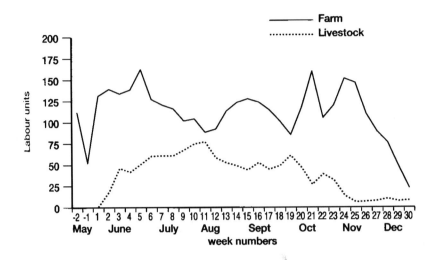

The KCSZ has a long historical record of choosing an alternative path – that of income *diversification* through craft specialisation, trade and short-term migration. Given the few data available, it is impossible to say in quantified terms whether, at the regional level, households depend more than before on such incomes; but this seems likely. Diversification may be conceived in steps of increasing detachment from crop production (Figure 3). However, strong circularities bind these steps back to the natural resource base. Investments, knowledge and networks may be necessary before embarking on diversification. Every rural household participates in some form of off-farm activity, and almost every adult, female or male. Permanent out-migration – the ending of a natural resource base to livelihoods – is suggested by the fact that long-term population growth tended to fall behind the rates of natural increase found elsewhere. It has been suggested that up to a half of natural increase may be accounted for in this way (Hill, 1977).

Figure 3: Stepwise livelihood diversification in a Sahelian environment
(Reproduced by permission of Routledge, Taylor & Francis)

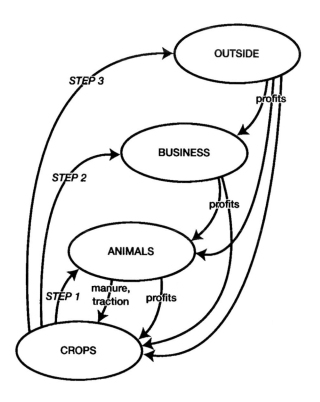

Table 2: Some implications of intensification

Investments	Cropping operations	Livestock operations
Land clearance	Seed selection and storage	Supervising grazing animals
Livestock fencing	Complex planting patterns	Maintaining corrals
Soil amelioration	Thinning, fertilising by stand	Cut-and-carry: browse, weeds, field borders
Tree planting and protection	Multiple weedings, ridging	Residue collection, cartage, storage, security; purchase of fodder, supplements
Terracing, stone lines, drains, ridging	Sequential harvesting rounds, cutting, laying stalks, drying, bundling	Water fetching, storage, well-digging
Storage structures, pens, poultry houses	Carting, storage	Milking, marketing
Small livestock (ruminants, birds, fish, etc.)	Threshing	Health and breeding

Kano City food markets, Nigeria

The huge demand for food commodities in urban Kano is not met primarily, or even to a major extent, from the KCSZ (Ariyo et al., 2001). Nevertheless, the city markets set the conditions within which rural producers must operate, most of them selling as well as buying food commodities at different times of the year. Moreover the city acts as a regional entrepôt, with movements of grains, legumes, roots and livestock products, as well as high value commodities such as kola nuts, following long-established patterns between north and south.

Inflation, the everyday experience of Nigerian consumers, disguised a steady downward trend in real food prices in Kano markets after 1973, the peak that was associated with the great Sahel Drought (Figure 4). The persistence of such a trend over three decades is noteworthy. Real livestock prices are not available for such a long period, but trends in the 1990s were also downward (Figure 5). Yet since 1960 the city's population has grown from about 250,000 by a factor of six or more. There have been repeated changes in nominal prices, input subsidy policy, import protection and marketing structures (Mustapha and Meagher, 2000), though food commodities have, for the most part, remained free of state intervention. Other costs, in particular fuel, have fluctuated wildly. There have been several major civil disorders. The downward trends are not explicable simply in terms of food imports, as they were maintained when import restrictions were in place, and the degree of import substitution for staple foods is quite limited.

Figure 4: Real millet prices in Kano markets, 1960–1997 (naira/tonne; base changed in 1969–70)

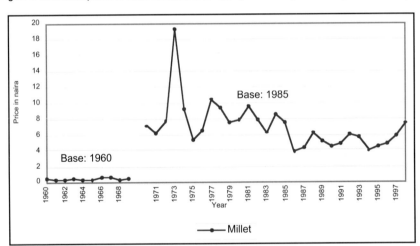

Figure 5: Index of real cattle prices in Kano markets, 1990–1998 (average per animal)

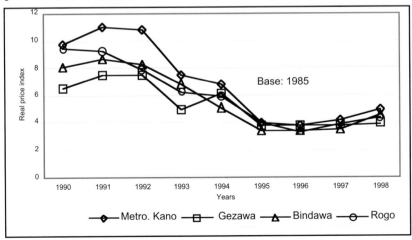

Although no systematic quantification of food sources was possible in the study (Ariyo et al., 2001), the evidence does not suggest that the source areas for Kano's grain and meat markets have undergone any major changes since a benchmark study in 1966–67 (Gilbert, 1969). Grain still comes mainly from the north-central part of the country and meat from the north and from neighbouring Niger, while root crops are imported from further south. Yet in all of these areas, the rural populations, and thus their subsistence requirements, have doubled, while average rainfall in the northern part of the hinterland declined by a quarter or a third from the 1960s to the 1980s.

Such a performance in the longer term is not only a testimony to the functional performance of the market system: it also points to significant adaptability in the productive sector. It is not consistent with expectations of increasing food insecurity, based on widely held perceptions of unsustainable natural resource management (under 'population pressure'). It is perhaps surprising that, given a general lack of street credibility (with long repeated allegations of hoarding, profiteering, inefficient infrastructure, ineffective regulation, the strangleholds of middlemen and other kinds of market failures), a rapidly growing and frequently stressed market system could deliver declining real prices to consumers over a long period. The same contradiction appears from long-term data series on the performance of the unjustly maligned Nigerian agricultural sector as a whole (Mortimore, 2003).

Maradi Département, Niger

This region, always a part of Hausaland (though remaining independent of the Sokoto Caliphate which overran the remaining emirates after 1803), is increasingly becoming inter-dependent with the Kano markets and the Nigerian economy (Mortimore et al., 2001). Although its southern *arrondissements* receive an average annual rainfall similar to that of northern Kano (ca. 400 mm), the department becomes increasingly arid towards the north, the official limit of rain-fed cultivation being passed at the 250 mm isohyet. To the north is the *zone pastorale*. The implications of long-term decline (from the 1960s to the 1980s) are correspondingly serious, and amplified by coarse, sandy, desert-edge soils of low natural fertility. Population densities decline along the same gradient, from >50 to <20 persons/km^2. Some settlements were established by the mid-nineteenth century at 50–60 km north of Maradi, but northern Maradi was mostly populated in a great rush of land-hungry migrants after the settlement of French colonial rule, extending up to the 'saturation' of the land frontier in the 1980s. To the south of the *zone pastorale*, cultivation accounted for 59% of the surface in 1975 and 73% by 1996 (Mahamane, 2001). The government's revision of land tenure arrangements to facilitate private appropriation *(Code Rurale)* created fresh enthusiasm to take land into cultivation, leaving very little residual pasture or woodland. According to a thorough analysis of natural resource management carried out in

1978–85, demographic and market pressures were responsible for widespread degradation of the soils and natural vegetation; moreover, 'commoditisation' seemed to be threatening the economic and social sustainability of the rural systems themselves (Grégoire and Raynaut, 1980; Raynaut, 1975; Raynaut et al., 1988). During the past forty years, agricultural policy has shifted through phases of export promotion or 'modernisation' (1960–1974), food 'self-sufficiency' financed with uranium revenues (1974–1984), and structural adjustment (from 1985: Hamadou, 2000).

Notwithstanding these and other prognoses of system failure, Maradi Département managed to maintain per capita output of cereals at levels well above estimated nutritional requirements in most years from 1964 to 1998, assuming that projected population data are correct (Figure 6).[1] A part of this requirement was supplied by extending the area planted from 1987 to 1995 (Figure 7), but before and after those years, the changes in area were not substantial enough to explain the achievement. The only alternative explanation is agricultural intensification, surprising though this may seem, where risk is high, yields low (often <100 kg/ha), and costs to market often high. A dis-aggregation of the northern (drier) and southern (wetter) *arrondissements* (Figure 8) shows that in the south, where land is scarcer, population densities higher and markets nearer, a positive yield trend may be emerging, whereas in the north, the extensive phase has not yet ended. In the south, there is more intensive interaction with Nigerian cross-border markets: livestock, human labour and tiger nuts are exported, while millet has been traded either way, depending on exchange rates and harvests. Increasingly, off-farm incomes have been sought in the more buoyant, urbanised economy of Nigeria. Such incomes are not spent entirely on consumption, as used to be assumed, but find their way into agricultural investments, as they do in north-west Nigeria (Iliya and Swindell, 1997). Once again, we cannot quantify this side of the equation. But with regard to natural resource management, there are suggestive indicators that a transition is occurring from an extensive, 'soil-mining' mode of production to an intensifying, more sustainable one, in association with a diversification of livelihoods. The findings suggested here are supported by local evidence of significant practices in land tenure, tree management, soil fertility management, cropping and agronomy at the village and farm scales.

---

1. The first census was in 1977, followed by another in 1988. Population projections forwards as well as backwards from these are provisional in nature.

Figure 6: Cereal (mainly millet) production in Maradi Department, 1964–1998 (kg/cap)

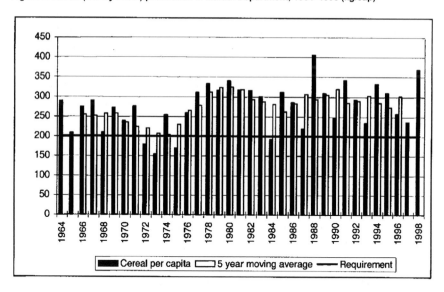

Figure 7: Areas planted to main crops in Maradi Department, 1979–1998

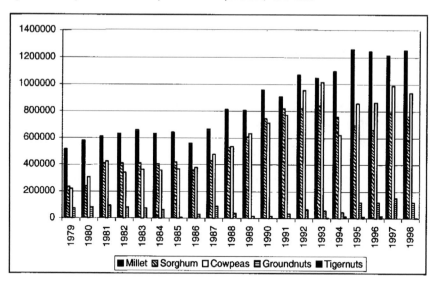

Figure 8: Yield trends in southern (Madarounfa) and northern (Dakoro) *arrondissements,*
Maradi, 1979–1998

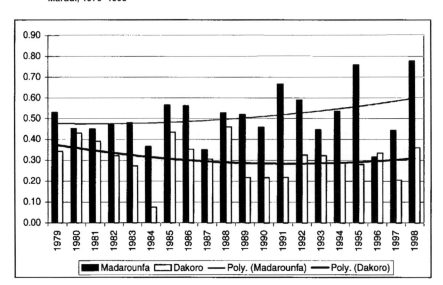

Social Resilience

The foregoing analysis may be brief, selective and superficial, but I believe that
these data are suggestive of new *narratives of achievement* that challenge the gen-
eralities that are often served up about Africa, are more specific as to time and
place (Scoones, 2001), and more valuable as pointers to policy than hypotheses
of system failure (Scoones and Toulmin, 1999). This is not to deny the possibility
that, in certain livelihood systems, indicators may suggest long-term decline rather than achievement (Davies, 1996).

Sahelian communities have become less mobile since land frontiers closed,
from twenty to forty years ago, as in Maradi, to more than a hundred years ago,
as in the KCSZ. The persistence of these communities is more remarkable in the
light of several decades of declining rainfall (though that may now have stopped),
rapid demographic growth, including increasing rural population densities and a
delayed transformation to declining agricultural labour forces, some degradation
of natural resources, and economic (if not also political) marginalisation. In a policy context where effective poverty-reduction strategies seem to be as elusive as
ever, it is worth asking whether or not this persistence, rather than being regarded
as an anomaly, represents a developmental outcome. Can we move beyond the
truism, 'The chief resource of the Sahel is its people' (Giri, 1988), to analyse the
nature and potential of social resilience?

An Empirical Approach

As already indicated, the persistence of dryland communities cannot be attributed to natural resource endowments.[1] Since these environments have not so far responded to high-input, high-yielding technological packages, they cannot in any general sense be attributed to a 'green revolution'. However, the role of technological change is ambiguous. Early maturing cowpeas in dry areas and hybrid maize in sub-humid areas have made a significant impact, but improving on local millet and sorghum varieties has proved difficult. The adoption of inorganic fertilisers has varied in both time and space and remains on average very low, owing to supply constraints. There has been a widespread adoption of animal-drawn ploughing and carting, a labour-saving technology that in some places has benefited from energetic promotion (e.g., Maradi) and in others has grown more spontaneously for fifty years or more (e.g., Kano). The risk attached to investment in new technologies is compounded by the environmental variability of drylands and by household poverty. Consequently, the role of productivity increases in agriculture is also ambiguous. Our data show examples of positive trends, but these were not found everywhere, nor at all times. A capacity is demonstrated, but an ambivalent performance indicates quite clearly that demand rather than supply factors tend to determine outcomes.

Basing the following discussion on empirical findings in the northern Nigerian Sahel (Mortimore and Adams, 1999), four analytical layers of social resilience can be hypothesised. In order of increasing depth, these are: knowledge, flexibility, adaptability, and values.

Knowledge Systems

Knowledge appears as an 'asset' under the terms of the 'sustainable livelihoods' literature (located in the last two of the 'five capitals': natural, physical, financial, social and human). However an accounting analogy does less than justice to the knowledge systems of dryland peoples. First, they comprise qualitatively different types of knowledge; indigenous, introduced, and hybrid (based on experimentation). Secondly, they are fluid and dynamic, constantly changing through imports, exports, neglect or intensification in response to the opportunities to use them. Thirdly, they are not so much a 'bank' as a cycle, analogous to soil nutrients, concentrated in some places (people), scarce in others, exploited in certain circumstances of age, sex, crisis or opportunity, and abandoned or fallowed in others – perhaps eventually eroded away from the 'knowledge catchment', perhaps awaiting rediscovery. Fourthly, although they evolved historically within

---

1. Few Sahelians have direct access to irrigated agriculture, except in the immediate vicinity of major rivers. These privileged areas cannot 'carry' the large populations living from rain-fed cultivation. Irrigation, contrary to popular belief, is also prone to risk and has been abandoned, for example, in most of the South Chad Irrigation Project in Nigeria, owing to dessication in the lake basin.

'dwelt-in' human ecosystems (Davidson-Hunt and Berkes, 2003), they expand rapidly in response to new opportunities outside the system, in particular, under contemporary conditions of economic integration and globalisation. For example, bi-local Nigerian livelihoods cutting across agro-ecological boundaries, rural–urban sectors, and distances of up to 1200 km received a boost during the historical conjunction of food scarcity and oil boom in 1975–85 (Mortimore, 1982; Mortimore, 1989). For communities living in drought-prone areas of northern Nigeria, critical knowledge 'assets' include, for example:

— *Using 'famine foods' derived from natural or domesticated biodiversity* for use in times of scarcity, drawing on indigenous knowledge (often women's), rights of access to natural resources, and family labour.
— *Using locally available cultivars, soil properties, moisture management techniques and evolved agronomic experience* to turn natural productivity to economic advantage on small farms.
— *Using information, support networks, acquired skills and rights of access to resources outside the local ecosystem,* by means of association, migration and 'nimbleness' in response to scarcity or opportunity, in a 'pulsating' and unbounded 'resource space'.

It is generally agreed that having (knowing) a diversity of options is the best insurance against risk, which in drylands frequently affects both income and food security. A diversity of options in the use of natural, economic, technological or social resources is a *desideratum* for households.

Flexibility

To pursue social resilience further, it is necessary to go beyond an 'asset' framework. Assets do not necessarily lead to successful strategies – something more is required. Given the variable behaviour of dryland ecosystems in terms of rainfall, soil moisture regimes, bioproductivity, plant communities and their use implications, household livelihoods depend on flexibility in the short-term (daily, weekly) allocation of resources, in particular labour. For example, flexibility is demanded by the need to deal with unpredictable events like a dry period during the rainy season (which may require replanting of crops, or decisions about alternative incomes or food), or pest attack, events which, turning up unannounced, call for rapid responses. Flexibility (Figures 1–3) is also needed to respond to unpredictable economic events, personal or health setbacks, or mortality (a recurring hazard in the growing season).

Flexibility is more than mere choice, though the range of choice determines its limits. It is more than economic opportunism, as social and psychological variables are involved. The opportunity costs of agricultural labour ensure that a flexible response in farming must be balanced against other demands. A normative strategy in the Sahel, for example, is the accumulation of food surpluses by producing more than anticipated requirements in the coming year, if possible several times more, thus smoothing consumption through time by amplifying variability in output between good and bad years. (Grain storage for several years is technically unproblematic in drylands.) But output maximisation may not be a pragmatic objective in some circumstances. And, of course, flexibility in the system does not necessarily imply equal flexibility in all households. Life trajectories in the villages show that social differentiation may be initiated by differential performance with regard to this variable.

Adaptability[1]

Farmers and other resource users in the Sahel do not simply respond to exogenous and endogenous change reactively within each growing (or dry) season. Their decisions, when considered in sequence, are cumulative and purposive, and therefore have a longer-term significance which reflects their understanding of longer-term and larger-scale changes. They are both rational and pathway-dependent – that is, each decision in a chain is influenced by both goals and previous decisions.

Adaptation in the household's system of managing its resources from year to year can transform its production systems (or its mix of livelihood-generating activities) in response to changing conditions. Although qualitative rather than quantitative in nature, adaptation measures 'performance' in the variable setting of the African drylands. Given the importance of farming and the shortness of the farming season, each season's outcome determines the starting point for the next year's decision chain. Adaptation thus describes the pathway or trajectory described by an individual or household livelihood. Over a series of years, a highly adaptive household must become stronger and a maladaptive one weaker (Figure 9).

Figure 9: Model of flexibility and adaptation (Mortimore and Adams, 1999)

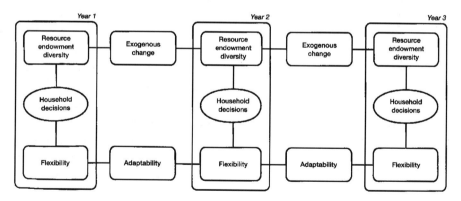

---

1. Davies uses a different characterisation of adaptation: 'whereas coping is a characteristic of structurally secure livelihood systems, vulnerable ones are characterised by adaptation', though she admits that 'one person's coping strategy may be another's adaptive strategy' (Davies, 1996: 58–9). I prefer to consider adaptation as a purposive, long- or medium-term change, and not to use the term 'coping' at all, as I do not consider it practicable to distinguish between strategies in terms of compulsion or choice, 'push' or 'pull'.

Adaptation is quite likely to be episodic, as circumstances demand certain kinds of action (such as during drought). It may be clustered in space, as the decisions taken within households differ from one place (such as a village) to another because of micro-environmental patterns. It may be clustered socially, reflecting income, ethnic or religious differences. But dynamism is its essence, and goals are continuously being revised in the light of current conditions. Adaptability has always been a feature of successful livelihood strategies in the Sahel, if not everywhere in the drylands, but in the late twentieth century it acquired a heightened importance and involved a wider range of activities as livelihoods were influenced by environmental, political, economic and social change. For example:

— *Exploiting growing internal food markets* in place of stagnant global markets for agricultural exports.
— *Exploring new employment opportunities* in growing urban areas, developing new networks, investing in urban *pieds à terres,* and eventually in property.

Values

Cultural or personal values are easily ignored in debates on economic development, yet (western) values provide the basis of new 'rights-based' approaches to poverty reduction and intergovernmental agreements about the Millenium Development Goals. Technicians tend to be even more dismissive of culture, which can be seen as a barrier to the uptake of new technologies. But market values have by no means completely supplanted values transmitted through cultural agency, and response to new opportunities is screened by such values, even if they are only residual, or often discounted in actual decisions. Flexible adaptation to livelihood opportunities, no less than the adoption of some new practice introduced by extensionists, could be constrained by a slow-moving dynamic or, on the other hand, facilitated by rapid change. Treating culture as a 'black box' is no longer adequate, and neither is an assumption that development involves a progressive absorption of market values and an elimination of everything else, as recursive militant Islamicism makes plain.

These are generalisations. On a much more specific level, two examples from the literature on northern Nigeria illustrate how swings in certain values may be interpreted in opposite ways by outsiders. The first of these is *monetisation,* the second *individualisation.* At a risk of over-simplification, these offer lessons as follows:

— *Monetisation: adaptation or a new bondage?* An influential critique of the penetration of markets into the fabric of rural society in West African export crop-producing areas during and after the booms of the 1960s saw 'monetisation' in terms of increasingly vulnerable livelihoods and greater risk to the conservation of natural resources (Copans, 1975; Franke and Chasin, 1980; Raynaut, 1976; Raynaut, 1977). When the Sahel drought struck northern Nigeria in 1972–74, a supposed, if sometimes romanticised precolonial 'moral economy', was thought to have disintegrated under the force of monetary pressures (Watts, 1983). Indeed, in Kano State in northern Nigeria, many informants questioned after the Sahel drought of 1972–74 expressed the view that 'the rich no longer help us as they did before', that is, before two or three decades of groundnut exporting had changed everything (Mortimore, 1989). Meanwhile, an inability to produce enough food had thrown rural people into an increasing dependency on the markets.

On the other hand, an upbeat view of the commercial acumen exhibited by ordinary farmers from the very inception of the Nigerian groundnut boom in 1911–12, and their energy in finding a 'vent for surplus', seemed to suggest a certain compatibility between the commercialised values of the Hausa, in particular, and the new global capitalism (Hogendorn, 1978). In Senegal, groundnut production for export, established even earlier by the French, was extended into new areas, especially during the 1940s and 1950s, by pioneering *daara* settlements under the authoritarian leadership of *marabouts* belonging to the Mouride brotherhood, an Islamic commercial system which expanded its influence into nearly every corner of the Senegalese economy (Cruise O'Brien, 1971). Such examples raise interesting questions about rapid adaptation in livelihood systems, not least: do cultural values impede or facilitate it, are new institutional formations necessary, and can economically beneficial outcomes be consistent with sustainable natural resource management?

— *Individualisation:* Another literature has described and analysed the individuation that followed in the wake of the monetary gains to be made from market participation. In the Hausa villages of northern Nigeria, it was hypothesised that such forces were undermining the institution of *gandu,* which in its main form is an extended family-based production unit in which the male head controls the land, inputs and outputs of the greater part of the farm, his sons (who, even if married and with children, continue to live with him) only staking a claim to relatively small plots given to them by their father through the subdivision of the main holding or purchase from outside. Market production was concentrated on these plots, as they could retain their profits. Even after a father's death, junior brothers might agree to retain unified management under a senior brother. In the 1960s, however, field evidence was interpreted to suggest a decline in the *gandu,* with sons preferring to break away from their fathers' control, and fathers being unable to secure plots for them in an increasingly tight land market (Buntjer, 1970; Goddard, 1973; Goddard et al., 1975). A contrary view argued that land scarcity prolonged sons' dependence on their fathers in densely populated areas, where big households might still be found (Hill, 1977: 180–99). Thirty years later the institution was by no means dead in the Kano area, where both economies of scale on collaborative ventures, and opportunities for specialisation in multi-dimensional household livelihoods, can be reaped from large, co-residential family 'corporations' (Mortimore and Adams, 1999:170–2). Tensions between the moral obligation to assist one's father and a desire for greater autonomy are not confined to this farming system. A trend, if any, needs to be distinguished from a developmental cycle, in which young men, once freed from their father's domination, set about establishing similar structures in the next generation.

West African dryland cultures value both autonomy and resilience. Such values may be rooted in certain fundamentals: such as the presence almost everywhere (until recently) of an open land frontier in a mainly rural world: an absence (for the most part) of inter-generational social stratification: and long traditions of geographical mobility, both migration to new living sites and circulation in the short term.

The sources of social resilience are found at three levels: in individual actions, through the family, and in community institutions. Actions that draw on human capital (knowledge, skills, health) under individual control, including such things as opportunistic behaviour, competition for power or profit, contract relations and self-development, are often assumed to be in the ascendent at the expense of family and community, being driven, of course, by the all-pervasive market. But families, who have been characterised as 'networks of implicit contracts' (Netting, 1993), continue to be the nexus of livelihood decisions made under the terms of continuous negotiation between members. Among these are decisions over the allocation of labour, the use of natural resource entitlements, productive investments and the sharing of benefits from primary production, in relation to natural resource-based livelihoods. Community institutions appear to be less important than the family, but this is or was not so everywhere, nor at all times. Community responsibilities include governing access to knowledge and passing it on, defending or negotiating rights, and regulating relations between winners and losers.

A Theoretical Approach

I have explored social resilience empirically in the context of African drylands. What connections can be made with theories of human-environmental relations? The term *resilience* is used in both ecological and interdisciplinary contexts to describe the ability of an unstable system to adapt to shocks or trends, if necessary by changes in population or specific composition, thus ensuring its continuity (Davidson-Hunt and Berkes, 2003; Gunderson et al., 1995; Holling, 1973). The concept of resilience is thus disequilibrial – that is, the persistence of an ecosystem is assured through adaptive changes in species composition or populations rather than by a return to equilibrium. Oscillations about a mean are, on the contrary, characterised as 'stability' (Blaikie and Brookfield, 1987; Mortimore, 1989). The environmental sciences long worked with equilibrial models, in particular with regard to understanding (and correcting) human impacts considered to be adverse. Disequilibrial models are now seen to have greater explanatory and normative value, for example on rangelands under highly variable rainfall, where a rational response is opportunistic stocking (Behnke et al., 1993). By extension, it has been proposed that farmers too must work in an opportunistic framework in African drylands (Mortimore, 1998).

Transferring the concept to social systems implies that an unstable but resilient system responds to external trends or shocks by adaptive change in certain parameters which may be permanent or temporarily irreversible. Social resilience may be characterised as the intelligence whereby matches are made between the co-evolving human and environmental systems, of which there are several models (Drylands Research, 2001; Robbins et al., 2002). Of all the myriad changes afoot in drylands, such things as regression from intensive to extensive farming, substitution of new crop varieties, transformation of natural woodland to permanent fields, replacement of rangeland grazing by residue feeding ('zero grazing'), change from rain-fed to irrigated farming, income diversification from agriculture, migration, urbanisation or the transformation of women's roles, education and employment need not be categorised as intrinsically positive or negative. To do so is to accept an equilibrial view, which, given the force of demographic and economic trends, is untenable in the long run.

With the broadening of economic horizons – which has been the experience of almost every 'dwelt-in' human ecosystem in Africa for a century or more – and the globalisation, not only of primary export markets but of labour and capital markets too, the scope of social resilience has extended rapidly in response to new sources of instability. Change may not always be popular, but whimsical global markets may demand it. In the 'post-Washington consensus' view, imperfections are recognised in the ways in which markets work, especially in relation to poor people (World Bank, 2003). Development theory and practice continue to stress what should be done to change things. However, it is easy to neglect what people do to adapt their own livelihood systems.

These models of change, which are characterised by continuous adaptation, go a long way 'beyond Malthus'. The determinism of Malthusianism stemmed from the rigidities of the supposed 'laws' on which it was based. Remaining within a framework of economic logic, alternatives are available which reflect different drivers – markets and technological change – as well as demographic growth (Boserup, 1990; Tiffen and Mortimore, 1994). These models describe change at aggregated levels of analysis and cannot be taken down to household or individual level: too much diversity and variability create 'noise'. But an adaptive model of change, such as social resilience as I have defined it, has the advantage that it can be used to interpret decisions at lower levels, where diversity and variability are taken into account within the conceptual framework. At higher scales, I suggest that the district-level data series presented in the first part of this paper represent outcomes, explicable in aggregate in terms of a neo-Boserupian transition to more intensive resource use. But at the lower levels they may be understood in terms of social resilience.

So what is scarcity? (See Introduction.) In an adaptive framework, the essence of scarcity is not a Malthusian lack of food, resulting from a failure of production (or of territory) to expand with population, but rather of adaptive options and of the means to use them. Of central importance here are the means to invest. Most debate on this theme, using a traditional definition of investment, assumes that poor people cannot afford to invest. However, public sector investment is a poor substitute, inadequate in scale to benefit more than a minority, and too easily undermined in its priorities and methods. Private investment by poor people, on the other hand, may have been under-estimated. In diversified rural livelihoods, funds can be transferred between sectors and strategies. Thus scarcity may be redefined as *disabled investment*. It might otherwise be described as *livelihood failure*. Livelihoods are not assets as such but outcomes of management – of asset endowments, of income streams, of competing claims, of uncertainty. They describe trajectories through space and time. Flexibility and adaptability are thus the keys to overcoming scarcity. Territory is no longer bounded in spatial terms, but in access – by such things as employment regulations, rent-seeking by providers, tariff barriers or immigration controls. Therefore, rather than achieving central control, enabling people to be flexible and adaptable in constructing and managing their livelihoods should be a cornerstone of policy.

References

Ariyo, J.A et al. 2001. "Long-term Change in Food Provisioning and Marketing in the Kano Region" in *Drylands Research Working Paper 34*. Crewkerne, United Kingdom: Drylands Research.

Behnke, R.H et al. (eds). 1993. *Range Ecology at Disequilibrium: New Models of Natural Variability and Pastoral Adaptation in African Savannas*. London: Overseas Development Institute.

Blaikie, P.M. and H. Brookfield. 1987. *Land Degradation and Society*. London: Methuen

Bohle, H.G. et al.1991. "Famine and Food Security in Africa and Asia". *Bayreuther Geowissenschaftliche Arbeiten* 15. 1991.

Boserup, E. 1965. *The Conditions of Agricultural Growth: The Economics of Agricultural Change under Population Pressure*. London: Allen and Unwin.

Boserup, E. 1990. *Economic and Demographic Relationships in Development*. Baltimore: Johns Hopkins University Press.

Brookfield, H. 2001. *Exploring Agrodiversity*. New York: Columbia University Press.

Buntjer, B. 1970. "Rural Society: The Changing Structure of the Gandu" in M. J. Mortimore (ed.) *Zaria and its Region: A Nigerian Savanna City and its Environs*. Occasional Paper 4: 157–169. Zaria, Nigeria: Department of Geography, Ahmadu Bello University.

Clay, E. and Stokke, O. 2000. *Food Aid and Human Security*. London: Frank Cass.

Copans, J. (ed.). 1975. *Sécheresses et famines du Sahel. 1, Ecologie, dénutrition, assistance. 2, Paysans et nomades*. Paris: Maspero.

Corbett, J.E.M. 1988. "Famine and Household Coping Strategies" in *World Development*, 16/9: 1099–1112.

Cruise O'Brien, C. 1971. *The Mourides of Senegal: The Political and Economic Organisation of an Islamic Brotherhood*. Oxford: Clarendon Press.

Davidson-Hunt, I.J. and F. Berkes. 2003. "Environment and Society through the Lens of Resilience: Toward a Human-in-Ecosystem Perspective" in F. Berkes, et al (eds), *Navigating Social-Ecological Systems: Building Resilience for Complexity and Change*: Cambridge: Cambridge University Press.

Davies, S. 1996. *Adaptable Livelihoods: Coping with Food Insecurity in the Malian Sahel.* London and New York: Macmillan and St Martins Press.

Downing, D.E. et al. 1989. *Coping with Drought in Kenya: National and Local Strategies.* Boulder, Colorado: Westview Press.

Drylands Research. 2001. "Livelihood Transformations in Semi-arid Africa 1960–2000: Proceedings of a Workshop Arranged by the ODI with Drylands Research and the ESRC in the series 'Transformations in African Agriculture". *Drylands Research Working Paper 40.* Crewkerne, United Kingdom.

Faye, A. et al. 2001. "Région de Diourbel: Synthesis". *Drylands Research Working Paper 23e.* Crewkerne, United Kingdom: Drylands Research.

Franke, R.W. and B.H. Chasin. 1980. *Seeds of Famine: Ecological Destruction and the Development Dilemma in the West African Sahel.* Montclair, New Jersey: Allanheld, Osmun.

Gichuki, F.N. et al. 2000. "Makueni District Profile: Synthesis". *Drylands Research Working Paper 11.* Crewkerne, United Kingdom.

Gilbert, E.H. 1969. *Marketing of Staple Foods in Northern Nigeria: A Case Study of Staple Food Marketing Systems Serving Kano City.* PhD Theis, Stanford University.

Giri, J. (ed.). 1988. *The Sahel Facing the Future: Increasing Dependence or Structural Transformation?* Paris: OECD.

Goddard, A.D. 1973. "Changing Family Structures among the Hausa" in *Africa,* 18: 207–18.

Goddard, A.D. et al. 1975. "Social and Economic Implications of Population Growth in Rural Hausaland" in J. C. Caldwell et al.(eds), *Population Growth and Socioeconomic Change in West Africa*, pp. 321–36. New York: Columbia University Press, for the Population Council.

Grégoire, E. and C. Raynaut. 1980. *Présentation générale du Département du Maradi*, Université de Bordeaux II, Bordeaux.

Gunderson, L.H. et al. 1995. *Barriers and Bridges to the Renewal of Ecosystems and Institutions.* New York: Columbia University Press.

Hamadou, S. 2000. "Politiques nationales et investissement dans les petites exploitations à Maradi". *Drylands Research Working Paper 33.* Crewkerne, United Kingdom: Drylands Research.

Harris, F. 1996. "Intensification of Agriculture in Semi-arid Areas: Lessons from the Kano Close-Settled Zone, Nigeria". *Gatekeeper Series 59* London: International Institute for Environment and Development.

Harris, F.M.A. 1998. "Farm-level Assessment of the Nutrient Balance in Northern Nigeria" in *Agriculture, Ecosystems and Environment,* 71: 201–14.

Hess, T.M. et al. 1995. "Rainfall Trends in the North East Arid Zone of Nigeria, 1961–90" in *Agricultural and Forest Meteorology,* 74: 87–97.

Hill, P. 1977. *Population, Prosperity and Poverty: Rural Kano, 1900 and 1970.* Cambridge: Cambridge University Press.

Hogendorn, J.S. 1978. *Nigerian Groundnut Exports: Origins and Early Development.* Zaria: Ahmadu Bello University Press.

Holling, C.S. 1973. "Resilience and Stability of Ecological Systems" in *Annual Review of Ecology and Systematics,* 4: 1–23.

Hulme, M. et al. 2001. "African Climate Change: 1900–2100" in *Climate Research,* 17: 145–68.

Iliya, M.A. and K. Swindell. 1997. "Winners and Losers: Household Fortunes in the Urban Peripheries of Northern Nigeria", in D. F. Bryceson (ed.), *Farewell to Farms: De-agrarianisation and Employment in Africa*, pp. 85–102. Leiden/Aldershot: African Studies Center/Ashgate.

Mahamane, A. 2001. "Usages des terres et évolutions végétales dans le département de Maradi". *Drylands Research Working Paper 27.* Crewkerne, United Kingdom: Drylands Research.

Mazzucato, V. et al. 2002. "Social Networks and the Dynamics of Soil and Water Conservation in the Sahel" in *Gatekeeper Series 101.* London: International Institute for Environment and Development.

Middleton, N. and D.S.G.e. Thomas. 1997. *World Atlas of Desertification*. 2nd edition. London and New York: Arnold.

Mortimore, M. 1982. "Framework for Population Mobility: The Perception of Opportunities in Nigeria" in J. I. Clarke and L. A. Kosinski (eds), *Population Redistribution in Africa*, pp. 50–7. London: Heinemann.

Mortimore, M. 1989. *Adapting to Drought: Farmers, Famines and Desertification in West Africa*. Cambridge: Cambridge University Press.

Mortimore, M. 1998. *Roots in the AfricanDdust: Sustaining the Sub-Saharan Drylands*. Cambridge: Cambridge University Press.

Mortimore, M. 2000. "Profile of Rainfall Change in the Kano-Maradi Region, 1960–2000". *Drylands Research Working Paper 25*. Crewkerne, United Kingdom: Drylands Research.

Mortimore, M. 2003. *The Future of Family Farms in West Africa: What can we Learn from Long-term Data?*, London: Drylands Research for the International Institute of Environment and Development.

Mortimore, M. and Adams, W. 1999. *Working the Sahel: Environment and Society in Northern Nigeria*. London: Routledge.

Mortimore, M. et al. 2001. "Department of Maradi: Synthesis". *Drylands Research Working Paper 39e*. Crewkerne, United Kingdom: Drylands Research.

Mustapha, A.R. and K. Meagher. 2000. "Agrarian Production, Public Policy and the State in Kano Region, 1900–2000". *Drylands Research Working Paper 35*. Crewkerne, United Kingdom: Drylands Research.

Netting, R.M. 1993. *Smallholders, Householders: Farm Families and the Ecology of Intensive, Sustainable Agriculture*. Stanford: Stanford University Press.

Oldeman, R. and R. Hakkeling. 1990. *World Map of the Status of Human-induced Soil Degradation: An Explanatory Note*. Nairobi: United Nations Environment Programme.

Raynaut, C. 1975. "Le cas de la région de Maradi Niger" in J. Copans (ed.) 1975.

Raynaut, C. 1976. "Transformation du système de production et inégalité économique; le cas d'un village haoussa Niger" in *Canadian Journal of African Studies*, X/2: 279–306.

Raynaut, C. 1977. "Circulation monétaire et évolution des structures socio-économiques chez les haoussa du Niger" in *Africa*, 2: 477.

Raynaut, C. et al. 1988. *Le développement rural de la région au Village – analyser et comprendre la diversité*, Bordeaux: GRID/Université de Bordeaux 2.

Robbins, P.F. et al. 2002. "Desertification at the Community Scale: Sustaining Dynamic Human-Environment Systems" in J. F. Reynolds and D. M. Stafford Smith (eds), *Global Desertification: Do Humans cause Deserts?*, pp. 326–56. Berlin: Dahlem University Press.

Scoones, I. and C. Toulmin. 1999. *Policies for Soil Fertility Management in Africa*, London: Department for International Development.

Scoones, I. (ed.) 2001. *Dynamics and Diversity: Soil Fertility and Farming Livelihoods in Africa*. London: Earthscan.

Somerville, D. 1986. *Drought and Aid in the Sahel: A Decade of Development Cooperation*. Boulder, Colorado: Westview Press.

Tiffen, M. and M. Mortimore. 1994. "Malthus Controverted: The Role of Capital and Technology in Growth and Environment Recovery in Kenya" in *World Development*, 22/7: 997–1010.

Tiffen, M. et al. 1994. *More People, Less Erosion: Environmental Recovery in Kenya*. Chichester, UK: John Wiley & Sons.

Trevallion, B.M. 1965. *Mtropolitan Kano: Report on the Twenty Year Development Plan 1963–1983*, London and Kano: Newman Neame for the Greater Kano Development Authority.

Turner, B.L.I. et al. 1993. *Population Growth and Agricultural Change in Africa*. Gainesville: University Press of Florida.

UNEP 1992. *World Atlas of Desertification*. Nairobi: Arnold for United nations Environment Programme.

Watts, M.J. 1983. *Silent Violence: Food, Famine and the Peasantry in Northern Nigeria.* Berkeley: University of California Press.

White, H. and Killick, T. 2001. *African Poverty at the Millennium.* Washington, D.C.: The World Bank.

Wiggins, S. 2000. "Interpreting Changes from the 1970s to the 1990s in African Agriculture through Village Studies" in *World Development,* 28/4: 631–62.

World Bank 2003. *Building Institutions for Markets: World development Report 2002.* Washington, D.C.: The World Bank.

The Making of an Environment

Ecological History of the Kapsiki/Higi of North Cameroon and North-Eastern Nigeria

Walter E.A. van Beek and Sonja Avontuur

Introduction

Since the writings of Boserup (1981) and McNetting (1993), smallholder agriculture has returned to research and planning agendas as something other than a cul-de-sac of development. The triangular nexus of land, demography and technology offers scope for various forms of intensification, land tenure and labour management, that is, for variation in agricultural practices beyond the simplistic and deterministic Neo-Malthusian metaphors. Land is no longer 'a resource of fixed quantity and quality that conditions both production and population size' (McNetting 1993: 278). With population growth as a relatively independent variable, the responses of farmers to these internal pressures and the transformation of markets, as well as the withdrawal of states, are products of cultural creativity in balancing possibilities, options and needs at the grassroots level.

This adaptive response to population growth brings about intensification and investment in land through irrigation, terracing, diversification, multicropping, manuring and other use of domestic animals (see also Zuiderwijk 1998). Variety is the name of the game, and multi- and intercropping, soil enrichment, mulching, agroforestry are all used in various mixes.

The aim of the following is to demonstrate two points in particular. The first is the flexibility of a population's response to its changing environment. The second is more fundamental. The debate of Boserup and McNetting with the neo-Malthusians implies a fundamental discussion between 'equilibrium' and 'exploitation' in ecological analysis. In the first paradigm, the relationship between population and habitat is dominated by negative feedback mechanisms such as population control, conservation measures – either directly or as a part of a less conscious cultural baggage – indigenous knowledge systems and investment in the productive environment. Netting's study is the best example of this.

The second, the neo-Malthusian paradigm, which is often invoked in conservation circles where worries about a loss of biodiversity abound, uses a positive feedback mechanism, such as the following:

population growth → agricultural intensification → habitat modification → increased production → further population growth plus loss of biodiversity etc. (Scoones 1999).

The first scenario is an optimistic one, according to which humans are wise enough (or experienced enough; or else 'culture' has grown wise) to reset the beacons when the tide goes out. In this scenario, a more sophisticated investment in the habitat, more specific knowledge and additional outlets for labour make for sustainability in a changing ecology. The second is the doomsday scenario, the old Malthusian legacy that is so hard to erase: population growth will exceed resource growth, and our old planet Earth is suffering from a plague of humans.

Our point is that both viewpoints are grounded in a series of dichotomies that have become questionable, namely those between nature and culture, man and habitat, and system and chaos. Recent work in ecology, the so-called 'new ecology' (Scoones 1999), tries to transcend these dichotomies. Croll and Parkin (1992) spoke about 'cultural understandings of the environment' as a dynamic factor, and Ingold (1992, 2000) tried to develop a new terminology with his 'affordances', his aim being to 'shift the focus of an ecological anthropology away from an equilibrial, eco-system-society-based research agenda towards individual responses to hazards' (Scoones 1999: 484). From the biological point of view, a similar shift occurred: 'We can no longer assume the existence of a static and benign climax community in nature that contrasts with dynamic, but destructive, human change' (Scoones 1999: 491). What have resulted from this are the notions of 'ecological engineering' and – on a longer time-frame – 'environmental histories', notions that are central to the cultural construction of the environment and the spatial-temporal construction of culture.

What follows here is therefore an attempt to create an environmental history of a particular environment-*cum*-culture, in order to show the mutual constitution of culture and environment. A group with a definite territory, an adaptive technology and intense local knowledge in an environment that seems stubborn and inhospitable, namely the Mandara mountains of North Cameroon, has been chosen to illustrate this. In recent years a considerable amount of research has been carried out here (van Andel 1998, Zuiderwijk 1998, Avontuur 1997, Boulet 1975, Boutrais 1984, Mueller-Kossack 1996, Seignobos 1982, Barreteau & Tourneux 1988, Sterner 1997). Most of the stages, starting from a moderate population density through increasing population pressure to full intensification can be seen in this area, with a subsequent shift to extensive agriculture when the population is moved to more open resources. The group in question is the Kapsiki-Higi[1] conglomerate, which straddles the border between Cameroon and Nigeria, on the central–western part of the Mandara mountains.

---

1. The Kapsiki have been studied by Walter van Beek in 1971, 1972–3, 1978, 1984, 1989, 1994, 1999 and 2003, financed by WOTRO (Netherlands Foundation for Tropical Research), Utrecht University, the Africa Studies Center and various other funds, with a total field stay of over two years, and by Sonja Avontuur in 1996 for six months, financed by the VSB foundation, Netherlands.

The Habitat

The Kapsiki habitat in Cameroon centres on a plateau at an altitude of 1000 metres, bordered by mountain ridges up to 1300 metres. The plateau itself, some forty by fifty kilometres square, is dotted with smaller and larger volcanic outcrops, which give the scenery a peculiar 'moonlike' atmosphere. On the western side, in Nigeria, where the group are called Higi, they live and cultivate on the mountain ridges as well as in the plains, expanding towards their Marghi neighbours. As we shall see agricultural practices vary with the type of field, but on the whole Kapsiki agriculture is quite characteristic of the area. Rain-fed Kapsiki agriculture produces sorghum, millet and maize as staples, intercropped with peanuts, Bambara nuts, beans and tiger nuts. Smaller crops include sweet potatoes, black potatoes, yam, couch, sorrel, tobacco, garlic, peppers and occasionally manioc. Fruit trees, pepper bushes and some sugarcane in wet places supplement their diet. The Kapsiki-Higi number about 200,000, the greater part in Nigeria. The population density is between 30 and 50 per square kilometre. Cattle and other livestock, goats and sheep, form an important feature of their agriculture. The cultivation of land and raising of cattle are both important to the value system of the Kapsiki, as well as to their symbolism.

As an old volcanic area, the Mandara plateau and hillsides are relatively fertile and can be cultivated on a permanent basis with few inputs and simple crop rotation. Water holes can be found all over the plateau and slopes, and although the slopes are not very easy to clear, weeds can be controlled relatively easy. Rains are more dependable in the mountains, which also retain water better. The mountain slopes demand some investment of labour, as they have to be terraced in order to be really profitable. The mountains are therefore well suited to labour-intensive horticulture by a small-scale population using simple technology and mixed husbandry.

The mountains have been inhabited for a very long time. Neolithic remains are quite numerous,[1] though the archaeology of the area is still being developed (David and Sterner 1987; MacEachern 1990). Neolithic axes are everywhere, serving often as ritual implements in the religions of the present day.[2] Until the late Neolithic, people seem mainly to have settled the plains, only a very sparse population entering the mountains. Rains were more plentiful, game more abundant, and in particular war and slavery were threats for the distant future. With the coming of the iron age at roughly AD 500 and diminishing moisture, the hills became more attractive, both as a safer area against external and possibly internal enemies, and for the iron ore which was found in the mountain gullies. The

---

1. Martin 1970: 1; David and Sterner 1987; van Beek 1978: 6.

2. This impression of long-term settlement is reinforced by evidence from palinography, food grains (David 1998) and iron and brass technologies (David and Robertson 1996). In his overview, MacEachern (1990) stresses the paucity of Neolithic sites (in contrast with artefacts).

mountains became both a refuge and a centre for iron production. Gradually the gravity of population shifted towards the mountains, where population density must have climbed slowly on the basic of a Neolithic form of exploitation from about 2000 BC, an iron technology from about 500 AD; brass seems to have arrived much later in the area, well into the second millennium of our era. The new technology facilitated an increased exploitation of the area, and sheep and goat husbandry became more important.

One sign of the length of occupation is the extensive terracing that is found everywhere in the mountains, especially in the north. Some groups, like the Mafa, no longer have any memory of making them and consider the major rock works to be the works of giant, stemming from the beginning of time (Martin 1970; van Santen 1993).

A major factor has been war. For a long time the Mandara mountains were a refuge from slave-raiding. Well before the onset of the Fulani *jihad* of the eighteenth century (Njeuma 1976), the Kapsiki must have populated the steep hillsides and the top of the granite outcrops that dot the plateau (van Beek 1987). Their villages were built, the compounds closely together, on the granite outcrops on what is now the Cameroonian side, and on top of the hills or on the steep hillsides in what is now Nigeria. Defence against mounted slave-raiders, whether Mandara, Baghuirmi, Kanuri, Bornu or Fulani, was of prime importance. Cultivation was feasible in the close vicinity of the mountain strongholds, either under close supervision from the village or in the relative safety of the inaccessible hillsides. Water was a problem, especially on the outcrops, but wells were found at the foot of most mountains.

Thus the Kapsiki lived in isolated villages on the hilltops. Not only were the hillsides a defence against foreign marauders, but the Kapsiki/Higi also fought each other at more or less regular intervals, as well as engaging in fighting within the village itself. Villages fought out their own wars between them (van Beek 1987; Otterbein 1968) and often captured slaves, who were usually ransomed by their kinsmen; a poor lineage, however, had to let its kinsman or -woman be sold beyond Kapsiki territory, into the hostile Muslim empires of Mandara, Bornu or later Yola. In the many fights within the villages poison was not allowed, nor could slaves be caught, since if there were casualties a blood-price had to be paid by the killer.[1] People therefore fought with clubs and sticks within the ward, and with knives and swords within the village, but in order to wound, not to kill. During most of Kapsiki history, the external threat, which did not have the sporting overtones of the internal fighting, was the more serious one. Muslim cavalries were on the whole a superior and better organised enemy (Barth 19857/8). Thus,

---

1. This never led to reciprocal feuding, however, through a specific mechanism in paying the blood price. Among the Kapsiki, the mother's brother of the deceased received the blood price, not his patrilineal kinsmen, which for the latter reduced the incentive for revenge killings, for which they would have to pay another blood price.

definitions of territory depended largely on the political situation. For our ecological history of the last century, therefore, we use political history divided into five relevant periods: before 1880, 1880–1920, 1920–1950, 1950–1980, and 1980 to the present.

Slaves and Spoils

During the first period, before 1880, slave-raiding, internal slave-hunting and external warfare must have been endemic, at least from the days of the Sokoto emirate, in the early nineteenth century (Denham and Clapperton 1826; van Beek 1988). Often these raids appear to have been large-scale Muslim expeditions that entered the mountains with a large force of cavalry. In many cases, the spirited defence of the mountain people was noted by outsiders. Just above the village of Kamale, an old earth ridge, reinforced with the ever-present stones, shuts off a narrow and steep gully, being at the same time a defence against slave-raiders and a limit to the cultivated fields. One sultan of Bornu died during a slave raid into the Mandara mountains, in 1863. Still, local losses must have outnumbered 'victories', even if the latter are better remembered.

In the period prior to 1880, the Kapsiki cultivated the slopes of the steeper hillsides and the sides of the outcrops where their villages were situated. The amount of intensification is hard to establish. The slopes of the main historical site of Mogode, *Rhungweδu*, show a considerable network of ridges and terraces, all dating from before 1880, somewhat like the Mafa area (Zuiderwijk 1998), but on a smaller scale. Agriculture for the Kapsiki must already have been associated with daring, bravery and courage: the bravest had their fields at the greatest distance from the safe haven of the hill-top village.

The general discourse on this period is couched in terms of a primordial family, invoking the image of a very small community on the ancestral mountain, during the times when the whole village could be housed on the three hectares of the mountain top. In the founding myth, the ancestral village was composed of one extended family with some incoming guests (van Beek 1978: 415), and the yearly sacrifice on this mountain recalls those days. In fact, the settlement at the top of the outcrop must be older. In the village of Mogode no sherds[1] younger than 350 years BP have been found on the old mountain top, meaning that the *Rhungweδu* mountain had already been vacated before the start of the eighteenth century. Probably most villages like Mogodé had already descended from their ancestral abodes for over a century, and it is safe to assume that prior to 1880 the threat of slave-raiding was much less severe than it would be later. The population had grown, people expanded over the gentle slopes that ring the plateau, and cultivation some distance away from the settlements became possible. In many cases,

---

1. Most sherds on *Rhungweδu* date back centuries, with a mean of 350 years BP.

claims to bush fields had been made in the years preceding the arrival of colonisation.

The earliest colonial period, 1880–1920, witnessed an increase in slave-raiding. The British colonial presence in Nigeria was already making its mark, as were the Germans in Kamerun. For the mountain dwellers these white people were far away, but the Fulani were not. Their dominance increased under the colonial presence. These were the days of slave-raiding Fulani dominated by Haman Yaji, a Fulbe chief of Maiduguri, who instituted a reign of terror in the mountains (Kirk-Greene 1958; Vaughan & Kirk-Greene 1995). From several bases, one of them close to Mogodé on the Kapsiki plateau, he carried out a virtually unending series of slave raids. This intensification of slave-raiding during the early colonial period has been noted for many parts of the Mandara mountains, as well as for other reclusive populations and slaving grounds (Fardon 1988). In a way, the colonisers, with their new armaments, upset the precarious balance of power in the mountains. Horses seem to have become more common (Smaldone 1977), and on the whole, after their initial 'pacification', the colonisers put their military might at the disposal of the indigenous rulers, or those who were seen as such, namely the sedentarised Fulbe. The markets for slaves, such as Mora, functioned undiminished. Even when the grand emirates were subdued by the incoming Europeans, the hunger for slaves was unabated (van Beek 1988). And of course firearms, though not absolutely superior to mounted cavalry, were an asset for a slave-raider. The impression is that, through the use of firearms, the raids became smaller but more frequent. Large cavalry forces no longer went deep into the mountains, and instead the Fulbe scourged the area through small-scale raiding. Three reasons can be found for this change. First, the centres of power were closer to the Mandara than they had been earlier: Yola, Kanuri and Baghuirmi no longer sent out their warriors on large-scale slaving expeditions, and Maiduguri, Mubi and Mora, all on the mountain perimeter, became the raiders' homes (cf. Vincent 1991). Guns may have been the second reason: raiders with guns enjoyed military superiority and did not need large numbers. Finally, the European presence precluded large-scale operations (Barkindo 1989).

The Kapsiki must have cultivated as close to their compounds as possible, as informants explicitly state. Agriculture in this period seems to be characterised by intercropping, manuring plots near the walls of the compound or within it, and the first intensive use of maize. Labour organisation was probably marked by increased individualisation of production. In the first part of the period, people still went off to the fields in groups in order to defend themselves; later this collective response to slave-raiding seems to have crumbled, and people started to leave the out-fields fallow and concentrate on the in-fields. As hit-and-run raids became more usual, stalking people very early in the morning and escaping with just a few slaves, collective responses to the problem were hard to organise (van Beek 1992b).

These decades marked the highest intensity of cultivation on the terraced slopes near the villages themselves. This first 'historical period', during which the coloniser gradually took control, was therefore quite atypical, one of a contraction of acreage instead of its expansion.

Peace in the Land

The following period, 1920–1950, is the first period of colonial rule. World War I had interrupted the colonising project, especially on the Cameroon side, where the Germans were defeated and their colony divided between the British and the French. The mountain peoples, like the Kapsiki, suffered in the struggle between the European nations, as for a number of reasons they tended to side with the Germans. First, they admired the fierce fighting strength of the Germans and chose what they thought were the strongest party. Secondly, more than the Germans, the French and English had tended (and would continue to tend) to rule indirectly through the local Fulbe elite; in siding with the Germans, therefore, the Mandara peoples were trying to avoid a renewal of Fulbe dominance. Of course, their backing the wrong horse resulted in fierce revenge on the part of the Fulbe. Later the threat of slavery subsided; the colonisers moved in, set up their administration and started to pacify the area in earnest, not just from the slave raids, but also from the internal fighting, which seems to have flared up strongly after the removal of the slave threat. Indeed, it was some time before these little wars ceased, in fact not until well after World War II. The last internal wars and skirmishes date from the late 1950s, and even into the 1970s occasional fighting broke out. Of course, the disruption of World War II itself, with its *levée en masse* of Cameroonian soldiers and the reduced attention given to internal government, did not exactly hasten pacification. By about 1950, the dominance of the Cameroonian and Nigerian colonial states had been sufficiently restored to bring the fighting to a close. One major innovation in this period was the institution of weekly markets, a phenomenon unknown to the area before the pacification, though now much appreciated.

It was therefore in these decades that the Kapsiki ventured out on to the plateau itself (van Beek 1989), cautiously at first, more boldly later. The first step was to establish wards some kilometres on to the plateau; the village of Mogode quickly grew from four wards in the centre to fourteen wards, which formed a large crescent on the plateau rim. Some small settlements on the very slopes towards Nigeria, one of the best protected against slave-raiding cavalry, were deserted at these times, as the more easy cultivation of the plateau offered better prospects. Though the old centre retained its political and ritual pre-eminence, the 'outlying wards', where people could live close to their new fields, became more extensively used for agriculture.

One stimulus has been the introduction of peanut cultivation, probably through the colonisers. *Arachis hypogea* was quickly taken up by the Kapsiki, for two reasons. It is an easy crop to rotate with the main staple, sorghum, and they were already familiar with a similar crop, the indigenous Bambara nuts (same species, different variety). The new peanuts occupied the same ecological niche and thus became the domain of the women, who had also cultivated the earlier varieties. The men had too many new fields in which to cultivate sorghum and millet to concern themselves very much with peanuts. An export crop from the start, Kapsiki women learned to use it in their sauces as well. Between the wars, peanut cultivation gradually spread throughout the Kapsiki's villages, furnishing the women with their first cash income. The former source of cash, the men's tobacco, did not grow proportionally and even declined.

This period therefore saw a rapid increase in the acreage under cultivation, for both the staple and peanuts. Many fields at modest distances from the village centre originate from this period, and thus many fields have been in the possession of patrilineal families for about three generations now. Maize, as the earliest crop, became more important as *soudure*, as the importance of small crops, cultivated in the immediate vicinity of the compound, dwindled.

The next period, 1950–1980, that of the 'mature colony' and first 'neo-colony', saw some changes in line with these developments. Pacification was completed,[1] and the people started to move around the area with greater freedom. The plateau and the plains in between the different villages were claimed for agriculture, and by about the end of the period 'no more bush', as informants put it, was available. Cultivation huts sprang up all over the plateau, and families dared to build individual compounds out of sight of the village wards. The government and some development projects introduced some changes, stimulating use of ox-drawn ploughs for plateau cultivation. Though this met with limited success, it became an established practice. Other experiments, like the planting of *mouskwari* sorghum, failed. On the plateau, especially in the vicinity of Rhumsiki, tourism increased (van Beek 2003), generating a demand for gardening: around the wet areas of the plateau in the neighbouring villages, people started to grow tomatoes, onions, radishes, lettuce and cabbages, stimulated by the particularly efficient manager at that time. Yet this only applied to a few individuals, mainly Christians who were taught this form of cultivation by their pastors.

Cattle also became more numerous. The Kapsiki had long kept a considerable number of cattle, and during this period the number gradually increased. They had their own brand of cattle that still predominated in their herds, but this slow-reproducing animal had to cede place to the Bos *indicus*, the Fulbe cattle. Yet in this period relations with the pastoral Mbororo Fulbe, who lived all over the plateau, grew more intense. Old scores having been settled, the Kapsiki and Fulbe moved into a kind of symbiosis in which the Fulbe herded the Kapsiki cattle together with their own, returning milk and manure to the agriculturalists.

---

1. The last war seems to have been between Mogodé and Sirakouti, in 1956 (van Beek 1987: 4).

The status of the Fulbe and the bush Mbororo was quite high, boosted by the support of the President of Cameroon, Ahmando Ahidjo, himself considered a northerner and a Muslim, and thus, in the eyes of the Kapsiki, a Fulbe. This period saw a clear growth of Muslim centres in the core of many villages, especially Mogode as the seat of the Lamido. As a *chef traditionnel*, he represented the government on the one hand, but still had enough political leeway to organise his court in accordance with traditional Fulbe style. Although he was a Kapsiki, he was a Fulanized Kapsiki. Fulanisation,or 'Fulbeisation' (Schultz 1984, van Santen 1993) became well known as a concept during this period. The Fulbe-ized Kapsiki set themselves up as merchants, first in peanuts, later to be supplemented by staple commerce. The civil war in Nigeria also provided considerable possibilities for commerce. Smuggling between the two countries, which is very easy for the Kapsiki, as they live on both sides of the border, became highly profitable: food and beer into Nigeria, enamel ware, gasoline and cloth into Cameroon. This period thus saw the establishment of Kapsiki traders, many from the central Mogode village, in the larger Mandara mountain area, as well as in Mokolo.

Agricultural labour became scarcer during this period; the extensification of agriculture increased the traditional bottlenecks in labour represented by the first and second weedings. One response was to break new ground in recruiting work parties more than had been done so far. Men organised the first breaking of a new field in large parties of twenty to thirty workers, with plenty of beer and food awaiting the party after completion. Labour was summoned by crying out in the night before the event, relying on the reciprocity of work done by others. The women, for their harvest and to a lesser extent for weeding, increasingly organised their own parties of about a dozen women from the neighbourhood; beans and especially peanuts were and still are harvested by working groups of women. The herding of goats and sheep, which are an important part of the Kapsiki's flocks, became something of a problem. Schools started to demand the attendance of the younger boys. Families with many children could afford to have one boy stay away from school and herd the goats and sheep, while the others went for education. Here the Kapsiki were helped by the decrease in child mortality that set in during this period. From a stable population up till the end of the 1960s with a fully traditional demographic pattern (high fecundity, high mortality; see Podlewski 1966), they entered the transition phase with a marked decrease in mortality, a situation that would also characterise the next period.

The Demographic Boom

The last period, since 1980, is one of the demographic increases of both humans and animals. In and since the 1980s, improved health care, together with improved water provision, with quite a few additional wells and pumps having been constructed by development aid, resulted in fewer early deaths. The hospitals in Sir and Mogode and the health posts in practically all villages improved the provision of vaccinations. The fight against malaria and epidemic meningitis was reasonably successful, while the threat of measles has been greatly reduced. Though demographic figures for the 1990s do not have the same precision as earlier ones (Podlewski 1966), the general trend is clear: the mortality rate is declining.

The mean number of living children has increased from 3.5 to between 4 and 5. Transition theory stipulates that increased fertility figures should follow decreases in mortality, though after a time lag. Figures for fertility are not available; the impression is some decline in fertility but not a large one. One field indication is the near disappearance of names with *meha* (literally 'old'), meaning the 10th, 11th etc. child, and suggesting that there is now a tendency to have fewer than ten pregnancies. Nonetheless any serious fertility decline is still far off, and Kapsiki society is fully exploding, with high fertility and decreasing child mortality.

The second demography concerns cattle. The mean number of cattle per household between 1973 and 1995 rose from 1.3 (van Beek 1978: 317) to 3.6 (Avontuur 1997: 44). This rise favoured the Fulani type of cattle, the classic long-horned humped *Bos indicus*, which almost characterises the West African savannah. The Kapsiki do have their own traditional brand of cattle, *Bos taurus*, short-horned, black-and-white cattle without a hump. These demand less food and fodder, and feed more readily on poorer grasses. Though the Kapsiki highly value their own type of cattle, they produce less meat for the market. Nonetheless, especially for ritual purposes, some proper Kapsiki cattle should be part of the herd (van Beek 1998). Herd increases were aimed at meat production, and the new flocks containing the *indicus* cattle consume considerably more grass and fodder than the older ones and as such bear heavily on the savannah vegetation.

The expansion of cattle-grazing, plus the expansion of agriculture, resulted in bringing almost all the plateau under either cultivation or grazing in the mid-1990s. One clear indication was the cost of roofing straw. In the 1970s almost all houses consisted of straw-roofed round huts, and bundles of roofing straw were almost never bought or sold. The usual way to roof a new hut was for the proprietor to collect the straw and then to call in his friends for a work party. Together the men plaited the straw rope for roofing, and produced the loosely tied straw lining for the roof. During the 1980s this changed. Long grasses suitable for roofing became scarce, and corrugated iron became a routine substitute. In the 1970s this was considered quite expensive, though 'modern' Kapsiki who had some cash like tailors or merchants had already started the trend. Only recently have people become aware of a receding water table, probably the result of fewer rains and more animals. One culprit, the Kapsiki indicate, are the eucalyptus forests which now dot the plateau through reforestation programmes. Though no exact measurements are available, surface water is becoming scarcer.

Agricultural Transformations

The whole of Kapsiki agricultural dynamics must be seen against a background of climate change. As elsewhere in west and central Africa, the climate seems to have become dryer. Mean annual rainfall in the period 1955–1969 was 1109 mm (Hallaire 1991: 20), and from 1970–1984 1012 mm. In Sir the mission measured a mean of 926 mm in 1992 and 1993. However, this decline in precipitation is not so clear. For instance, the 1994 figure greatly exceeded these figures, with over 1400 mm of rain. As elsewhere, drying up implies not just less rain, but more erratic rainfall, with wild fluctuations. Also, the rains now tend to fall somewhat later in the year, especially the heavy rains in the middle of the season, which have shifted from July and August to just August. Nonetheless, in 1994 as in 1972, most households could produce enough for their own needs, at least enough staple, sorghum, millet and maize (called 'sorghum of the Marghi', their neighbours in Nigeria). Some poor families have to rely on kinsmen and neighbours for their needs, but this is the exception rather than the rule. Nonetheless subsistence accounts for 62% of the crop production, the remaining 38% being sold in the market. Although Kapsiki society may no longer be *'la société qui suffit à elle même'* (Podlewski 1966), as it was in the early 1960s, the subsistence orientation is still quite marked. People are used to consuming what they produce and are loath to produce a cash crop that they do not consume themselves (Avontuur 1997: 27). No farmer places a priority on cash crops. According to Avontuur, crop yields in 1994 indicated that 32 out of 38 families examined produced enough staple to feed themselves, while 6, equally distributed over the mountains and the plateau, were short of staple. However, most of these were blacksmith families, who easily make up for a lack of harvested crop, while the others produced enough plaited utensils (mats, chicken fowls etc.) to buy the rest of the staple they needed. Two families are in dire straits. One is a settled cattle-less Mbororo (Fulani) family, where the husband refuses to cultivate ('not his way of living'), and the wife, while occupying herself in agriculture, cannot make up for this. The other two are old people, living with a small grandson or granddaughter. They rely on the kinship network to be fed (Avontuur 1997, 29). Though quite individualistic, the Kapsiki still honour these requests, albeit somewhat grudgingly. Poor people are routinely described as 'lazy', just about the worst accusation possible (cf. van Beek 1987). In 2003 this tendency is still recognisable.

The Kapsiki fully recognise the variations in soil fertility, such as those produced by volcanic remains: the soils on the slopes, they say, is the 'shit of the mountain', yet fertile as such. The plateau itself varies from red laterite to loamy black soils, with occasional rocky patches. Also, the plateau sports river gullies as well as some permanent waterholes. On the whole, the Kapsiki recognise the plateau fields to be less fertile than the slopes and more prone to weeds. Fallow periods need to be longer on the plateau (cf. de Steenhuijzen Piters 1995).

Thus the two main ecotopes, the mountain slopes and the plateau, offer spe-cialised niches for various crops. The main crops, sorghum and maize, grow on both, with some ecotopical variation for the many varieties of sorghum: red on the poorer soils, the high-yielding yellow variety on the mountain slopes. Maize needs the richer patches anyway, and is often grown close to the homestead in or-der to profit from household refuse and to guard against thieves taking it just be-fore harvest. Pearl millet, yams, tobacco, garlic and macabo (in small quantities) grow better on the slopes, yellow sorghum, peanuts and beans better in the mountains. On the plateau, by contrast, the 'wetter' crops thrive, namely sweet potatoes, black potatoes, sugarcane (near open water), rice, manioc and fruit trees, the latter near seasonal rivers. As Kapsiki villages spread out over the fields, especially in the last phase of history, an increasing number of them aim to culti-vate fields both in the mountains and on the plateau. Though those that move out on to the plateau try to retain their earlier fields on the mountain slopes, this dual strategy is easier for those who stay in their mountain homes and open up fields on the plateau.[1] The reason is clear: claims to the plateau fields are less de-tailed and less dense than those to the mountain fields (cf. van Andel 1998).

The Kapsiki invest little in manure for the fields, but they practise mixed crop-ping to a large extent. Maize and sorghum are intercropped with beans, sesame, sorrel, peanuts, okra, pumpkin and bambara groundnuts. Monocropping, though always on a small scale, is adopted for tobacco, eggplant, rice, tiger nuts, sugar-cane, garlic, sweet potatoes and black potatoes. It is realised that intercropping in-creases fertility and decreases weeding. Trees such as *Acacia albida* and *Ficus ingens* should remain in a field to enhance fertility. Other trees are for timber on-ly, and shade is not considered important for plant growth. The timing of burn-ing off the fields right after the harvest is somewhat puzzling; the dry Harmattan does not allow nutrients to be infiltrated, and the only result is to render the fields unusable for cattle-owners, which in fact is one of its motives.

Just as important as soil type is the angle and presence of rocks. All slopes are strewn with rocks, both large and small, and they can only be cleared and culti-vated by gathering the stones into terraces, which is obviously also a measure against run-off. The plateau fields are much less rocky and do not require exten-sive terracing. Thus, for the cultivation of all mountain fields the hoe is by far the most suitable instrument, whether with a pointed blade on the most rocky fields, or with a wider blade at the foot of the hills. On the plateau the hoe is being re-placed by ox-drawn ploughs, which were introduced in the area in the late 1970s, though adoption of this new technique has been very slow. The cost of feeding the oxen and the disappointing results led to many of those who had adopted it early on to abandon the plough, eat the oxen and return to hoe cultivation. Grad-

---

1. In Roufta the mountain inhabitants had 40% of their fields on the plateau, while the plateau inhabitants had 14% of their fields in the mountains, all in the village of Roufta (Avontuur 1997: 24).

ually, a smaller plough drawn by donkeys was introduced, with better results. In 1972 only four farmers in Mogode were using a plough (out of a population of 1800). In 1994, in the more remote village of Roufta, about four out of ten farmers own a plough. Yet although people like to cultivate with a plough, they recognise the loss of soil fertility that a plough may cause (it is said to 'bury' the fertile top-soil), and insist that in many cases the soil has to be 'healed' by reworking it with the hoe. Everywhere, plough cultivation reflects the polarisation of wealth in the village: the rich men own plateau fields and are able to use ploughs. Total investment in agriculture has not risen, whether as investment in land or in implements. The total amount of ploughs, oxen and other investments is still very low. Everywhere the basic type of agriculture has remained the same, namely the hoe-type of horticulture that has characterised African cultivation for so long. One reason for this persistence of the old tried and tested technology is the environment itself, another backdrop of the whole century of agricultural activity we are discussing.

One technology that did change agriculture is the coming of the grain mill. At the end of the 1970s some enterprising outsiders introduced grinding mills in the villages. After some misgivings from the men that machine-ground sorghum did not taste good, the women quickly settled the question by using the device en masse. The 1980s saw a gradual expansion of the mills, and in 1994 almost all villages had access to one. In 2003 some excess competition was threatening to emerge between mills. The main change was the impact on maize cultivation. Maize had been a *soudure*, a modest crop serving as a first harvest, to bridge the gap until the main sorghum crop. The maize kernels were not well suited to the hand-driven stone mills of the Kapsiki, and the women disliked grinding maize. The coming of machine mills changed all that. Maize became a major crop that was easy to cultivate, with a good yield per hectare and an early harvest.

Strategies for Adaptation

Tenure is changing in the direction of more individual ownership. Title to land in principle, and to a large extent in fact, follows patrilineal kinship organisation: clan, lineage, sub-lineage. In principal land belongs to those who have cleared it, a general rule still in operation on the fringes of the village territory. However, on the slopes all fields have been cleared for several generations, at least three, while on the plateau recent decades have seen the division of new fields, usually determined by first clearance. In principal, therefore, the land belongs to the patrilineal descendants of those who cleared it. Though living dispersed throughout the ward and beyond the village wards,[1] the lineages and sub-lineages still control most of the fields. In 1994 and 2003 about half of the fields had been inherited, about the same proportion as in 1972. What had changed were the gifts given in return for loans. In 1972 these still amounted to some pots of beer, or herding the lender's animals for a time. By the 1990s, borrowing land had become more complicated. A field is considered to have been borrowed so long as the full amount of gifts to the lender has not been paid in full. Besides the beer, money, goats and utensils were also given, and then on a regular basis. Without new gifts, the field might be taken back. This new trend shows most clearly when a field has been borrowed to build a compound, as often happens. Without gifts each year, the builder of a house may be thrown out of it by the owner of the land. One inducement actually to do so would be the increased fertility of the plot after several years of accumulating household refuse. In the 1970s this was unthinkable: building and living had clear priorities over cultivation. Fields can also be rented, in which case an agreed sum is paid beforehand. House plots were often being bought in 2003, because of the possibility of conflict. Gradually, the bulk of court cases have shifted from brideprice to land issues, especially those linked to habitation.

Sales of fields have increased only slightly in recent decades. In 1994 only 6% of fields were bought; sale was possible but discouraged in the 1970s, as it still is in the 1990s. Often, the sale of land is an indication of tensions between agnatic kinsmen, brothers, half-brothers and lineage brothers. In the Kapsiki social system the (sub)-lineage cannot prevent one of its members from selling land, even though he is taking it out of the lineage's total stock of land. Often, therefore, the other members decide to buy it back. This is still the case, though increasingly the land is being bought back by individual lineage members, which provides a clear individual title contractually. The accumulation of land in the hands of individuals still is a long way off, but the tendency is there. Finally, borrowing land against sizeable counter-gifts is not that far removed from the actual sale of land. Even when borrowing was 'cheap', the lines between borrowed and owned fields tended to become blurred, especially when loans were inherited over generations. Then both the actual limits of the fields and the kind of title involved became unclear. The present tendency towards individual ownership has led to clearer boundaries.

Throughout the past three decades, differences in wealth between Kapsiki have increased. Cattle is becoming monopolised in the hands of fewer and fewer individuals. Especially in roadside villages, many Kapsiki have taken up commerce. Smuggling, trading in peanuts and recently trading in cattle have produced a small Kapsiki merchant class in the Mandara area, both within and outside Kapsiki territory. They routinely invest in cattle, bringing herds from the Diamare plains into the mountains to add to the Kapsiki herds. Kapsiki who have

---

1. The village of Roufta, site of Avontuur's research (1997), is something of an exception in this respect, since the clans, lineages and sub-lineages follow territorial lines, each ward being associated with a particular clan. Migration here means a gradual change in clan affiliation. In the practice of land tenure, this reinforces the claims of the patrilineal units, even though they are not composed strictly in accordance with the patrilineal ideology, due to immigration.

made a career as officials also invest in cattle, which they keep on the plateau, guarded by their younger kinsmen.

Raising livestock for cash has also become more important in recent decades, at least for some. The number of people owning one or two cows has not grown (Avontuur 1997: 34; van Beek 1978: 316) and hovers at around one third. More people were cattle-less in 1994 than in 1972. In the latter year, however, the richer cattle-owners had more than five cattle, while in 1994 about the same proportion of people had more than sixteen. The number of goats and sheep doubled between 1972 and 1994, with a tendency towards more goats and fewer sheep. Donkeys were scarce in 1972, but had become omnipresent by 1994, mainly to draw ploughs. Within the family, the situation has hardly changed at all. In principal the men own the livestock (except poultry), though a woman can also invest her earnings in livestock, and then she may own cattle, sheep or goats. However, selling them is another matter, as this is the husband's task, either for his own profit (just as he may sell her peanut produce for his own benefit) or for hers. However, he runs serious risks if he pursues his own advantage too much, first, because his wife may leave him, and secondly because all the neighbours will know what is happening, and a man enriching himself from his wives' livestock is not much respected.

Diversification is not new, but it is clearly happening. By far the greatest amount of time is still spent on agriculture, by both men and by women. Though men also spend some time on stock raising and the women on household activities, agriculture easily ranks first in the expenditure of time and energy. Also, agriculture provides the first cash income. Almost all households earn money by selling crops, though the differences between households are considerable. The most important cash crop, as in the whole region, in fact, is peanuts. For women who sell their own produce, peanut sales comprise 69% of their income, the rest coming from other small crops, such as other nuts, okra or garlic. Income sources for men are more diversified: in 1994 Roufta peanuts amounted to 13% of their income, tobacco 16%, sweet potatoes 12%, sugar cane 12%, and cassava 13% (Avontuur 1997). The largest slice of income for men derives from stock sales (37%). This has therefore not changed lasting recent decades, as in 1972 the proportion of income by cattle sales was at the same level (van Beek 1978: 44). However, a large proportion of men's agricultural sales comprise the products of their wives, such as peanuts and cassava, and men depend on their wives' labour for the cultivation of sweet potatoes. Produce tends to be sold immediately after harvest. Farmers would obtain better prices if they could wait for prices to go up towards the end of the dry season, but most of them do not have enough cash reserves for school fees, taxes and the debts they have incurred during the cultivation season. Again, the more wealthy farmers can make more of their produce by waiting for the market to rise.

Alternative earnings from agriculture have always been quite important and are becoming more so. All women trade, and most men do so too, at least occasionally. Most women brew and sell *mpeldi*, the white Kapsiki beer brewed by women. In 1972 this brought them about 70 per cent of their cash income, a figure that had not declined in 1994. Towards the turn of the century women started to brew the red variety, which was formerly reserved for male production, as a market product with great success. One main advantage for the women is that they can keep the profits from beer themselves; their husbands never have access to it. Only when they invest in livestock do things change. Beignets and other small foodstuffs are also a favourite women's produce for sale, usually at the weekly market. Besides crops and cattle, men sell plaited straw products (ropes, baskets, mats, even granaries). Other men supplement their agriculture by working as tailors or butchers or trading in soft drinks and industrial beer from Nigeria. Small products, such as dried fish, medicines, kola nuts, the occasional bottle of whiskey, cigarettes, salt, sugar, soap or matches, can be traded by anyone, though some people set up a proper shop on market days. For many, a box of matches or sweets is an excellent excuse to go to another market, visit another village, and spend the meagre earnings on samples of the local beer. In 1972 as in 1994 (Avontuur 1997: 49), the men were complaining that ultimately all the money ends up in the hands of the women. That, at least, did not change, though women's control over any form of invested capital, such as cattle, did not change much either.

Most non-farm production, such as house building, roofing, plaiting, basket weaving (this may be specialised work), is intended for the use of the household and is not marketed. The exception, all important in Kapsiki society, is the work of the blacksmiths (van Beek 1992a), to whom working in iron (though not smelting; see Sterner 1997), burials, drumming and other music and many medicinal tasks are relegated as specialists, for which they have to be paid. Blacksmiths' wives make pottery and have their own medicinal specialisation, often for children. This caste-like group, which combines labour specialisation, endogamy and ritual obligations with notions of pollution, might be called 'general specialists', and they have strong associations with death. They were richer than the average non-smith (*melimu*) Kapsiki in 1972, and to all appearances still were in 1994 and 2003. Though Islamisation has made some dents in their marital isolation, allowing some of their girls to marry into Fulanised Kapsiki families, the distinction between the two groups has hardly shifted at all over 25 years.

The Making of an Environment

Thus processes of intensification and expansion see-saw through Kapsiki agricultural and political history. The general trend is one of labour economics: intensification occurs only if required, if external circumstances make more extensive methods unfeasible.

The Kapsiki try to harvest as much produce as possible per unit of labour. As long as land is not scarce, this is a viable strategy. The tendency towards expansion has been most marked on the plateau, especially with those who can plough. The gradual increase in the number of ploughs, as already noted, represents a shift towards expansion, as in fact all plough agriculture is done on the basis of the fallow system. Some five to eight years of fallow are deemed sufficient to restore fertility, counting on the resilience of the volcanic soils in particular. Ploughs, then, are used to increase area cultivated with the same amount of labour, especially for weeding. The risk of soil degradation becomes clear at this juncture (Avontuur 1997: 46), but the main option still seems to be to increase the acreage under cultivation, not to invest in the soil. The consequences of a possible scarcity of water are not as yet clear.

When required, intensification seems to have happened in the past, both during the intense periods of slave raiding, and for specific crops, such as those cultivated for the hotel. In this respect, the Kapsiki do not have any problem with the technicalities of more intensive agriculture, and they seem to switch quite easily from one approach to the other, but only if required or if it is profitable to do so. Thus Kapsiki society will continue for some time to follow a course towards the polarisation of wealth, favouring a few, but disadvantaging most. Then intensification should be adopted due to population pressure, which is definitely increasing (cf. van Oostrum 1993).

Obviously the territory available to the Kapsiki is limited, for what are their options for expansion of the area under cultivation? To the north, east and south, Kapsiki country is hemmed in by groups with at least similar population densities. To the south the Hina and Bana are in a similar situation to the Kapsiki, while expansion towards the north is blocked by the massive population of the Mafa. In the Nigerian west, the Higi are moving into the plains of the Margui population. However, the international border represents a restriction: Nigeria does not welcome too many immigrants, and relations between the two countries are tense. After all, the very area where the Kapsiki and Higi live is one of the disputed border zones between the two countries.

However, adapting to changing times also changes the environment. Several factors have repeatedly changed the ecology. Climatic changes, with a gradual reduction in moisture and more erratic rainfall, are an independent variable, but most factors for change are cultural. Political insecurity, for instance, and the constant threat of war and raids, have drastically influenced interaction with the environment. Knowledge and technology have had an impact as well, such as changes in cultivars, like peanut cultivation and the rise of maize, and the occasional flourishing of horticulture. Moreover the introduction of the plough, though still on a small scale, not only means more outfields being used as acreage, it also creates a sharper distinction between types of fields: flat, without stones, versus the mountain slopes. Obviously this technology is changing both the fields themselves and their water management.

A fourth factor is labour, hence demography. The most spectacular environmental change is, of course, terracing. Like their neighbours in the area, the Kapsiki have changed the face of the hillsides. Though not as intensively as the Mafa, they have changed run-off patterns, creating a new niche for both plant cultivation and non-cultivars. In turn, the terraces require maintenance, as water erosion and cattle tend to disrupt them. Thus changes in the environment influence cultivation and labour input.

Husbandry has been a crucial input. Goats and sheep seem to have been a continuous presence without much dynamic impact, but cattle-herding has changed. Though the Kapsiki *Bos taurus* has long had a presence in the mountains, the arrival of the Fulbe, bringing their own brand with them, has undoubtedly intensified cattle-herding. Thus, from the late eighteenth century the plateau has been grazed much more extensively. This increased the exploitation of the plateau, and in fact changed the typical *brousse* into pasturage. This relationship with the pastoral Fulbe has been quite dynamic, and the ethnic distinction between the two sides of the ecological picture – agriculturalists and pastoralists – has proved highly fluid, changing the characteristics of the 'bush'. (van Beek 1998).

Incorporation into a market economy has redefined the territory further, with the special characteristic of being straddled on an international border, with tourists finally coming to *le pays Kapsiki* and paying for the aesthetic enjoyment of a part of the landscape that for the Kapsiki was neither interesting nor productive (van Beek 2003).

We return at this point to the debate of Boserup and Netting with the 'Malthusians'. First, in the case described here the physical environment has proved flexible, at least sufficiently so to allow for a dynamic cultural definition and to provide for different degrees of land-use intensity: environment and culture continue to determine each other in the ecological history of these mountains. The final question is whether this flexibility has any inherent limits. Recognising the mutual interdependence between the environment and the human adaptive response, varying scenarios for the future become feasible. The first question is how far the malleability of the environment can be stretched. Both the physical geography, including rainfall, and the political situation provide limits to flexibility. A further reduction in rainfall will affect the ecology, for instance, as will the political futures of both countries, Nigeria and Cameroon. But other limiting factors are important. Market characteristics, logistics and – certainly demographics will bear their mark. Considering other cases from the Mandara mountains (Zuiderwijk 1998, van Andel 1998) or from elsewhere entirely (McNetting 1993), and taking into account Kapsiki ecological history, options for intensification, diversification and other adaptive strategies are still very much present for the Kapsiki and will undoubtedly lead to different definitions of the environment. But the difference between 'equilibrium' and 'exploitation' will become less and less marked, as the more recent periods of this ecological history have in fact shown. Ecological engineering, from terracing to gardening and from cultivar selection to intensive manure application, makes this opposition less relevant. An increasing variety of individual choices for the Kapsiki, an increased awareness of the long-term ecological costs and benefits accruing from adaptive responses and a heightened degree of interaction with external forces will increasingly cause the two paradigms to merge.

Bibliography

van Andel, A. 1998. *Changing Security: Livelihood in the Mandara Mountains Region in North Cameroon.* Leiden: African Studies Centre, Research Report 57/1998.

Avontuur, S. 1997. *Livelihood Strategies and Land Use: A Study on the Influences of Changing Livelihood Strategies on the Land-Use System of the Kapsiki in North-Cameroon.* Utrecht: Department of Anthropology Publ. 18.

Barkindo, B.M. 1989. *The Sultanate of Mandara to 1902.* Wiesbaden: Steiner.

Barreteau, D. and H. Tourneux, H. (eds). 1988. *Le milieu et les hommes: Recherches comparatives et historiques dans le bassin du lac Tchad.* Bondy: ORSTOM.

Barth, H.1857/8 *Reisen und Entdeckungen in Nord- und Zentral Afrika in den Jahren 1849–1855,* Vol. 5, Gotha.

Beek, W.E.A. van, 1978, *Bierbrouwers in de bergen: de Kapsiki and Higi van Noord-Kameroen en Noord-Oost Nigeria.* Utrecht: ICA.

_____ 1987. *The Kapsiki and Higi of the Mandara Mountains,* Prospect Heights: Waveland Press.

_____ 1988. "Purity and Statecraft: The Fulani Jihad and its Empire" in W.E.A van Beek (ed.), *The Quest for Purity,* Pp. 144–182.The Hague/Berlin: Mouton

_____ 1989. "The Flexibility of Domestic Production: the Kapsiki and their Transformations" in P. Geschiere and P. Koonings (eds), *Proceedings Conference on the Political Economy of Cameroon.* Research Reports no. 35, Tome II, pp. 613–46. Leiden: African Studies Centre.

_____1992a. "The Dirty Smith: Smell as a Social Frontier among the Kapsiki/Higi of North Cameroon and North-Eastern Nigeria" in *Africa* 2 (1), pp. 38–58.

_____ 1992b, "Slave Raiders and Their People without History" in J. Abbink & H. Vermeulen (eds.), *History and Culture; Essays on the Work of Eric R. Wolf.* Pp. 53–71. Amsterdam: Het Spinhuis.

_____ 1998. "Les Kapsiki et leurs bovins" in Seignobos, C. and E. Thys (eds), *Des taurins et des hommes: Cameroun, Nigéria.* Pp. 15–39. Paris: ORSTOM.

_____ 2003. "The African Tourist Encounter: Effects of Tourism in Two West-African Societies" in *Africa,* 73, 3.

Boserup, E.1981. *Population and Technological Change: A Study of Long-Term Trends.* Chicago: The University of Chicago Press.

Boulet, J. 1975. *Magoumaz: Pays Mafa (Nord Cameroun), étude d'un terroir de montagne.* Paris: ORSTOM.

Boutrais, J. et al. 1984. *Nord du Cameroun: des hommes, une région.* Paris: ORSTOM, Mémoires no. 102.

Croll, E. and D. Parkin (eds). 1992. *Bush Base, Forest Farm: Culture, Environment and Development.* London: Routledge

David, N. 1998. "The ethnoarcheology and field archeology of grinding at Sukur, Adamawa State, Nigeria" in *African Archaeological Review* 15 (1): 13–63.

David, N. and I.G. Robertson. 1996. "Competition and Change in Two Traditional African Iron Industries" in P. R. Schmidt, (ed.), *The Culture and Technology of African Iron Production.* Pp. 128–44. Gainesville: Florida University Press,

David, N. and J. Sterner. 1987. "Mandara Archaeology Project 1984–1987" in *Nyame Akuna* 29: 2–8.

Denham, D. 1826. *Narritive of Travels and Discoveries in Northern and Central Africa in the Years 1822, 1823 and 1824.* London.

Fardon, R. 1988. *Raiders and Refugees: Trends in Chamba Political Development, 1750 to 1950.* Washington: Smithsonian Institution Press.

Hallaire, A. 1991. *Paysans montagnards du Nord-Cameroun: les monts Mandara.* Paris: ORSTOM.

Ingold, T. 1992. "Culture and the Prescription of the Environment" in Croll, E. and D. Parkin, (eds), *Bush Base, Forest Farm: Culture, Environment and Development.* Pp. 39–56. London: Routledge.

___ 2000. *The Perception of the Environment; Essays in Livelihood, Dwelling and Skill.* London: Routledge.

Kirk-Greene, A. H. M. 1958. *Adamawa Past and Present: An Historical Approach in the Development of a Northern Cameroons Province.* London: International African Institute.

MacEachern, A.S.1990. *Du Kunde: ethnogenesis in North Cameroon.* PhD thesis, University of Calgary.

Martin, J.-I.1970. *Les Matakam du Cameroun: essai sur la dynamique d'une société pré-industrielle.* Mémoires ORSTOM 41. Paris: ORSTOM.

McNetting, R. 1993. *Smallholders, Householders: Farm Families and the Ecology of Intensive, Sustainable Agriculture,* Stanford: Stanford University Press.

Müller-Kossack, G.1996. "The Dughwede in NE Nigeria: Montagnards Interacting with the Seasons" in *Berichte des Sonderbereichs 268, Bd 8,* pp. 137–70.

Njeuma, M.1976. *Fulani Hegemony in Yola (Old Adamawa), 1809–1902.* Yaoundé: CEPER.

Oostrum, K. van 1993. *Sustainable Land-use and Social Change: A Study on Ecological Knowledge, Soil and Water Management and Social Change of the Mafa in North Cameroon.* Report 25. Leiden: CML.

Otterbein, K.F. 1968. "Higi Armed Combat" in *Southwestern Journal of Anthropology* 24: 195–213.

Podlewski, A.M. 1966. *La dynamique des principales populations du Nord-Cameroun (entre Benoué et lac Chad).* Cahier Orstom, Sc. Hum. 3. Paris: ORSTOM.

Santen, J.C.M. van 1993. *They leave their Jars Behind: The Conversion of Mafa Women to Islam (North Cameroon).* Leiden: VENA.

Schultz, E.A. 1984. "From Pagan to Pullo: Ethnic Identity Change in North Cameroon" in *Africa* 54 (1): 46–64.

Scoones, I. 1999. "New Ecology and the Social Sciences: What Prospects for a Fruitful Engagement?" in *Annual Review of Anthropology,* 28: 479–507.

Seignobos, C. 1982. *Nord-Cameroun, montagnes, hautes terres.* Paris: Ed. Parenthèses.

Smaldone, J.P. 1977. *Warfare in the Sokoto Caliphate: Historical and Sociological Perspectives.* Cambridge: Cambridge University Press.

Steenhuijsen Piters, B. de 1995. *Diversity of Fields and Farmers: Explaining Yield Variations in North-Cameroon.* Wageningen: AUW.

Sterner, J.A. 1997. *The Ways of the Mandara Mountains: A Comparative Regional Approach;* London: SOAS.

Vaughan, J.H. jr. and A.H.M. Kirk-Greene (eds).1995. *The Diary of Haman Yaji: Chronicle of a West African Muslim Ruler.* Bloomington: Indiana University Press.

Vincent. J.-F. 1991. *Princes montagnards du Nord-Cameroun: les Mofu-Diamaré et le pouvoir politique.* Paris: Harmattan.

Zuiderwijk, A. 1998. *Farming Gently, Farming Fast: Migration, Incorporation and Agricultural Change in the Mandara Mountains of Northern Cameroon.* Leiden: CML.

Agro-pastoral Conflicts in the Tikar Plain (Adamawa, Cameroon)

Quentin Gausset

Introduction

Conflicts between agriculturalists and pastoralists in Africa are often interpreted as resulting from competition over resources that have been made increasingly scarce by growths in population and cattle. The argument builds on the Malthusian assumption that more people lead to agricultural expansion, while more cattle lead to pastoral expansion. At some point there is a clash between the two forms of development, and conflict ensues. The neo-Malthusian approach also suggests that population growth above the carrying capacity of a piece of land leads to the degradation, even 'desertification', of land and pasture, which only enhances further the pressure on resources and conflicts (Anderson and Woodrow 1998: 284; Grainger and Tinker 1982: 11, 21, 34; Hussein 1998: 60–61; Jacobson 1988: 12–13; Kates et al. 1977: 276; Oxby 1999: 233–4; Spencer 2000: 19–22; Stryker 1989: 91). Thus, agropastoral conflicts are often explained by population growth leading to fewer resources and to more conflicts over them. In the following I shall argue that, in Adamawa, the province of Cameroon with the lowest density of population, the presence and intensity of agropastoral conflicts are not caused by population pressure, but rather by complex social, political, cultural and historical factors, which will be discussed in the present paper.

Agro-pastoral conflicts, if left unresolved, can turn into bloody riots (Bassett 1988; Hagberg 2001; Hussein 1998). In December 2001 and January 2002, on the Mambila plateau (Nigeria), more than a hundred people were killed and more than 20,000, mostly Fulbe, displaced to seek refuge in Cameroon, mainly in the area where I was doing fieldwork. This conflict wiped out most rural Fulbe settlements over an entire region. The aim of this article is not to explain the conflict which erupted on the Mambila plateau,[1] but rather to analyse the causes of agro-pastoral conflicts in the Tikar plain (in south-western Adamawa, Cameroon), a region which borders the Mambila plateau in Nigeria and which has been used

---

1. The situation on the Mambila plateau is quite different from what is found in the Tikar plain. One major difference is that the former is characterised by high densities of human and cattle populations. Another difference is that collective land has been privately enclosed by herders. This process has been pushed so far that it has led to the spoliation of some farmers' land (Boutrais 1995: 1094–98; Hurault 1998). Finally, the political situation in Nigeria is generally quite different from that found in Cameroon (Dare 1997; Levin 1997; Lovejoy and Williams 1997).

in the past thirty to forty years as a transhumance destination during the dry sea-son. Although the Tikar plain has a much lower density of population than the Mambila plateau, it is also the theatre of agro–pastoral conflicts that might very well become violent if nothing is done to diffuse the existing tensions. It is there-fore crucial to understand the roots of agro-pastoral conflicts in this region.

The Adamawa plateau was originally inhabited by local agricultural popula-tions. It was conquered during the first half of the nineteenth century by the Fulbe and their local allies and came under the rule of sultanates that were part of the Sokoto empire. Until the European colonisation, the main economic re-source of the Fulbe sultanates was slaves, who were captured from the local pop-ulations by the Fulbe and their allies and exported to Yola and Sokoto (Burnham 1996; Büttner 1967; Hurault 1975; Johnston 1967; Kirk-Greene 1958; Lacroix 1952; Mohammadou 1966; 1978; 1981; 1991; VerEecke 1994). After German colonisation, the slave trade was abolished, although domestic slavery continued to exist until late in the 1950s. Cattle replaced slaves as the main economic re-source of the region (Siran 1980: 55). The Adamawa plateau is indeed extremely well suited for cattle-herding. The plateau has high annual rainfall (1500 mm on average in Banyo) and a low population density, estimated to be less than ten per-sons per square kilometres in 1970 (*Atlas du Cameroon* 1971), and less than five persons per square kilometres in Banyo (Hurault 1969: 964). It has an altitude above 1000 metres, which has provided relative protection against tsetse flies and bovine trypanosomiasis, although the plateau has never been totally free from it (Boutrais 1995: 1134–42). Adamawa is mainly covered by woody savannah, with gallery forests along the many rivers that water it. It is thus well suited for both cattle-herding and savanah agriculture. The zones of cattle-herding used to be limited to the plateau and characterized by transhumance, during which the cat-tle grazed close to the permanent Fulbe houses during the rainy season, going fur-ther south in search of new pastures during the dry season.[1] This movement pushed the herders further and further south each year, until they reached the end of the plateau in the 1950s.

Cameroon's rain forest starts in the plains that are found to the south of the plateau, a few hundred metres lower in altitude. Until recently, the plains were considered to be unsuitable for-cattle herding due to the prevalence of tsetse flies and trypanosomiasis. However, with the improvement of extension veterinary services and the use of fly repellent for cattle, from about forty years ago, pastoral pioneers have progressively dared to spend the transhumance period in the plain.[2] In the Tikar plain, which is the focus of this paper, this strategy has proved very

---

1. Most herders living on the plateau practice agriculture during the rainy season (see also Boutrais 1994b), including the Mbororo, the so-called 'nomadic Fulbe', and they have established long-term land rights.

2. A similar change happened in other regions; see, for example, Boutrais (1994a); Waters-Bayer and Bayer (1994); Blench (1994); Adebayo (1997)

profitable and a huge success among herders, who continue to go further south each year searching for new pastures. This paved the way for the Tikar plain to become a transhumance destination during the dry season, a factor which became important for the pastoral industry in this part of Adamawa. The dates of the beginning and end of transhumance in the plain are decided by the prefect of Banyo, in order to ensure that there are no cattle in the plain during the rainy, and main agricultural season. The local, non-Fulbe population herds small ruminants such as goats and sheep, but virtually none of them keeps cattle, at least not themselves, since the cattle owned by local farmers is usually kept by cattle-herders based on the plateau. Thus, during the rainy season, all the cattle, as well as the agro-pastoral conflicts, are found on the plateau, and it is only during the dry season that agro-pastoral conflicts are found in the plain (and on the plateau, as some cattle spend the dry season there).

Figure 1: Cameroon

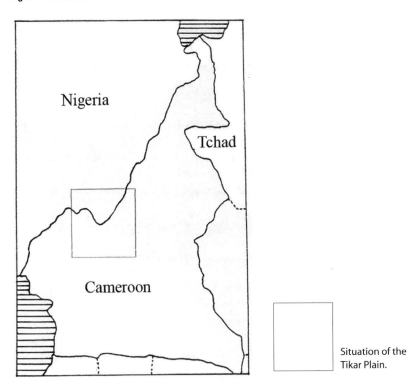

Situation of the Tikar Plain.

Figure 2: The Tikar Plain

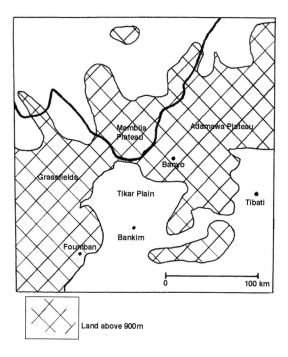

Proximate Causes of Conflict

Agro-pastoral conflicts are relatively new in the Tikar plain, having started only about thirty to forty years ago, and are interesting to study, as a satisfactory solution has not yet been found for them. The proximate causes of conflicts generate tension between the two populations, which can easily become violent. Every year, some farmers and herders beat or injure each other with sticks, knives, machetes, or even guns. Although human deaths are fortunately still extremely rare, the killing of cattle and the intentional destruction of farmers' property (fields, plantations, granaries) are regular occurrences. The causes of these conflicts are seen differently, according to the origin and occupation of the informants.[1]

---

1. As will be clear in the following, we are not dealing with 'management problems' (arguments over the choice of alternatives among individuals with the same goals and interests) or 'disputes' (involving competing, but negotiable interests, and issues of gain and loss), but with real 'conflicts', which involve the development of the individual or identity group, and are thus bound up with non-negotiable human needs and question of identity (Burton and Dukes, in Cousins 1996: 45–6).

Direct Causes of Conflict as Seen by Agriculturalists

Cattle often move unsupervised, especially at night, when they may eat planted or harvested crops; since the transhumance happens during the dry season, the cattle eat cassava and dry season maize and damage coffee plantations. Cattle also eat maize from granaries. As the fields are often far from the present-day villages, which were resettled along the main road in the 1950s, many villagers build their granaries in their fields. When cattle find these granaries, they may feed on the stored food and finish it off in a matter of two or three days. If the farmer is not properly compensated, he and his family must struggle until the next harvest to avoid starvation. The main problem for farmers is that pastoralists are often reluctant to compensate them for damage done by cattle, resorting to various methods to avoid having to do so (see below). When cattle move unsupervised, it is most often early in the morning when the herders are still asleep and when the grass has dew, which is supposed to make food more palatable for the cattle. Agriculturalists want cattle to be fenced in at night, but pastoralists resist this, since they see early morning grazing as an important part of the cattle diet (see also Boutrais 1995: 732).

The presence of cattle and pastoralists in the plain disturbs existing agricultural strategies. Pastoralists light bush fires anywhere at any time during the dry season, in order to encourage grass re-growth for their cattle. This burns fallow fields (thus preventing forest re-growth and shifting cultivation) but sometimes also granaries, houses, or even coffee plantations and people. Cattle eat the grass in fallow fields, thus preventing forest re-growth. This, coupled with bush fires in fallow fields, forces farmers to go further away to cut forests if they want to practice shifting cultivation, or to begin practising savannah cultivation. Finally, cattle trample down the earth, making it more difficult to cultivate.

Direct Causes of Conflicts as Seen from the Pastoralist's Point of View

The frustration of pastoralists is based in part on agriculturalists expanding their fields into areas which were formerly used as pastures, and more specifically as kraals (rest camps) where cow dung is concentrated. They take advantage of the pastoralists' presence without giving them any compensation for it (elsewhere, people are willing to pay cattle-herders to establish their kraals in the fields, so as to benefit from the dung). Moreover, some agriculturalists have begun to create fields in the savannah, a long-term threat against the amount of pasture available. Agriculturalists try to prevent pastoralists from having access to areas where they have many fields in order to protect these fields. This is resented as a restriction on freedom of movement – an essential feature of nomadic pastoralism (Swift 1977: 462).

Pastoralists blame agriculturalists for refusing to fence in their fields, unlike people on the plateau. They also resent the fact that people in the plain are not as submissive to Fulbe authority as those living on the plateau. But the most serious complaint of the cattle-herders is that some agriculturalists are poisoning their cattle by various means, including spraying pesticide for coffee on pastures.[1]

Ultimate Causes of Conflicts

Although the proximate causes of the conflicts described above are significant triggers, we must go further and find the ultimate causes of conflicts, an issue that needs to be addressed if conflicts are to be resolved. It is often argued that the ultimate cause of agro-pastoral conflicts is the scarcity of resources, which are made even scarcer due to population growth and environmental degradation (Anderson and Woodrow 1998: 284; Bennett 1991; Cousins 1996: 44–45; Grainger and Tinker 1982: 11, 21, 34; Homer-Dixon 1994; Hussein 1998: 45; 60–61; Jacobson 1988: 12–13; Oxby 1999: 233–34; Spencer 2000: 19–22; Stryker 1989: 91; Tonah 2000: 557). This neo-Malthusian perspective argues that scarcity and population growth lead to vicious circles of over-exploitation and the degradation of resources. However, I shall argue that scarcity cannot explain the origin of agro-pastoral conflicts in the Tikar plain. First, if the resources are seen in objective terms, there is place for much more cattle and many more fields in the region. Secondly, seen as a relative concept, scarcity depends on the perception and uses of resources (see also van Beek in this volume), which must be understood in relation to the socio-political context which creates it.

Objective and Relative Definition of Scarcity

One can define scarcity as an insufficiency (objective lack) of existing resources in order to sustain the livelihoods of the people who use the resource. This definition of scarcity is linked to the concept of carrying capacity, namely that, given a certain technological level, a limited territory can only sustain a limited number of cattle and people. This definition thus builds on the Malthusian perspective that, beyond a certain threshold, resources will not be sufficient to feed the growing population that relies on them, thus triggering famine, wars, migration or the over-exploitation of resources. Agro-pastoral conflicts are thus interpreted as signs announcing that such a threshold has almost been reached, or has already been passed. However, we cannot say that resources are scarce in the Tikar plain. People and cattle are not starving and are not forced to migrate in order to survive. On the contrary, the area is seen as having a great potential for development, both agricultural and pastoral, and both pastoralists from the north and agriculturalists from the southwest are swarming in to seize these agricultural and pastoral opportunities. So far, nobody has been prevented from creating new fields or spending

---

1. Agriculturalists are believed to kill cattle either in revenge for having had their fields destroyed (either by the cattle that is killed, or by other cattle which could not be caught on the spot), or just because of their supposed craving for meat (Muslim Fulbe do not eat meat from a cow which has died without being slaughtered but rather give it to the local Christian population).

the dry season period of transhumance in the plain. Each year, the number of pastoralists and agriculturalists who choose to do so increases greatly, and there still seems to be room for more.[1] It is clear to every pastoralist that the dry season conditions (the amount of grass and water) are far better in the plain than on the plateau. Therefore, given current strategies and technology, one cannot say that resources are scarce or that the carrying capacity has been reached in the Tikar plain. It could be argued that the great increase in agriculture and grazing is putting resources under pressure and causing more conflicts (see, for example, Blench 1994: 208). However, this can be questioned on several grounds. First, the evidence for it is shallow (Hussein 1998: 39–57). Secondly, archival material tends to show that agro-pastoral conflicts were already serious and frequent decades ago (Breusers et al. 1998: 365–8). In our case too, agro-pastoral conflicts arose in the plain as soon as cattle started to spend the dry seasons there, when population densities were much lower than today. So even if population pressure could explain an increased frequency (as local people claim) and intensity of conflicts (which remains to be proved), it is unable to explain the *existence* of agro-pastoral conflicts in the Tikar plain.

Since an objective definition of scarcity is not very useful in the Tikar plain, it might be more interesting to use a relative definition of scarcity as a perceived inadequacy between existing resources on the one hand and existing needs on the other. People develop strategies to maximise not just the material aspects of their resources, but also their health, free time, reproduction, social capital, etc. If resources are limited and people's desires unlimited, there is always (everywhere and at all times) a perceived inadequacy between the amount and geographical situation of resources and human needs, hence the constant quest for new places, new resources, new technologies. The spatial distribution, limited nature of resources and imperfections of knowledge and technology unavoidably imply the lack of fit between resources and needs, as well as relative scarcity, leading to restricting access to resources through the development of rules, rights, ownership and tenure systems.

In the context of the Tikar plain, despite the fact that there is still room for many more farmers and cattle-herders, most people, both pastoralists and agricul-

---

1. The annual growth of the cattle industry in Cameroon was 7.5% on average between 1996 and 1999 (Moutou 2002). Due to the lack of reliable statistics, the number of cattle in the Banyo district is difficult to estimate. Statistics are usually based on the number of cattle covered by vaccination campaigns. However, many herders do not vaccinate all their cattle. Some want to keep their property secret and evade taxation, and others do not trust the effectiveness of vaccination, partly due to serious mistakes made by the veterinary service in the past. It is really only in times of serious epidemics (i.e. too late) that people vaccinate all their cattle, but this is not a good time either to estimate cattle numbers, as another strategy against epidemics is to move the cattle into regions which are not subject to it. Despite these shortcomings in assessment, it can be said that the increase in cattle remaining in the plain during the dry season is much higher than the national average growth of cattle, since for some years now, the transhumant cattle have come not only from Banyo, but also from Tibati and the Mambila plateau in Nigeria.

turalists, think that there are already too many fields or too many cattle in the plain. In other words, they think that the lack of fit between resources and needs is increasing. Any increase of cattle or fields will make it more difficult for existing farmers and herders to maintain their standards of living. Nobody doubts that there is room for many more cows to spend their transhumance in the plain and surviving it, but more cows will mean less grass per cow. The current question is not how many cows can survive in the plain, but rather how fat and healthy they will be if there are more cows sharing the same resource. It is not how many people can practise agriculture, but rather how many can continue practising shifting cultivation in forested areas and how many will be forced to practise savannah cultivation. At present, people perceive the limited amount of grass as limiting the well-being of their cows, not their numbers. Conversely, the limited amount of forest remaining is perceived as limiting the amount of shifting cultivation and coffee plantation, not the number of farmers. People do not think in terms of a fixed carrying capacity (how many cows or people can survive somewhere), but rather in terms of relative carrying capacity (looking at the well-being – the fit between needs and resources – of cattle and people).

It should be stressed that the perceived increase in relative scarcity is first and foremost seen as being caused by people who share the same livelihood strategy. It is the increase in herders and cattle numbers which is seen as the main threat to other herders, and the increase in farmers using forests which is seen as the main threat to shifting cultivation. However, although conflicts among herders or among farmers do exist (see, for example, Gausset, forthcoming), they are much less frequent and much less violent than agro-pastoral conflicts. Moreeover, since relative scarcity should be better suited to explaining conflicts among farmers or among herders than between farmers and herders, we need to go beyond territory and scarcity in order to explain agro-pastoral conflicts. In the following, I shall argue that the ultimate causes of conflicts are linked to the conflicting co-existence of different perceptions and uses of the same resource, different systems of management, different systems of power and justice, and different cultural and ethical perspectives.

Conflicting Perceptions and Uses of the Same Resources

Farmers and herders have different and conflicting perceptions of what constitutes a resource, which are linked to different uses. First, grassland is the main resource of pastoralists, but it is seen as hunting ground, fallow land or potential agricultural land by agriculturalists. Second, while the movement of cattle is an integral part of transhumance, it is exactly what threatens the success of agriculture. Cattle start moving at night, when the herders are usually still asleep. Agriculturalists perceive the movement of cattle as a threat to their fields and harvests (especially early in the morning, when agriculturalists are also still asleep). Third, the fields, which are the main resource for agriculturalists, are seen by herders as restricting the movement of cattle. Fourth, agriculturalists rely mainly on shifting cultivation and coffee plantations. Forests are transformed into either coffee plantations or maize fields, which are cultivated for a few years in succession before being left fallow for from five to eight years. Savannah fields are scattered in the landscape, according to opportunities perceived in the different soils and locations. For pastoralists, however, keeping land fallow is a waste of resources, and unfarmed land should be grazed at any time, especially if this will prevent the regeneration of bush and maintain the grass. Shifting places all the time and making scattered fields in the landscape is to invite trouble when cattle are grazing freely. Fifth, bush fires are an integral part of both pastoral and agricultural life. Pastoralists light bush fires randomly at almost any time of the dry season to hasten the re-growth of grass, to make sure that there are always some patches of new fresh grass growing. Agriculturalists see these random bush fires as a nuisance, since they spoil fallows and threaten bush granaries. Agriculturalists themselves burn cleared forest or fallow fields, usually at the end of the dry season, under strict control so that it does not spread to other areas. Burning for hunting purposes is practised, but not close to agricultural areas. Thus both agriculturalists and pastoralists set fire to the grass in the bush, but they do this in different ways and for different purposes.

In short, the same resource can be used very differently by different people. What is seen as a resource by herders (grass, movement, random bush fires) is seen as a nuisance by farmers, and vice versa (fields, fallow, and forested areas). There are therefore conflicts of perceptions and interests, due to the conflicting co-existence of different modes of production.

Conflicting Systems of Management, Rights and Ownership

Each system of resource use is linked to a system of rules that is accepted within the community. When the same resource is used and perceived differently by different communities, there is inevitably a conflict between the different *systems of management* (strategies, rules, rights) that are developed by the different actors.

From the farmers' perspective, anybody who is allowed to do so by the local chief can acquire rights over land by transforming it for agricultural purposes, that is, clearing the bush or the forest to establish a field. Rights over land continue to be held even when it is left fallow for many years – nobody can farm it without asking the permission of the person who cleared it. However, in the view of the pastoralists, any piece of land which is not farmed can be grazed and burnt without asking the permission of the agriculturalist 'owner'. Pastoralists feel that they have the right to graze their cattle anywhere as long as the cattle do not damage crops or harvests. Nobody owns pastures, and anybody can establish himself anywhere. However, if pastoralists like a certain place, they tend to come back there in the following years. In course of time, herders begin to think that they have the acquired a right to continue grazing where they have already done so for many years. This right is contested by agriculturalists, who do not ask for permission to create new fields in it.

One way of preventing cattle from spoiling fields is by fencing either the cattle or fields. Agriculturalists want cattle to be fenced in at night, so that they do not wander around unsupervised when people are sleeping (which is when most of the problems occur). When they are suffering from crop destruction, they utter the following sentence again and again: 'Is the field moving to meet the cattle or is it the cattle that move into the field?', thus placing the responsibility on the pastoralists, who have failed to look after, or fence in, their cattle. Pastoralists, on the other hand, want fields and granaries to be fenced in. For them, it does not make much sense to fence in something that moves, like cattle; it makes much more sense to fence what does not move, namely fields.[1] Moreover, they consider grass with dew eaten early in the morning to be very important for the diet and health of their cattle, and they are not ready to wean them off of it. However, they resent the attempt of some farmers, and even some pastoralists, who try to keep their cattle free from contact with other herds, to prevent cattle from going into some areas by fencing access to that area (at a ford, for example). These fences are often broken down by pastoralists, who do not accept this kind of restriction on their movements.

Another way to prevent damage to fields is to guard the cattle or the fields at all times. It is usually accepted that cattle should be guarded at all times. The problem is that it is a very tough job. The herder has to sleep in a straw hut in the bush and may have to walk dozens of kilometres per day. A herder may get tired during the day, fall asleep while his cattle are resting, and not notice when they start moving again. Or he can fail to wake up at 4 am to follow his cattle when they start to move. Moreover, many herders are hired by rich cattle-owners, and some are not serious or reliable about their work, given the miserable salary they receive for an extremely tough life in the bush, which does not induce them to behave in a more responsible manner. This problem is in itself very complex and should not be underestimated (Bassett 1994). Some owners hire two herders, one to be responsible for cattle during the day, the second at night. Or else they share the responsibilities: the herder is responsible for damage done by cattle during the day, while the owner is responsible for damage done at night. Many Fulbe watch their own or their father's herds, and are usually more careful. However, they may also participate in feasts and rituals, which keep them away from their unattended cattle for a number of days. As a result of the poor supervision of cattle, many farmers are forced to spend significant amounts of time watching their fields, plantations or granaries, an additional burden that they strongly resent.

---

1. Fencing a field is often not enough to prevent damage to it. Strong bulls often destroy fences made of wood and bamboo to eat cassava in a field or maize in a granary, with other cattle following the bull into the breach thereby created. Barbed wire seems to be more efficient, but most farmers cannot afford it.

The state, for its part, tries not to become involved in the management of these issues and to limit itself to some very general principles. Officially, the state owns all the land that is not titled (i.e. basically all the land outside of urban areas), although the local population can enjoy its usufruct. Anybody has the right to harvest the fruits of his labour, and whoever threatens this, as happens when cattle destroy a harvest, or when a chief takes back land cultivated by a migrant before he has harvested his fields, places himself in the wrong and must pay compensation for the damage done. As a rule, the state recognises the right of anybody to establish himself anywhere in order to make a living. This means that it recognises the right of pastoralists to graze their cattle anywhere that is not being cultivated (including in fallow areas). But it also means that they recognise the right of farmer to create new fields in former pastures. The state considers the plateau to be primarily a pastoral zone and thinks that farmers should fence their fields, but it also regards the plain as primarily an agricultural zone and thinks that herders should fence their cattle. However, this is just advisory and is not enforced as such. Thus, the state tries to be fair to everyone, and tries not to give precedence to any particular group. The state defends first and foremost the right of free movement, which benefits everyone but is equally frustrating to all and creates tensions.

Conflicting Structures of Power and Justice

Conflicts between different systems of rights and management, based on different uses and perceptions, are legal conflicts and imply politics. They depend on who has the power or authority to define and enforce the rules on ownership, to define the rights and duties of people, and to manage conflicts. There is a clash here between three different political systems.

First, the local agricultural populations have local chiefs in every village, who rule over the land in the village (Gausset, forthcoming). These sacred chiefs (see Gausset 1995, 1997) organise rituals to ensure fertility and resolve conflicts and distribute the land to both local and foreign farmers. Although a foreigner is expected to make a gift to the chief, the land that is given cannot be sold on. Once the land is no longer in use, it comes back under the authority of the chief, who can then hand it on to another person. Just as farmers must ask the chief for permission to create a new field somewhere, the chief expects migrant herders to ask him for permission before they establish themselves anywhere with their herds. Although this is indeed customary practice (see also Adebayo 1997: 98), herders seldom ask the permission of the local chief. As most herders are Muslims and most local chiefs Christian (Gausset 1999, 2002), as the local chiefs are officially under the authority of the sultan, and as the sultan owns many herds of cattle, the herders prefer to go directly to the sultan to ask his permission to graze in the plain.

The second structure of power is based on the Fulbe sultan ruling over a sultanate (including the Tikar plain) that was carved out around 1830 by his ancestor (Gausset 1998, 2003). He is the only 'paramount chief' ('chief of first degree') in the department and is recognised by the administration as the highest traditional authority, above the local chiefs. However, his power is relatively weak in the Tikar plain, an area used to be seen mainly as a reserve for slaves, and which lost its attractions for the sultans when the slavery was abolished at the turn of the twentieth century. The sultans renewed their interest in the plain when it became an important are of transhumance some thirty to forty years ago. The primary resource of the sultan are the 'gifts' of cattle made by his people as well as by the foreign cattle-herders who ask his permission to establish themselves in his sultanate. He also receives an important proportion of the Islamic *zakat* (a certain percentage of the cattle herds are supposed to be given each year in charity), which is given to him instead of being given directly to the poor (Dognin 1981). Thus the sultan is one of the biggest cattle-owners of the area (see also Boutrais 1994b: 178). His wealth depends directly on the amount of cattle which graze in his sultanate, since he receives some of them either as gifts, as part of a 'traditional taxation' system (*zakat*, a tax on inheritance), or through more or less forceful extortion from foreign herders staying in his sultanate. Since the sultan is considered to have a strong personal interest in herding and is still associated with the institution of slavery, his authority is strongly contested by the local populations of the Tikar plain and their chiefs (Gausset 2003).

Thirdly, there is the state, which officially has a monopoly of land ownership, force and taxation, and is supposed to represent all Cameroonian citizens equally and to defend the freedom of movement of all Cameroonian citizens. The state monopoly of force and taxation is contested by the sultan, who benefits from some forms of taxation and has a private 'army' to help him rule his sultanate. The state monopoly over land is contested by the local chiefs, who claim to be the only ones entitled to redistribute land, as well as by the sultan, who claims to be the only one able to allocate grazing rights. Freedom of movement is contested by both the sultan and the local chiefs, who want migrants to accept their local rules before establishing themselves anywhere. Some local chiefs also try to limit the number of migrants moving into an area when these threaten to outnumber the local population. There is thus a conflict between three different kinds of power. Local chiefs claim that they are the only ones who can give permission for others to stay on their territory. The Fulbe sultan makes the same claim in respect of allowing pastoralists to stay anywhere in his sultanate. The Cameroonian state claims to own all non-titled land and to allow anybody to establish himself freely wherever he wants. All three types of power partly recognise, as well as partly challenging, the authority of the other. The co-existence of, and competition between, traditional and state rules is also a problem in other parts of Cameroon, as well as of Africa generally (see also Benjaminsen and Lund 2002; Cousin 2000; Hagberg 2001; Hilhorst 2000; Little and Brokensha 1987: 194).

When it comes to justice, conflicts are ideally supposed to be solved in customary courts, of which there is a hierarchy ranging from dignitaries, to chiefs of
third rank, to chiefs of second rank, to the sultan (the chief of first rank), who is
a kind of customary court of appeal. The state system parallels the customary system and has its own hierarchy. The state structure exists in parallel to, and works
as a kind of court of appeal for, the customary courts, as conflicts which are not
solved by the customary structure must be referred to the state system. One problem with the customary system is that the local chiefs and the sultan do not base
their rulings on the same customs: in particular, the sultan uses, among other
principles, Islamic law. A second problem is that the two customary power structures and the state structure receive different kinds of support from the population. The local farming population usually supports its traditional leaders. The
migrant farmers usually accept the authority of these traditional local leaders, although they are more ready to go to state courts than the local farmers. The Fulbe
and pastoralists usually support the sultan. Although conflicts should ideally be
heard first by the local chief and then by the sultan, the herders usually reject the
authority of the local chiefs, and the farmers usually reject the authority of the sultan. The roots of the problem are cultural and historical. The local populations
used to be raided for slaves and have never recognised the authority of the sultan
over them. On the other hand, the Muslim Fulbe look down on the local chiefs
since they are non-Muslims and former slaves, and they do not recognise their authority.[1] As a consequence, agro-pastoral conflicts are usually brought before the
state courts.

In order to bring a case to the state court, the plaintive must first find a potential culprit. A case requires first evidence. For a farmer whose field has been
damaged, the best way is to catch the herd in his field and to follow it until it takes
him to its owner. If it is not possible to catch the cattle in the field, one can try
and follow the tracks left by the herd, and hope that the owner will accept the
charges or will still be there (many herders move away as soon as they realise that
their herd has caused serious damage somewhere). Some farmers become furious
when they find cattle in their field and would them with their machete. It is then
up to the herder to find whoever has hurt his cattle and ask him for damages. If
a cow is hurt in a field (breaks a leg, dies, or is injured by the farmer), the herder
can blame the farmer for the damage incurred. Second, the court procedure requires damages to be assessed. If the two parties cannot agree, the extension officers for agriculture and animal husbandry come together and estimate the
damages. The cost of this assessment falls on the plaintive. Third, there is the
judgement, in Bankim or Banyo. This can take a long time if the evidence is not
sufficient, if the forms of procedure are not respected, etc. Fourth, once judgement has been given (assuming there is no appeal), the culprit must repair the

---

1. In Adamawa, there is no joking relationship which might diffuse tensions between the Fulbe
and local populations, unlike what is found in some other parts of West Africa.

damage incurred by the victim. The transfer of money can be delayed if the loser does not accept his defeat.

All these different steps take time, energy and money, and leave plenty of room for corruption. One of the parties might try to bribe those acting in the case, in order to influence the outcome, or else the administrative actors can delay or block the process until one party pays what is required to move the case forward. Cameroon being perceived as one of the most corrupt countries in the world (according to Transparency International), bringing a case to court costs money – and the higher one goes in the hierarchy, the more expensive it becomes. As a result, those who win a case are usually not the most righteous, but rather the richest. And, given that one head of cattle can be sold for as much as the total annual income of a farming family, the richest are usually the herders. Farmers can seldom compete with herders over money. This gives great confidence to herders in refusing to pay fair compensation for the damage done by their cattle (see also Harshbarger 1995, cited in Hussein 1998). Even when cattle are caught red-handed, the owner might say 'I know that my cattle have done damage, but I won't pay. You can bring me to court if you want'. They know that they are likely to get away with it because farmers do not have the means to bring them to court, and even if they do, the herders are likely to be more successful in bribing the gendarmes, the extension officers, the clerks or the judges. Otherwise they can promise to pay and never do so, even after being required to do so by the chief or a court order.

Farmers often complain that herders prefer to pay much more in bribing officials than in repairing the damage done to farmers (see also Adebayo 1997: 105–6). This behaviour is partly related to the cultural prejudices that exist between Fulbe herders and local farmers. Many Fulbe look down on local people and cannot accept that their 'slaves' should ask for reparation and bring them to court. They prefer to pay more in bribes and to teach them a lesson by reminding them who has the power, rather than admit to their own wrongdoing. Another reason for avoiding payment is to claim that the locals have previously killed or wounded their herds in some way or another (by theft, spraying pesticides, etc.), and that the damage to fields done by their cattle does not begin to balance the loss that they suffered earlier.

If people have the feeling that they cannot get justice, that their rights are not respected, that they are exploited, they may well take the law into their own hands by deciding to have recourse to 'the justice of the machete', or to 'the justice of the match', thus destroying each other's property or, in more extreme cases, beginning to kill one another and chase one another away on a large scale, as happened recently in Nigeria. People are then drawn into a spiral of violence that goes on reinforcing itself. In these conflicts, herders, who have a weaker attachment to the land and who are extremely vulnerable if their herds are attacked, are likely to be the losers and to be chased away.

To sum up, local actors cannot agree which traditional authority, the local chiefs or the sultan, is in charge of managing resources and the conflicts. They then appeal to the state court system, which can always short-circuit the customary legal system, but which is both unable (because lacking human and monetary resources) and unwilling (because too corrupt) to solve the problem. In this situation, those who have the upper hand are those who have the money, usually the herders. This feeds the frustration of the farmers, who increasingly have recourse to violence. For a time, using violence only brings them even more trouble in court. But as the frustration builds up, it can suddenly degenerate into extremely violent regional riots, in which farmers often end up having the upper hand. As can be seen, present-day agro-pastoral conflicts do not have much to do with the so-called 'scarcity of resources', but are rather linked to a conflict of power and to a perceived lack of justice.

Conflicting Ethics: Who Should Come First?

One cannot address the question of ownership, power and justice without asking the questions, who *should* own the resource, who *should* have the power, and who *should* bear the cost and reap the benefit of resource distribution. The questions of ethics and environmental justice are central to this discussion. In their turn, they are linked to broader debates about individual versus collective rights, and indigenous rights versus equal rights. When new migrants establish themselves in great numbers somewhere, should migrants adapt to the existing system of management? How much should they be allowed to change the local practices? Who should reap the benefits and bear the costs of the changes they bring with them?

The use of the Tikar plain for transhumance during the dry season, which started about forty years ago, has brought about many changes. Although everybody, including the herders, agree that in theory the latter should bear the costs involved, in practice costs are, to an important extent, borne by the farmers. Farmers experience crop damage in their fields and seldom get proper compensation for their loss (they can even lose much more if they decide to bring the case to court). They must also expend more effort in cultivating soils that have been made hard by trampling, and more time and energy either fencing their fields and granaries, or watching them constantly to chase away wandering cattle. Many pastoralists do share these costs by paying compensation for the damage and by fencing – not the cattle at night, however, but rather the fields and coffee plantations in the vicinity of their camp (then taking the barbed wire with them if they move elsewhere). However, some refuse to cooperate and thus create a lot of tension, although even these reluctant herders bear part of the cost through the growth in the violence directed against cattle and pastoralists.

As for who benefits from the arrival of cattle in the plain, herders are obviously the main winners. It is often argued in the literature that there is a symbiosis between farmers and herders (for a review, see Hussein 1998: 17–20): farmers obtain meat and dairy products, as well as manure and draught power, in exchange of their agricultural products, and everybody benefits (Hussein 1998: 17; Swift 1977: 461; Tonah 2000: 552; Waters-Bayer and Bayer 1994: 222–4). This might be true in areas where farming and herding have been integrated together for a long time, but this is not at all the perception that local actors have of the situation in the present case (see also Boutrais 1995: 722). Farmers repeat constantly that 'You can survive on eating maize only but you cannot just eat meat without maize', or 'You can eat maize without meat in the sauce', insisting on the fact that while pastoralism is unnecessary, everybody, including pastoralists, relies on agriculture.[1] The number of farmers who drink milk and can afford beef is relatively small in rural areas. People prefer to rely on fish, their own chicken or on game meat, which is still relatively abundant. The production of meat is aimed at supplying southern Cameroon rather than the local markets, which often have to be content with sick or injured cattle. Cattle are never used for their draught power or for transport in the area. As for manure, this is concentrated in the kraal, and those who benefit from it are those who can farm these areas once the herders have left (see also Boutrais 1995: 761). Those farmers who are ready to pay pastoralists for their cattle manure are almost exclusively migrant Muslim farmers: local farmers do not think of entering into this type of arrangement. Another possible type of symbiosis is when farmers keep cattle and entrust it to Fulbe herders (Breusers et al. 1998; Oksen 2000: 63–71; Tonah 2000). This was tried by some local farmers in the 1980s, when the price of coffee was high and farmers had money to invest; it is still one of the investment strategies of the local elite. However, many farmers have been deceived by herders running away with their cattle or cheating them by telling them that their cattle had died. As local people say, 'When a cow dies, it is always the farmer's cow', or, 'If a cow gives birth to a female calf, it is always the Fulbe's cow. If the calf is male, it is always the cow of the farmer.' Farmers who own cattle have difficulties in distinguishing individual cows; they are not as interested in them as they should be, and they are at the mercy of their shepherd's good will and honesty, which is often questioned (see also Adebayo 1997: 107; Breusers et al. 1998: 369).

In short, when comparing costs and benefits, most farmers claim that they were, and would be, better off without the presence of cattle in the plain. This is not just a narrative hiding strong ties between the different groups (cf. Breusers et al. 1998); there is almost no integration between herding and farming in the area, and the two groups are extremely polarised towards one another. One of the reasons restricting the possibility of integration is that no cattle spend the rainy season in the plain. This is forbidden by prefectoral order and is a rule that is welcomed by the farmers, as it prevents a lot of agro-pastoral conflict. At the same

---

1. This would explain why herders usually live close to farmers, as they depend on them for access to markets and food products, despite the fact that this proximity might increase agro-pastoral conflicts (see also Boutrais 1995: 730).

time, however, it prevent local farmers from benefiting more from the presence of cattle. So far, the mixing of herding and farming is seen as the cause of all problems, and most of the solutions advanced aim to separate the two activities as much as possible by limiting transhumance to the dry season, fencing out cattle, determining zones reserved for pastures, etc.

Thus most farmers clearly reject the supposed symbiosis between farmers and herders as a myth. They claim that herders both depend on and benefit from farmers much more than the other way round. And they claim that it is farmers who bear most of the cost of the introduction of cattle in the area, since they lose their crops and do not receive proper compensation for this. They are not opposed to the presence of cattle in the plain as long as they do not have to change their agricultural practices and do not have to bear the costs of their being there. They define themselves as autochthonous and feel that, if there are costs, they should be borne by the migrants. The saying, 'Is the field moving to meet the cattle or is it the cattle that move into the field?' can be applied to the pastoralists themselves. No farmer asked the herders to use the plain for transhumance: it was the herders who moved into the plain. Farmers think that migrants should therefore adapt to local practices and respect the local structures of power and justice: if they bring new problems with them, they should be the ones to bear the costs involved.

In facing these problems, the Cameroonian state tries to apply the same rules to all its citizens. In order to build up a feeling of national unity, the state supports the principle that all citizens have equal rights and freedom of movement. Anybody should be able to establish himself anywhere in Cameroon, regardless of his religion, ethnicity, race, etc. Monopolies over land ownership and power are used as methods to reach this aim and prevent Cameroonian citizens being discriminated against locally. However, although they are well intended, the 'equal rights of individuals' defended by the Cameroonian state are, in practice, inefficient, unrealistic, creating conflicts and, at some level, unethical.

First, the position of the state is inefficient, as it insists on the right of people to establish themselves anywhere without really defining which management system should apply –the local one or the one introduced by the newcomers – let alone being able to define its own management rules. There exist a few rules regulating bush fires and dates of transhumance, but nothing on tenure rights. The state's apparatus and its law are ill equipped to deal with all the land conflicts that come from the confrontation between migrant and local populations having very different livelihood strategies. It is, moreover, too understaffed and too corrupt to work properly. It would be much more efficient to empower the local traditional chiefs and to declare that migrants must accept local rules.

Secondly, state claims and policy are not realistic, as everybody in Cameroon expects traditional chiefs to be responsible for distributing resources and to determine who can establish themselves where. Even civil servants, who are often born and educated in villages or small towns, know and accept that chiefs rule over their territories. They also know that challenging this rule can create much trouble. So, in practice, although the state supports freedom of movement and uses the argument that all the land is state land, it nevertheless acknowledges the authority that traditional chiefs have over their territory, at least as long as this authority is not challenged locally (by migrants, for example). The state turns a blind eye to local ways of managing tenure rights through the local chief (even though this challenges the state's monopoly of land ownership), but also turns a deaf ear when the authority of local chiefs is challenged by migrants (see below). The problem in the Tikar plain is that there are two traditional authorities each claiming this right, the local chiefs and the sultan. These two institutions, which are supported by different populations, have been in conflict since the mid-nineteenth century. Far from recognising this, the state operates with a hierarchy of power that does not work in practice: the sultan is supposed to rule over the chiefs of the plain, although actually he has little authority over them.

Another problem is that when migrants challenge local authority and management rules, the state treats them on an equal footing with the indigenous population. This creates more conflicts than it solves, as it both encourages and rewards migrants to challenge the existing balance of power. Securing the rights of migrants without defining their duties – that is, saying that anybody can establish himself anywhere without saying whether they have to respect the local traditional authority – is a *de facto* challenge to traditional authority and local management rules, giving a free hand to migrants to challenge the local rules and power structures, and encouraging permanent renegotiations of rules, and therefore permanent conflicts between indigenous and migrant communities.

Finally, allowing migration without allocating clear responsibility regarding who is to manage the resource or defining who should bear the cost of migration can create an unfair situation in which the local people end up being deprived of their resources (or, more importantly, of control over their resources) by newcomers. The empowerment of local chiefs and communities would ensure that they keep control over 'their' own resources. This would not prevent the local immigration of herders (representing the free circulation of Cameroonian citizens), but would make sure that the newcomers adapted their strategies to the local rules, without challenging the local system of ownership and balance of power. Local empowerment would avoid local communities having to bear an unfair load of the costs incurred from the changes introduced by the newcomers, and it would also allow them to solve problems according to their own rules, hopefully allowing them to find acceptable solutions to agro-pastoral conflicts and to avoid resorting to violence to reach the same ends.

Conclusions

The conflicts described in the present chapter are not restricted to the Tikar plain, but bear a striking resemblance to what is found in the highlands of Bamenda and Banyo (Boutrais 1995: 722–71 and Hurault 1964), although the conflicts in these two areas have unfolded in the very different context of a much higher density of human and cattle populations, a permanent cattle presence and a different balance of power between farmers and herders. As the Tikar plain has a low population density and a large unfulfilled potential for the development of agriculture and cattle-herding, population pressure cannot explain the many conflicts that exist between farmers and herders. The cause of agro-pastoral conflicts is rather to be found in its social, cultural and political aspects. What constitutes a resource or an important strategy for some represents a waste or a nuisance for others. The difference in perceptions and in the use of resources is closely associated with differences in the definition of ownership, rights and management. Claims to fallow land are not recognised by pastoralists, and claims to grazing land are not recognised by agriculturalists. People cannot agree on what should be fenced and watched, cattle or fields, or on who should do this, the herders or the farmers. The question of ownership, rights over and the management of resources leads inevitably to the question of power. A significant problem is that farmers follow their local chiefs and do not recognise the authority of the sultan. Conversely, pastoralists follow the sultan and do not recognise the authority of the local chiefs. The state is supposed to arbitrate in local conflicts, but its legislation is not well adapted to this role, and its staff are not numerous enough and often too prone to corruption to be able to solve problems satisfactorily. Finally, the question of power is closely linked to the question of ethics, and to the debate that is going on in Cameroon over the tensions between the principle of freedom of movement versus indigenous rights. Few people accept being outnumbered by foreigners when this means that they have to bear the costs that are linked to migration, change their agricultural practices and lose power over their traditional resources. The state might be able to dampen agro-pastoral conflicts in the Tikar plain by making sure that proper compensation is paid if damage is done and by empowering local traditional authorities in their role as resource managers. As this is far from being the case today, given that the current situation is close to lawlessness, there is every reason to be pessimistic about the future outcome of these conflicts.

Bibliography

Adebayo, A.G. 1997. "Contemporary Dimensions of Migration among Historically Migrant Nigerians: Fulani Pastoralists in Southwestern Nigeria" in *Journal of Asian and African Studies* 32 (1–2): 93–109.

Anderson, M.B. and Woodrow, P.J. 1998. *Rising from the Ashes: Development Strategies in Times of Disaster*. London: Intermediate Technology Publications.

Atlas du Cameroun 1971. Yaoundé: Institut de recherches scientifiques (IRS).

Bassett, T. 1988. The Political Ecology of Peasant-Herder Conflicts in Northern Ivory-Coast. *Annals of the Association of American Geographers* LXXVIII (3): 453–72.

___ 1994. Hired Herders and Herd Management in Fulani Pastoralism (Northern Côte d'Ivoire). *Cahiers d'Études Africaines*, 133–135, XXXIV (1–3): 147–73.

Benjaminsen, T. A. and C. Lund 2002. "Formalisation and Informalisation of Land and Water Rights in Africa: An Introduction" in *The European Journal of Development Research* 14 (2): 1–10.

Bennett, O. 1991. *Greenwar: Environment and Conflict*. London: Panos Institute.

Blench, R. 1994. "The Expansion and Adaptation of Fulbe Pastoralism to Subhumid and Humid Conditions in Nigeria" in *Cahiers d'Études Africaines*, 133–135, XXXIV (1–3): 197–212.

Boutrais, J. 1994a. Pour une nouvelle cartographie des Peuls. *Cahiers d'Études Africaines*, 133–135, XXXIV (1–3): 137–46.

___ 1994b. Les Foulbé de l'Adamaoua et l'élevage: de l'idéologie pastorale à la pluri-activité. *Cahiers d'Études Africaines*, 133–135, XXXIV (1–3): 175–96.

___ 1995. *Hautes terres d'élevage au Cameroun*. Paris: ORSTOM.

Breusers, M. et al. 1998. Conflict or Symbiosis? Disentangling Farmer-Herdsman Relations: The Mossi and Fulbe of the Central Plateau, Burkina Faso. *Journal of Modern African Studies*, 36 (3): 357–80.

Burnham, P. 1996. *The Politics of Cultural Difference in Northern Cameroon*. Edinburgh: Edinburgh University Press.

Burton, J. and Dukes, F. 1990. *Conflict: Practices in Management, Settlement and Resolution*. New York: St Martin's Press.

Büttner, T. 1967. "On the Social-Economic Structure of Adamawa in the 19th Century: Slavery or Serfdom?" In W. Markov (ed.) *African Studies,* pp. 43–61. Leipzig: Karl Marx Universität.

Cousins, B. 1996. "Conflict Management for Multiple Resource Users in Pastoralist and Agro-Pastoralist Contexts" in *IDS Bulletin* 27 (3): 41–54.

___ 2000. Tenure and Common Property Resources in Africa. In C. Toulmin and J. Quan, eds., *Evolving Land Rights, Policy and Tenure in Africa*, pp. 151–79. London: IIED.

Dare, L. 1997. "Political Instability and Displacement in Nigeria". *Journal of Asian and African Studies* 32 (1–2): 22–32.

Dognin, R. 1981. L'installation des Djafoun dans l'Adamaoua Camerounais. La Djakka chez les Peul de l'Adamaoua. In C. Tardits, ed., *Contribution de la recherche ethnologique à l'histoire des civilisations du Cameroun*, Vol I., pp. 139–57. Colloques Internationaux du CNRS, No 551. Paris: CNRS.

Gausset, Q. 1995. Contribution à l'étude du pouvoir sacré chez les Wawa (Adamawa, Cameroun). *Journal des Africanistes* 65(2): 179–200.

___ 1997. *Les avatars de l'identité chez les Wawa et les Kwanja du Cameroun*. PhD Thesis, Université Libre de Bruxelles.

___ 1998. "Historical Account or Discourse on Identity? A Reevaluation of Fulbe Hegemony and Autochthonous Submission in Banyo (Adamawa, Cameroon)" in *History in Africa* 25: 93–110.

___ 1999. "Islam or Christianity? The Choices of the Wawa and Kwanja of Cameroon" in *Africa* 69(2): 257–78.

___ 2002. "The Spread of Islam in Adamawa" in T. Bierschenk and G. Stauth (eds), *Yearbook of the Sociology of Islam* 4, pp. 167–85. Münster: LIT.

___ 2003. "From Domination to Participation: The Politics of Religion and Ethnicity in Northern Cameroon" in N. Kastfelt (ed.), *Scriptural Politics: The Bible and Koran as Political Models in the Middle East and Africa*, pp. 185–202. London: Hurst

___ forthcoming. "'Our Land is not for Sale'. Land Tenure and Land Conflicts among the Kwanja (Adamawa, Cameroon)" in B. Derman et al. (eds), *Conflicts over Land and Water in Africa*.

Grainger, A. and Tinker, J. 1982. *Desertification: How People make Deserts, how People can stop and why they don't*. London: Earthscan.

Hagberg, S. 2001. "A l'ombre du conflit violent: règlement et gestion des conflits entre agriculteurs Karaboro et agro-pasteurs peul au Burkina Faso" in *Cahiers d'Études Africaines*, 161, XLI (1): 45–72.

Harshbarger, C.L. 1995. *Farmer-Herder Conflict and State Legitimacy in Cameroon*. DPhil thesis, University of Florida.

Hilhorst, T. 2000. "Women's Land Rights: Current Developments in Sub-Saharan Africa" in C. Toulmin and J. Quan (eds), *Evolving Land Rights, Policy and Tenure in Africa*, pp. 181–96. London: IIED

Homer-Dixon, T.F. 1994. "Environmental Scarcities and Violent Conflict: Evidence from Cases" in *International Security* 19 (1): 5–40.

Hurault, J. 1964. "Antagonisme de l'agriculture et de l'élevage sur les hauts plateaux de l'Adamawa (Cameroun). Le lamidat de Banyo" in *Etudes rurales* 15: 22-71.

___ 1969. "Eleveurs et cultivateurs des hauts plateaux du Cameroun" in *Population* XXIV: 963–94.

___ 1975. "Histoire du lamidat de Banyo" in *Comptes rendus trimestriels de l'Académie des Sciences d'Outre-Mer*, XXXV(2): 421–65.

___ 1998. "Land Crisis on the Mambila Plateau of Nigeria, West Africa" in *Journal of Biogeography* 25: 285–99.

Hussein, K. 1998. *Conflicts between Farmers and Herders in the Semi-arid Sahel and East Africa*. Norwich: University of East Anglia (Overseas Development Group and School of Development Studies).

Jacobson, J.L. 1988. *Environmental Refugees: A Yardstick of Habitability*. Worldwatch Paper 86. Washington, D.C.: Worldwatch Institute.

Johnston, H.A.S. 1967. *The Fulani Empire of Sokoto*. London: Oxford University Press.

Kates, R.W. et al. 1977. Population, Society and Desertification. In Secretariat of the United Nations Conference on Desertification, ed., *Desertification: Its Causes and Consequences*, pp. 261–317. Oxford: Pergamon Press.

Kirk-Greene, A.H.M. 1958. *Adamawa, Past and Present*. London: Oxford University Press.

Lacroix, P.F. 1952. Matériaux pour servir à l'histoire des peuls de l'Adamawa. *Etudes Camerounaises* V (37–38): 3–61 and VI (39–40): 5–40.

Levin, M.D. 1997. The New Nigeria: Displacement and the Nation. *Journal of Asian and African Studies* 32 (1–2): 134–44.

Little, P.D. and Brokensha, D.W. 1987. "Local Institutions, Tenure and Resource Management in East Africa" in D. Anderson and R. Grove (eds), *Conservation in Africa: People, Policies and Practice*. Pp. 193–209. Cambridge: Cambridge University Press.

Lovejoy, P.E. and Williams, P. A.T. 1997. "Introduction: Displacement and the Politics of Violence" in *Journal of Asian and African Studies* 32 (1–2): 1–4.

Mohammadou, E. 1966. "Introduction historique à l'étude des sociétés du Nord-Cameroun" in *Abbia* 12–13: 233–71.

___ 1978. *Fulbe Hooseere: les royaumes foulbé du plateau de l'Adamaoua au 19ième siècle. Tibati Tignere, Banyo, Ngaoundere. African Languages and Ethnography, VIII*. Tokyo, Institute for the Study of Language and Culture of Asia and Africa (ILCAA).

___ 1981. "L'implantation des Peul dans l'Adamawa (approche chronologique)" in C. Tardits (ed.), *Contribution de la recherche ethnologique à l'histoire des civilisations du Cameroun*. Vol. I, 229–47. Paris: CNRS.

___ 1991. *Traditions historiques des peuples du Cameroun Central, Vol. II. African Languages and Ethnography*, XXIV. Tokyo: Institute for the Study of Language and Culture of Asia and Africa.

Moutou, A. 2002. *Cameroun : Rapport pays sur les problèmes de population, stratégies et interventions dans le cadre de droits et de santé de la reproduction*. Douala: Institut Panafricain pour le développement – Afrique Centrale (IPD-AC).

Oksen, P. 2000. *Cattle, Conflict and Change: Animal Husbandry and Fulani-Farmer Interactions in Boulgou Province, Burkina Faso*. Ph.D. Thesis, Roskilde University.

Oxby, C. 1999. "Mirages of Pastoralist Futures: A Review of Aid Donor Policy in Sahelian Pastoral Zones" in *Review of African Political Economy*, 89: 227–37.

Siran, J.-L. 1980. "Emergence et dissolution des principautés guerrières Vouté" in *Journal des Africanistes*, L (1): 25–57.

Spencer, P. 2000. "Pastoralism and the Growth of Civilization in the Sahel: Islam, Evolution, or the Tragedy of the Commons?" In H. Sørensen et al. (eds), *Natural Resources and the Muslim Traditional Culture in the Sahel-Sudan Region*. Pp. 17–29. Copenhagen: University of Copenhagen (North/South Priority Research Area).

Stryker, J.D. 1989. "Technology, Human Pressure, and Ecology in the Arid and Semi-Arid Tropics" in In H.J. Leonard (ed.), *Environment and the Poor: Development Strategies for a Common Agenda* Pp. 87–109. New Brunswick: Transaction Books.

Swift, J. 1977. "Sahelian Pastoralists: Underdevelopment, Desertification, and Famine" in *Annual Review of Anthropology*, 6: 457–78.

Tonah, S. 2000. "State Policies, Local Prejudices and Cattle Rustling along the Ghana-Burkina Faso Border" in *Africa* 70 (4): 551–67.

Transparency International: http://www.transparency.org

VerEecke, C. 1994. "The Slave Experience in Adamawa: Past and Present Perspectives from Yola (Nigeria)" in *Cahiers d'Études Africaines*, 133–135, XXXIV (1–3): 23–53.

Waters-Bayer, A. and Bayer, W. 1994. "Coming to Terms: Interactions between Immigrant Fulani Cattle-Keepers and Indigenous Farmers in Nigeria's Subhumid Zone" in *Cahiers d'Études Africaines*, 133–135, XXXIV (1–3): 213–29.

Transhumance, Tubes and Telephones: Drought Related Migration as a Process of Innovation

Kristine Juul

Scarcity is often connected with territoriality and boundedness. However, the migration of environmental refugees is not regarded as a solution to the problem of the imbalance between population pressure and scarce resources. Rather, population movements across territories have been perceived as a mechanism for spreading over-exploitation and degradation. As part of a general perspective of crisis and disaster, drought-related migration has been perceived first and foremost as the ultimate exit option for drought-ridden herders who are trying to avoid total destitution, while resource conflicts are seen as the immediate result of increasing pressure on a limited resource base.

Findings from northern Senegal collected over a period between 1988 and 2002 do not confirm this gloomy picture of a production system in crisis. In this case, drought-related migration acted as a catalyst for change, as the drought refugees on their move southwards were forced to develop new and more efficient herd-management strategies, which in the end also benefited the indigenous population in the area of settlement. Due to the skilful ways in which these entrepreneurial migrants adapted to the new situation, in many ways the post-drought period turned into period of increased opportunities. Although many conflicts were played out over access to water and pastures, this was less because of scarce resources than over social and political control.

The Decline of Pastoralism, or Drought as a 'Revelatory Crisis'?

Many authors write of pastoralism within a scenario of crisis (see Baxter, 1993; de Bruijn and van Dijk, 1995; Markakis, 1993), and of the 'decline of pastoralism' as an unquestionable, almost irreversible fact. But as Dietz has shown (1993: 85), they seldom define what they mean by decline: Is it decline in the absolute number of people who can be regarded as pastoralists, or rather decline in the relative contribution of pastoralism to pastoral communities? And is this happening because of 'de-pastoralisation' on the part of some households, or because of a growing importance of the non-pastoral aspects of the economy of the households? Alternatively, is what is involved the absolute and structural decline of the number of animals in the pastoral area, due to either drought or loss of grazing lands?

The term 'crisis' might be considered a more appropriate concept than 'decline' because it allows for the possibility of recovery. But as pastoralism may be conceived of as a model of management in an unpredictable environment, it may be hard to find periods in which the term is not applicable. Considering the Fulanis of the Ferlo, it would appear that the uncritical adoption of a 'crisis scenario' is unlikely to generate very fruitful insights into the processes of transformation that are taking place in northern Senegal. For, if the effects of drought on the livelihoods of the local population are only perceived within a perspective of crisis, then the decline of pastoralism will tend to be regarded as an unquestionable and almost irreversible fact. And when the impact in terms of decline is taken for granted, further scrutiny of the adaptation of drought-ridden herders to their new environment becomes unwarranted and unnecessary.

The unilineal result of this model also presents a number of methodological problems. As 'drought refugees' are reduced to the role of passive victims, almost a residual category, little scope is left for uncovering the unexpected and innovative ways in which drought victims may react to and/or take advantage of new situations. Moreover, if the adaptive capacities of the local population are ignored, a number of local skills and management techniques will be rendered invisible to researchers and policy-makers. As a result, not only are interesting opportunities to study the resilience and adaptive capacities of pastoral societies lost, but research also turns a blind eye to the rapid development that characterises the recent history of many Sahelian countries (see, for example, Morton, 1994: 60–92). Indeed, migration as an exploitation of (new) opportunities is a long-standing tradition in West Africa and has had positive repercussions not only for pastoral productivity, but also for agricultural expansion and the development of trade. As many areas are characterised more by scarcity of labour than scarcity of land (Berry, 1989) an influx of foreign herders or farmers has often acted as a catalyst for the development of new productive activities. This was the case in northern Senegal, as will be shown below.

Assessing the implications of such processes of migration requires a far more open-ended perspective than that offered by the conventional natural resource management framework. One such alternative is provided by Jacqueline Solway's article of 1994, where the effects of the 1979 and 1987 droughts in Botswana are analysed in terms of *revelatory crises*. Instead of perceiving drought solely in terms of crisis and decline, she analyses drought as a disruption of conventional routines, which enables actors to innovate in respect of production techniques and to alter existing power structures.

The notion of a 'revelatory crisis' derives from Marshall Sahlins (1972) and describes a situation in which socio-economic patterns are sufficiently interrupted by droughts or the like to expose contradictions in the existing order that may have been latent or contained prior to the drought. Solway's point, in line with this, is that external factors such as famines or droughts provide perfect scapegoats, since all social dislocations and sufferings may be attributed to these phenomena, while underlying internal problems, such as unequal access to resources and power relations, may be left unacknowledged and therefore unconfronted. Through its disruption of existing routines, drought may instead act as a pretext allowing actors to create innovations in normative codes (Solway, 1994: 473).

In this way, drought becomes a time of experimentation, when taboos may be violated and moral codes flaunted. This is a period when manifestations that were previously considered unacceptable may become accepted. According to Solway (1994: 473), drought paradoxically exposes contradictions and deteriorating conditions, while at the same time allowing them to be concealed and mystified. In this respect it is likely to lead to accelerated rates of social change. Consequently, the perception of droughts as revelatory crises provides us with the means for understanding droughts as periods not only of constraints, but also for new opportunities.

Negotiating Property and Access to Resources

One of the issues that one is likely to confront in relation to situations of drought is the question of property and the sharing of central resources such as water and pastures. In many African societies, relationships pertaining to shared access to resources like water sources play a significant role in binding the community together in ongoing networks of rights and obligations.

As has been stressed in a large number of articles on tenure issues in Africa (Berry, 1989, 1993; Peters, 1992, 1994; Solway, 1994), local concepts of property facilitate reciprocal use, since rights to property are simultaneously individuated and dispersed. While most items may be identified with an individual, a larger kin group will usually enjoy some sort of use rights. This is not to say that there is no difference in access, but rather that property exists in a continuum. A process of commodification may therefore grant greater legitimacy to the rights of the individual or the narrow group of owners, but these rights are still not total. For, while one person's claim may take precedence over others, this does not preclude the others from making claims, nor does it negate the legitimacy of these claims. As Solway stresses, such a system obviously invites redefinition, negotiation and a constant series of counter-claims among kin (Solway, 1994: 482–4).

Depending on their location within the politico-economic structure, farmers and herders have different and sometimes competing interests in and interpretations of the legitimacy of claims to property. Whatever their claims, local conceptions of property still make a variety of contradictory claims legitimate, while denying them requires a rationalisation that is rarely universally accepted. According to Solway, it is under such circumstances that a locally recognised crisis, such as a period of drought, may present an opportunity to redefine the range and priority of property relations and claims. In this situation the drought becomes the licence or moral pretext for a denial of communal claims, which would have been considered antisocial before the drought.[1] If we analyse drought from the perspective of revelatory crisis, a less one-dimensional image of the processes of adaptation to the post-drought situation in northern Senegal may be discerned. This perspective stresses the multiple and often contradictory courses that development in the region has taken, while leaving open the possibility of counter-hypotheses.

The first section of my description of the case study below examines how drought and drought-related migration have contributed to increased productivity in the pastoral production systems of the Ferlo. This is followed by a second section analysing how drought was used by certain strata of the population to justify exclusive rights to crucial resources.

Drought As an Opening for New Opportunities

When talking about droughts as revelatory events, we may usefully distinguish between 'watershed events' and 'events of articulation'.[2] In the context of drought, watershed events are those where changes in meaning and practice have reached a point where it becomes obvious that production patterns will not go back to 'normal' pre-drought conditions once the rains resume. This was the case with the severe droughts of 1972–73 and 1983–84. In contrast to this, the dry years of 1991–93, which will be discussed further on in the article, may be regarded as 'events of articulation'. Here the lasting effects upon the production system were limited. Instead opportunities to question existing power structures and to adapt them to a new emerging order were enhanced.

The two devastating droughts of 1972–73 and 1983–84 profoundly altered the production systems of northern Senegal. Among the areas that were hardest hit by the failing rains was the Senegal River Valley. Here the impact of the droughts was twofold. On the one hand, it spurred a process of sedentarisation, since a large number of herders who had suffered very heavy livestock losses during the droughts were left with few options other than the use of an irrigated plot. As a result, irrigation was boosted considerably between 1975 and 1988, and irrigation schemes sponsored by the state, external donors or the villagers themselves mushroomed along the valley. Indeed the post-drought period turned out to be the peak expansion period for irrigation along the Senegal River.

---

1. In Solway's example, the local emerging commercial elite have used the drought as a pretext for withdrawing their economic resources from the pool available for communal purposes, as part of a shift from wealth in people to wealth in things. Drought may also provide an opportunity or a point of entry for the state to insert itself in the life of citizens in new and unexpected ways, for example, as a consequence of the instrumental effects of drought-relief measures. For a discussion of such instrumental effects of development aid, see Ferguson, 1990.

2. See also Sally Falk Moore's distinction between events with diagnostic qualities and events of articulation (Moore, 1994: 365).

On the other hand, this paved the way for a dramatic increase in mobility among those herders who had a sufficient number of animals left with which to maintain a pastoral life-style. For these herders, the combined effects of poor rains and the proliferation of irrigated agriculture had created increasingly difficult conditions for livestock production along the Senegal River Valley. This pushed them towards the abandonment of their previous, fairly sedentarised agro-pastoral life-style. A large number of them therefore pulled up their roots and moved south towards the more abundant rangelands of the southern Ferlo.

While many studies have come to the unhappy conclusion that herders have been forced out of their area of origin by drought and agricultural expansion, fewer have dealt with how the migrants have fared in the area of their reception. The modalities according to which these herders have adapted to new circumstances therefore remain largely undocumented.

This is remarkable, not least because the outcome of the massive post-drought migration in Senegal turned out to be very different from what had been anticipated. Contrary to expectations, post-drought migration in this case acted as a catalyst for technological innovation among those herders who had been forced to move. This led to a minor revolution in range management strategies, to increased herd productivity and to a dramatic rise in prosperity among newcomers and first-comers in the area of reception. The single most important factor contributing to this success was in fact a spill-over effect from the irrigation process, namely the recycling as water containers of huge rubber inner tubes from the tyres of bulldozers and other heavy machinery used in the preparation of the large irrigation schemes.

The Inner Tube and the Donkey Cart

The importance of this innovation is closely related to the structure of the pastoral space of northern Senegal. This is organised above all by boreholes placed at distances of approximately thirty kilometres from one another. Since the water table in most parts of the Ferlo region is several hundred metres below the surface, diesel pumps make water available to pastoralists and their herds all year round. This enables them to stay in the grazing lands of the Ferlo even after the surface water has dried up. These deep wells, dug mainly by the colonial administration in the mid-1950s, therefore occupy a central position in pastoral resource management.

A major difficulty during the dry season consists in simultaneously ensuring optimal fodder conditions and limiting energy losses linked to the effort to reach the water sources. As the dry season progresses, the distance between the wells and the fresh and untrampled pastures increases. If cattle are grazed further than fifteen to twenty kilometres from the well, too much energy is spent on getting to the water. For sheep and goats the maximum distance is somewhat less.

Among the indigenous herders of the Ferlo region, the dry-season strategy consists in moving the camps to a distance of five or six kilometres from the deep well once the natural pools have dried up. The animals are then grazed in a centrifugal movement, reaching pastures still further away as the dry season progresses. Local herders must therefore reckon with significant energy losses by the end of the dry season, when animals become weak and skinny, and thus difficult to sell at reasonable prices.

When the drought refugees from the Senegal River Valley, the so-called FuutankoBe,[1] arrived in the southern part of the Ferlo region, they were forced to attack the problem in a radically different way. Aware of their marginal position as foreigners in an area still marked by the adversities of the drought, they tried to avoid conflicts with the settled population setting up their camps on marginal pastures, at a good distance from the boreholes. This required a solution to dealing with the problem of energy losses. In this situation the recycling of old rubber inner tubes from cars and tractors into water containers showed ingenuity, since, when laid on a donkey cart, these tubes, which tended to become larger and larger once their potential was recognised, could transport large quantities of water (300, 600, even 1000 litres) over long distances. This considerably reduced the constraints related to watering, enabling the newcomers to live closer to the fresh and untrampled pastures at a distance of up to twenty kilometres from the wells. The radius of pastures accessible to the herds was now considerably enlarged when compared to the 'centrifugal grazing strategy' employed by the more sedentary households.

At present, most pastoral households have at least one cart, often two or three.[2] They are used primarily to transport water and for travelling. In cases of transhumance they are also used to carry younger and older members of the family and to transport luggage, poultry, water and sometimes industrial feed concentrates to ensure the proper feeding of the animals. Carts also enable herders to transport the newborn lambs or sick animals, which are unable to make the journey otherwise. In this way, they help to limit losses related to migration considerably.

While the adult animals continue to water at the borehole every second day, the ingenuity of the new system consists in sparing the youngest and the sick animals the long and arduous trip to the well. Placing the camp far from the well means that the young animals that graze in the vicinity of the camp are assured access to fresh pastures. In this way the herd is provided with optimal fodder con-

1. Since the area of the Senegal River from which the migrating herds originate (*la Moyenne Vallée*) is called Fuuta in FulBe, herders from the area are called FuutankoBe, the people of the Fuuta. The FuutankoBe herders are also referred to as *egge-egge*, from the term *eggol*, meaning those who are always on the move (Ba, 1986: 137).

2. In 1994, pastoral households (*galles*) in Bouteyni possessed an average of 1.62 carts. 18 of the 33 households examined by Thébaud had at least one cart, while the richest households had from 3 to 6 (Thébaud, 1994: 24).

ditions, a situation which is maintained through frequent movements of the camp during the dry season, while the distance from the water point is kept constant. The result is a substantial decrease in mortality and an increase in calving rates and other parameters of herd productivity, for which reason the tube is often referred to as 'the secret of the Fulani'.

A precondition for the 'triumph of the tube' was the distribution of horse and donkey carts among the herders. During the 1970s the cooperative movement made attempts to introduce carts as part of a general attempt to mechanise the rural sector. The results had nonetheless been meagre, and by the beginning of the 1980s the number of pastoral households with a cart at their disposal was extremely limited (Santoir, 1982: 30). Between 1975 and 1991, however, the number of carts increased tenfold (Santoir, 1994: 251), from one per 24 households to one cart and a horse for almost every second household. This booming period coincided with the massive migration of the FuutankoBe herders, for whom the carts became a *sine qua non* for the development of new herding strategies. Once it had been introduced, the local herders quickly adopted the system. As Santoir notes, this rapid adaptation is particularly noteworthy, since these rather substantial investments had to be made in the midst of a drought period without any external assistance.

Young herders filling up their tubes at the water reservoir.

From Cattle to Sheep

The full ingenuity of the new water transportation technique is perhaps best understood when linked with the development by FuutankoBe herders of a highly specialised herding system based on the raising of sheep rather than cattle.

As described widely in the literature on pastoral production systems, drought rehabilitation strategies tend to be based on the diversification of income strategies when herd depletion is limited by non-pastoral activities such as agriculture or wage labour. The surplus from these activities may temporarily be invested in sheep and goats. The aim of such investments is that once such small-stock has reproduced sufficiently, the offspring are exchanged for heifers, thus contributing to the reconstruction of the cattle herd.

By contrast, the rehabilitation strategy adopted by FuutankoBe herders has been one of specialisation. Rather than diversify the household economy into agriculture or wage labour, they have embarked on a very labour-intensive herding system based on the raising of sheep and to a lesser extent of goats. The goal of this strategy is to keep herd reproduction as high as possible by increasing mobility in order to ensure fodder availability throughout the year. In this way herd composition is adjusted to suit the new and more difficult ecological conditions, since a large part of the fodder requirements of sheep and goats can be met by letting them browse on tree products which are less affected by failing rains. The shift towards sheep was also motivated by the higher reproduction rates of small stock and by a substantial rise in the market value of sheep in particular.

This shift in herd composition towards the large scale rearing of small-stock was only made possible by the improved watering and grazing conditions. For whereas flock sizes in the traditional system tend to be limited by the difficulties of simultaneously meeting pasturage and watering requirements, the tube and the donkey cart enabled herders to move closer to distant pastures. This allowed them to keep far larger flocks of sheep than had been possible earlier. But while the tube and cart system helped to limit losses of animals, it is important to stress that the new system of water transport is extremely labour-intensive. As a result of increased labour investments in surveillance and water transportation, little space is left for supplementary income-generating activities.

Increased Mobility and New Grazing Techniques

The strategy was, however, only possible with a high level of mobility. Hence the tubes and carts have been essential, not only in connection with the transportation of water, but also in relation to travelling, as they contribute to lowering the constraints on pastoral mobility. As newborn lambs can be transported on wheels together with industrial foodstuffs, the benefits of moving to more abundant pas-

Newborn lambs transported
under the wheels of a cart.

tures will often outweigh the risks associated with mobility,[1] which is no longer
related only to situations of drought.

A direct result of the technological innovation resulting from the tubes is that
the number of herders migrating regularly over longer distances has increased considerably. As transhumance has become less risky, it is predominantly the search
for fodder plants that motivates FuutakoBe herders for extensive nomadisation
several hundred kilometres south of their usual zone of interest to the Gambian
border. As one herder stated: 'Many things have changed for pastoralism since
1973.

This is due to the arrival of the donkey carts, the water inner tubes and the industrial feed concentrates.[2] All three ease mobility.

The strategy of specialised sheep-rearing has proved to be an extremely viable
one. Thanks to better drought resistance and the shorter reproduction cycle of

---

1. The risks related to nomadisation involve animals getting lost on alien ranges, disease and mortality among exhausted animals, lack of appropriate water and fodder conditions, and increased
investment of labour in the surveillance of animals in alien areas.

2. The use of agro-industrial by-products and feed concentrates to supplement the poor pastures at
the end of the dry season is another example of herders' 'unwrapping' of selected project interventions. Feed concentrates were originally promoted by various livestock projects as a means of
improving milk production and increasing fertility. They are now widely used by herders. In
most cases, however, they are not used systematically but mainly given to weak and sick animals.
In a survey carried out in 1989 by the author in collaboration with O. Touré, 58% of herders
indicated that they used agro-industrial by-products and feed concentrates. Only 15%, however,
indicated that they spent more than 50,000 CFA (i.e. 1000 French Francs) a year on this.

sheep, herders originating from the Fuuta area were able to recover their losses very quickly, and today most of them have flocks far larger than their pre-drought size.[1] Among FuutankoBe herders residing in the south of the Ferlo region, it is not unusual to see herds of 400 to 700 or even 1000 sheep and goats. Indeed, their strategy of specialisation was such that many of them now are forced to diversify their economic strategies, first by investing part of their surplus into cattle, which is less demanding in terms of surveillance, and later into shops and real estate in nearby cities, as it becomes impossible to mobilize sufficient manpower to look after more animals and larger flocks.[2]

Increased Mobility as a Win–Win Situation

Since this successful strategy has been widely copied by the original inhabitants, the result is that livestock population, stock composition and geographical distribution have all been substantially modified over the last two decades.[3] According to the widely held orthodoxies on overgrazing, it might be assumed that the increased number of animals browsing on the range would lead to overgrazing. Nonetheless, migrants and sedentary herders alike recognise the positive impact of migrant herds, since they not only contribute to the opening up of new land for pasture, but also help to improve the quality of the range.

As mentioned above, the 'newcomers' usually settle far from other herders and at considerable distances from the borehole in order to find pastures that have not been trampled. Thus they often penetrate into areas that were formerly dominated by dense bush vegetation. According to the herders, in such areas sheep tend to clear the bush by browsing, so that high quality pastures can come up with the

---

1. Unfortunately no studies of flock sizes before 1972–73 are available. An unpublished summary of the different studies carried out on herd compositions made by Santoir sums up the following results: In the Senegal River Valley studies of herd composition after 1975 report average small stock flocks of 30.9 head per household (Blanc/SEDES, 1975 in samples taken downstream in the valley, Santoir, personal communication); 40.6 head (samples from Mbane and Thille Boubacar, Santoir, personal communication); 21.3 head (Matam, Santoir, 1979); and 35.1 head (Senegal River Basin, Santoir, personal communication). Tourrand and Direction de L'Elevage (DIREL) estimate drought losses of small stock in the two drought periods at between 30% and 50% (Tourrand, 1989: 4 and data from DIREL Statistical Unit).

2. As an example of the booming of retail shops, the village of Barkedji, which at my first visit in 1989 had two shops, had more than 35 in 2002. In the main town of Dahra Djoloff there is now a wealth of shops, of which, interestingly, more than ten of the largest are owned by FuutakoBe herders.

3. According to figures from the National Office of Livestock (Direction de l'Elevage, DIREL), the growing importance of sheep and goats in the southern part of the Ferlo has resulted in an increase of 162 % in the small stock population in the Department of Linguère from the predrought level of 1971 to 1993. Until 1968 cattle exceeded small stock in numbers in the northern half of Senegal (Linguère Departement). This is in contrast to the situation today, where one finds 35 head of cattle per 100 head of small stock in Senegal north of Gambia (Santoir 1994: 234) Because of their higher market value, sheep are preferred to goats.

next rains.[1] At present nothing seems to indicate that the increased number of animals grazing in the southern part of the Ferlo is leading to range deterioration. On the contrary, the new facilities for water transportation are enabling herders to spread their animals over a larger area, thus permitting formerly under-used pastures to be exploited. Range deterioration is therefore likely to be insignificant in comparison with agro-pastoral and more sedentarised production systems, where animals are concentrated around the village.

However, it is also worth noting how the meanings and values attributed to certain objects or strategies have changed over time: in the process, those pastures that are located furthest away in the bush shifted from having limited value to becoming some of the principal objects of conflict. Once the potentials of the new water transportation system were fully grasped, the strategy of settling in the bush as far away as possible from the well turned into a winners' strategy, where it was foreign owners living closest to the untrampled pastures who had managed to position themselves most favourably in the on-going competition over fodder resources. Far from any first impression that this was an act of conflict-avoidance and marginalisation, the ability to set up a camp far from the well has turned into one of the prime markers of the successful strategy put into practice by drought refugees. This strategy is still being refined, the latest fashion being a large iron cistern on wheels manufactured by the local blacksmiths, through which the volume of water transported may be further increased while ending the inconvenience of rubber tubes exploding, which represents many hours of lost effort in terms of hauling water and travel time.

As will be discussed in further detail below, this influx of a large contingent of mobile and very specialised herders has not taken place without conflicts. This does not alter the fact that, in the case of Senegal, drought, acting as a catalyst for technological innovation, has given a substantial boost to pastoral production. However, by giving rise to a new class of very rich pastoralists, the majority of whom are to be found among the FuutankoBe population, this technological innovation has also contributed to altering existing social relations in the area. This will be the focus of the following section.

The Politics of Adaptation and the Adaptation of Politics

Among those studying pastoral societies, there is a tendency to naturalise mobility and towards analysing it mainly in terms of its physical characteristics, as a journey from one point to another. However, as the Indian anthropologist Agrawal

---

1. Research over nine years in the GTZ project of Widou Thiengoly in the northern Ferlo confirms these statements. In this project, the regeneration of pastures turned out to be lower in areas under controlled and reduced grazing pressure than in areas submitted to 'normal' grazing. In years of consecutive good rainfalls (such as 1988, 1989 and 1990), controlled low grazing proved directly harmful to pastures (see Tluczykont, 1991: 41).

has pointed out, writing on Raika pastoralists in Rajastan: 'Movements through a landscape also depends on the ability to find one's way in a thicket of dynamic property rights regimes in land'. (Agrawal 1998: 12)

In the second section, therefore, the focus is on how the newcomers have managed to adapt their economic and political strategies to the new opportunities offered by the post-drought situation. The focus is now on the processes through which these drought refugees have managed to negotiate access to water and land with a group of competing actors with whom they entertained at best very distant relationships. The difficulties which this process entailedmay be captured in the following quotations.

> There is much more jealousy now than was the case in 1983–84. It is now, when the locals have started to copy the newcomers and have large herds themselves, that the problem of rivalry arises. (FuutankoBe herder, Djagueli, Feb. 1993.)

> It is very difficult to prohibit people from using the well and the pastures solely by law. There are no rules to apply. Although wells are private property, its difficult to limit access. The only way is to block access to the water. If the well contains little water, the foreign herders are likely to abandon the area within a short time, but if the well has plenty of water it is almost impossible to persuade people to go elsewhere. (Rural councillor, Bembem, Feb. 1993.)

As these statements show, one immediate effect of post-drought rehabilitation and of the growing prosperity of the newcomer population was that conflicts between the two parties increased in number and intensity. For while adaptation to the new pastoral production system proved manageable and highly successful, it also brought about new exigencies in terms of realignments of political authority and of rights to and control of resources.

Little documentation is available concerning relationships between strangers and locals before the large-scale droughts of the 1970s and 1980s. It is therefore difficult to assess in retrospect whether the level of conflict has increased substantially since the arrival of the first drought refugees. However, interviews carried out on the subject do leave a clear impression that although conflicts and contradictions were, and still are, recurrent phenomena in the pastoral communities of the Ferlo region, the general porosity and latent mobility[1] inherent in these communities has helped to ensure a relatively peaceful influx of the first wave of foreigners. The extent this impressive achievement was revealed when I tried to assess the number of newcomers in five villages and found that the proportion settled on a regular basis in the vicinities of the villages amounted to between 30% and 70% of the popu-

---

1. Population movements are no new phenomenon either to the Sahel in general or to the Ferlo region. Closer scrutiny of the genealogy of those claiming to be 'locals' or 'first-comers' often shows that they have occupied their present territory for only a few more years than the so-called 'strangers'. On the other hand, those labelled as 'newcomers' have in many cases been regular users of a particular deep-well for nearly 20 years.

lation.[1] To this should be added a large but varying number of nomadising herders passing through to villages on shorter or longer visits during the dry season.

However, this situation of amity derived just as much from the submissive attitude of the FuutankoBe herders, who chose to keep a low profile vis-à-vis the local population. In order to avoid conflicts, they camped mainly in remote areas and (at least temporarily) endured the malice of the 'first-comer' population.

But as prosperity and wealth in animals increased, so did the competition for the available resources. Since the beginning of the 1990s, the normative codes of Fulani solidarity seem to have come under increasing pressure. According to these codes, water and pastures are open to anyone, and denial of access to strangers is considered shameful. For in a drought-prone area like the Ferlo region, climatic hazards and crisis conditions are recurrent phenomena that may force anyone to camp in alien territory.

From the 1990s on, ever fiercer claims to exclusivity have been made by the first-comer population. Increasingly, these herders are asserting their rights as indigenous inhabitants, as part of a general upsurge in distinctions between 'locals' and 'strangers'. At the same time, the former migrants, who have entered into a phase of economic consolidation, are trying to convert some of their newly acquired wealth into social capital in order to increase their political authority and extend their control over productive resources. As a result, tension and rivalry between the two groups today run higher than during the early drought years.

Despite the feelings of the actors involved, few of these struggles involve the participation of local representatives of the state apparatus. Indeed, these struggles over political alignments are seldom conducted as direct clashes. Instead they are part of a long-term war of attrition over the meanings ascribed to key statuses, principles, codes and customs. As a result, many of these struggles tend to pass unnoticed by people other than those directly involved.

A prominent example of such 'noiseless' struggles has been attempts to enforce exclusive rights by denying access to water or similar acts directed towards limiting the scope for manoeuvre of alien herds (as expressed in the quotation above). Often the motivation for such acts is not shared by the population as a whole, for which reason this type of social manoeuvring is likely to be hampered by local conceptions of rights and obligations. Limiting access to alien herds therefore requires a skilful reinterpretation of the existing normative framework. In the case of post-drought Ferlo, the situation of scarcity created by the shorter, localised drought of 1991–92 was therefore a convenient opportunity for political and social adjustment to a new reality.

---

1. This assessment was carried out in the villages of Barkedji, Naoré, Djagueli, Fourdou and Ranerou. For a more detailed account, see Juul 1999.

Drought as an Opportunity for Situational Adjustment

Between 1991 and 1993, failing rains in the northern Ferlo for two successive years propelled a new wave of migration from the Senegal River Valley to the less affected areas of southeastern Ferlo. As early as the beginning of the rainy season of 1991, when it became clear that there would not be enough rain, the most live-stock-rich herders from the Senegal River Valley started moving to join their kin in the southern Ferlo. The animals were moved at a steady pace, giving them the opportunity to graze and recover at the various boreholes or wells on the way. At certain wells this resulted in a tripling of the number of animals that had to share the meagre pastures available.

Obviously this created anxiety among the local population, who foresaw that they would be forced to migrate themselves once the large foreign herds had stripped the area of fodder. Transhumance for these often relatively poor agro-pastoralists is often rather problematic, since it makes great demands on labour and logistics. More importantly, perhaps, it is likely to hamper other supplementary activities that may provide crucial income to the household economy.

In addition to the immediate threat of fodder shortage, anxiety arose among the indigenous population that this new contingent of migrants would also settle in the area on a more permanent basis, a situation that could further change the balance of power and threaten the privileges of the settled elites. In an attempt to reserve the meagre resources for themselves, new methods of limiting access to pastures were tried out.

Although these techniques varied, they were primarily aimed at making the watering of large (alien) herds as difficult as possible. At some of the relatively shallow wells, the pump was blocked so that water had to be drawn by hand. At the deep artesian boreholes, where water is inaccessible without a pump, instead the well committees obstructed the connection between the reservoir and the animals' drinking troughs. This forced herders to draw water directly from the reservoir and to water the often very large herds from a few oil drums cut in half. Consequently, the time and effort spent in watering the animals increased significantly.

The most frequent way of discouraging herders from settling, however, was to charge alien herds exorbitant watering fees. In the course of the 1991–92 drought, migrating herders in the southern Ferlo unanimously reported excessive taxing policies or direct denial of access. Many herders claimed to have spent large amounts of money bribing the various well committees or paying sums equivalent to the cost of a full month of watering at their usual well just to use the watering facilities of certain wells for a few days.[1] For many well committees, the influx of strangers

---

1. One of my informants claimed to have paid 2,500 FCFA at the borehole at Naoré for 15 days, 4,000 at the well at Bem-Bem for 4 days, and 10,850 at the borehole at Loumbi Aly Tedy for one month of watering.

therefore turned into a new profit opportunity, as the excessive taxing of alien herds contributed to increasing turnover many times over, leaving many indigenous herders to cease their payments completely.

Such opportunities for profit-making were also exploited by some of the locally elected councillors, who abused their authority in order to make transhumant herders pay for the right to install themselves in the pastures. This illicit commodification of the right of settlement was apparently carried out under different 'legal' guises of a 'fine' paid to the councillor. Nevertheless it was yet another example of attempts to commodify former sharing arrangements (free movement on the range) and to give such transactions a legal pretext and thus make them more socially acceptable.

Until this moment the local elites enjoyed a clear monopoly of local politics. But as newcomers felt increasingly squeezed by the discriminating policies, they started to react. Despite being dispersed over the territory, they managed to organise a delegation to take their protests to the government in Dakar. By drawing on their religious network through the Tidjane Muslim Brotherhood, they were able to obtain access to the Minister of Interior and have him intervene on their side of the conflict. This was all the more remarkable, as the Minister was close related to the settled elite in the area, someone who largely owed his political career to the electoral support of the settled Fulani population of the region. Now he sided the FuutankoBe herders by denouncing the illegal practices of overtaxing strangers and by stressing the state ownership of, and free grazing rights over, Senegalese territory. In this way he overruled local attempts to regulate access to resources, while forging an alliance with a new rising and economically successful group of herders, who could later prove to become important allies. This breakthrough for political influence on the part of the 'newcomer' population has been used extensively since then.

The remarkable ability of local politicians and other pressure groups to short-circuit the official process of decision-making by involving politicians at higher levels in order to defend particular local interests has been described by several authors. Blundo (1998) and Juul (1999) have noted the extraordinary ease with which politicians from relatively low levels of party politics have been able to gain access to the central stages of Senegalese politics. Technological innovation has also been significant here. While obtaining access to centres of political influence previously demanded the dispatching of a delegation of people to present their case to various political connections in town, the introduction of public telephone booths in most of the borehole villages in the wake of the 2001 elections seems further to have limited the distance between the 'low' and 'high' levels of Senegalese politics. These telephones quickly developed into important channels for the dissemination of rural protest, as local politicians (FutankoBe and indigenous) do not hesitate to call the politically most influential individuals, such as the Minister of Internal Affairs, if decisions are taken at local level of which they do not approve. As can be seen from the picture below, it is not uncommon to

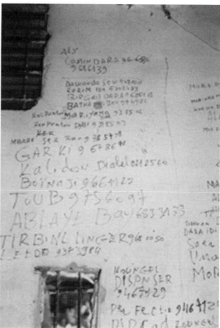

Telephone booths have spread remarkably over the Ferlo region since the late 1990s. The right-hand picture shows the walls of one of the booths, with important numbers such as the hospital *(dispenser)* and firebrigade *(birgad dara)*, as well as those of central politicians such as Daouda Sow and Karim Ba.

find the names and numbers of the most prominent Fulani politicians listed on the walls of the public telephone booth alongside other convenient numbers such as the police station and the hospital, so that any emergency situation can be handled through direct connection with the most powerful person at hand. Obviously such telephone calls seldom do the job alone, but are followed up through other urban connections to ensure that the message has been properly understood.

Exclusive Rights and the Heterogeneity of Interests

> The problem is the lack of rain, not the arrival of foreign herders. But there are too many herds now. If more arrive the pump won't be able to provide sufficient water. (President of the well committee of Jaen Fuuta, 1992).

Local herders in general are rather ambivalent about the various attempts to exclude transhumant herds. As can be seen from the quotation above, many competing justifications for the denial of access are offered, ranging from presumably 'neutral' technicalities related to the fragile state of the worn-out mechanical borehole equipment or a 'disinterested' reference to the lack of rain, to far more biased references to an 'excessive number of animals'.

But hostile attitudes towards strangers are far from uniform. In reality, the transgressions of the Fulani norms of hospitality mentioned above are not invariably acceptable to the population as such. Many local herders have expressed their concern about the ill-treatment of foreigners:

> Closing off the wells is not proper behaviour. The calamities which have forced these people to move might affect us next time. Besides, where there are many people, there is also more happiness. (President of the well committee, Loumbi Sanrabe 1992)

Neither the denial of access to watering facilities, the differential and excessive taxing of the migrating herds, nor the attempts to commodify the right to camp on the open range complies with the customary norms and regulations of local resource management. They also infringe the legal framework covering watering and grazing facilities, which stresses free and equal rights of access for all Senegalese citizens. Claiming exclusive rights to resources that have previously been free to all has therefore required considerable effort on the part of the local elites in constructing moral pretexts permitting transgressions of the accepted norms of Fulani solidarity. Their attempts are further complicated by the contradictory and ambiguous positions of the local population.

The cry for exclusive rights is primarily raised by the politically strongest groups of herders and agriculturalists. It is among these groups that the discourse of scarcity has been promoted most energetically in order to justify restrictions on the use of common resources such as water and pastures. Thus these groups have tried to adjust the system in their favour. For while high degrees of permeability and free access to water and pastures are preconditions for a mobile, extensive livestock system, the indigenous system of production has been moving towards increasing sedentarisation ever since the installation of boreholes in the 1950s. This system evidently favours the development of more exclusive rights. For these groups, mobility no longer takes precedence as a risk management strategy. Exclusive rights, where pastures are restricted to a limited group of users, could turn out to enhance their potential for engaging in more pragmatic herding strategies.

But even among the local elite, the call for exclusivity is ambiguous and indeterminate. Among these groups, foreigners represent not only competition and constraints, but also new income opportunities. In general the arrival of economically powerful foreign herders has increased prosperity and provided an important boost to the economic life of the villages. Local trade in livestock, often an important supplementary activity of the local agro-pastoralists, is encouraged, as are the weekly markets. Sales of grain by peasants to non-cultivating strangers have increased, as has the turnover of the local shops. New income opportunities are generated, as local youths are contracted by the rich herders as paid herders, just as a wealth of services and gifts are exchanged to improve relationships between the two parties.

Even more important are the substantial subsidies that the newcomers provide towards the running costs of the deep wells. With the arrival of a large number of livestock-rich herders, the turnover of the local well committees in charge of the operation and maintenance of the boreholes has increased dramatically. A lack of accounting transparency has facilitated informal agreements in favour of the in-digenous herders, leaving many wells to be financed almost exclusively by the ex-orbitant taxes imposed on FuutankoBe herds. This system, which more or less exempts the first-comer population from paying watering fees, has obviously helped to make the arrival of a large number of foreigners more acceptable to the indigenous population.

This also reflects the new political role of the well committees. Although the latter have no official authority with regard to regulating access to adjacent pas-tures, the low water table ensures that access to pastures is controlled by those controlling the watering facilities. But the well committees do not just hold the key to controlling local grazing resources. Due to the rapidly growing funds col-lected as watering fees, they have also become a important source of profit, and as such a means of gaining political power for those who control them. In this way, well committees have turned into vital institutions in local political life and are used as such by the local political elite. As the funds of the well committee are crucial assets for local elites with political aspirations, attempts to restrict access to high-paying strangers are no longer so intensive. Instead new alliances may be forged with newcomers, who in certain cases have been able to play very skilfully on these rivalries, trading representation on the committee for political support at election times.

Thus as conflicts over local resources become politicised and intermingled with larger political goals, the conflicts generated by post-drought migration tend to be related less to competition over presumably scarce pastoral resources than to struggles to gain control over political key institutions such as the well com-mittees. This therefore becomes yet another example of how objects of struggle may change in the process of adaptation.

From Claims for Open Access to the Enforcement of Private Property: The Changing Attitudes of 'Older' Migrants

Perhaps the most interesting expression of post-drought rehabilitation and adapta-tion has been the ways in which the attitudes and perceptions exhibited by certain layers of newcomers have changed during the process. Claims for exclusive rights are no longer expressed solely by the settled indigenous population, but are increas-ingly being made by 'older' Fuutanke herders. As part of their adaptation to chang-ing conditions and new opportunities, moral rules and old solidarities among these well-established newcomers are being transformed. Increasingly, they are support-ing attempts to limit the number of transhumants settling around 'their' boreholes. In this way, they are discreetly seeking to limit the access of those of their relatives from the Fuuta who have only recently managed to rebuild a sufficiently large herd and who are now ready to start copying the production strategies of their prosper-ous kin. Through the continuous moulding and circumvention of Fulani norms of solidarity, some of the former drought refugees seem to be turning into fierce defenders of the right to exclude 'newcomers' from the local resource base as were the so-called first-comers.[1] Although in general FuutankoBe herders have tried to protect resources governed a open access regimes, this does not demonstrate any stronger propensity among them towards collectivity than what may be found among the first-comer population. Rather, it reflects the perception of immediate needs. For in reality some of the most successful attempts to secure individual access to the range have been by newcomers. The most striking example here is the digging of private wells as a means of securing of individual property rights to part of the range. Such operations obviously involve not only considerable investment,[2] but also considerable political skill in obtaining a licence for drilling. Nevertheless, private wells have been sunk in the south-eastern Ferlo by rich FuutankoBe herders in several localities (some of which are located within the boundaries of the national game reserve, although settlement here is legally confined to the existing boreholes).

What is interesting is how the FuutankoBe herders, who are otherwise fierce defenders of free grazing rights, apparently adhere to restrictions where their own wells are concerned. Asked whether such a well would not attract other users, one of the new well-owners replied that he had been granted not only rights of exclusivity to his private well, but also to the pastures in a radius of 5 kilometres surrounding it. As mentioned above, such actions involve clear violations of both Islamic and customary law, as well as transgressions of national law. Herders' assertions of property rights not only to the well itself but also the adjacent pastures therefore constitute a revealing re-interpretation of norms. The allegation, and the precision with which the extension of rights was described, might well derive from an optimistic interpretation of existing regulations, which prohibit the creation of fields within a distance of a kilometre around the wet season ponds.[3] Interpreting this as a right to control the adjacent pastures is yet another example of the changes in mentality and the transgressions of moral codifications, which, according to Solway, are likely to take place in a period of readjustment after a drought. For the appeal of such wells is not merely the need for more secure wa-

---

1. It may be convenient here to stress that even among these herders, the genealogy of 'indigenousness' and belonging may in many cases be less solid than might be expected. In the village of Ranérou, for example, one group of the fiercest opponents to the strangers, the cattle-rich FafaBe herders, had only arrived in the village at the beginning of the 1970s, just before the drought.

2. According to the examples provided, the price of a well in this area ranges from 600,000 to 1 million CFA. Three such private wells have been located by the author, but according to the *souspréfet* of Ogo, the number of FuutankoBe herders who have obtained permission to dig private wells is far larger. At present an investigation is being carried out into the illegal issuing of permits within the national game reserve.

3. The idea that control over a source of water also confers control over land within a certain radius of the well may also stem from the many mapping exercises and delimitations of resource regimes and 'pastoral units' (*unités pastorales*) currently popular among development projects (such as PAPEL and PRODAM) working with the same logic in the area.

tering facilities: the attraction lies just as much in its status as a *man-made* well, a feature which lends itself more readily to being claimed as exclusive property.

This need, felt by newcomers, to ensure future access to productive resources by claiming them as private property seems to be increasing as newcomers increase their prosperity. During my latest fieldwork in May 2002, I found that many of the richest and therefore also most mobile herders were actively engaged not only in digging wells, but also in building brick houses in their dry season camps. As in most cases these camps were located in gazetted areas, both the wells and the brick-houses were clearly illegal constructions. The motive for these considerable investments seems to lie more in their symbolic attributes as signs of settlement and belonging through investments in the land than in any increase in tendancy towards a more sedentarised lifestyle. The brick houses and the wells – which in several cases provide quite insignificant amounts of water due to the well-known scarcity of easily accessible aquifers – and the considerable investment involved in construction and in bribing the authorities underscore how these infrastructures serve as 'monuments of integration,'[1] whose primary purpose is to make it more difficult for local authorities to evict the newcomers from the land. As such they are symbols of a new stage in the ongoing struggle between old and new elites respectively to limit, or extend and strengthen, acquired rights of occupation.

The Establishment of Exclusivity: A Unidirectional Movement?

In areas characterised by drought and high mobility, identities and group solidarities tend to emerge or dissolve according to the opportunities available. Thus 'ethnic' identities are constantly being reconstituted. Labels like 'FuutankoBe', 'migrant' or 'stranger' have helped to give the drought refugees of the Senegal River Valley a group identity they did not have before. During the current process of economic and political consolidation among the majority of these herders, a new situation has been created in which these solidarities seem to evanesce and be replaced by other types of alliance, for example, with part of the settled local elite.

Nevertheless this movement is not unidirectional, and newcomers still straddle the divide between different forms of identity according to what is more convenient in the specific situation. It was by stressing their situation as foreigners deprived of their rights to move freely over the range that they established the basis of their present success. Once 'firmer' rights have been granted through official recognition or the enforcement of 'private property-like' rights to land adjacent to private wells, other concerns than free grazing and watering rights have tended to take precedence. Nonetheless, it is still by referring to their group identity as

---

1. The phrase 'monuments of integration' is borrowed from Ferguson (after Nielsen 1999), who uses the term 'monuments of development' to describe symbolic acts or constructions made by local communities in order to signal modernity and a willingness to 'be developed' to donors.

'those who contribute most to the running costs of the well' that they can lay claim to representation on the well committee and other similar institutions. Likewise, the tendency towards increased sedentarisation is paralleled by a tendency towards increased mobility, a situation that applies to first-comers and newcomers alike. Thus claims to more exclusive rights are likely to continue to coexist with claims in favour of free access to pastoral resources.

Stressing the continuous straddling of herders between different types of identity points to a slightly different interpretation of the role of drought than that proposed by Solway. Where Solway states that drought accelerates and renders visible what have previously been latent processes and, in a somewhat uni-lineal interpretation of the revelatory process, stresses how the vitality of shared-use entitlements is being undermined as a result of long-term structural changes towards commodification, privatisation and class-formation (1994: 492), the case of Senegal seems to point towards a far more ambiguous and fluid situation, in which several trends are at work at the same time.

It is true that the acquisition of land by individuals and the commodification of former sharing arrangements are becoming common; but this does not confirm a general trend towards the individualisation or privatisation of hitherto communal resources. Apart, perhaps, from the cases of 'spontaneous privatisation' of the range surrounding the private wells, few of the incidents outlined above point towards individual acquisition, but instead they are intertwined with more 'reciprocal' arrangements.

Conclusion

As shown above, the case of post-drought Senegal does not fit in with a crisis scenario, nor does it suggest that pastoralism is in decline. There is neither an absolute nor any structural decline in the number of animals. Instead of a depastoralisation of household economies, development seems to favour adaptation towards a more specialised, mobile and labour-intensive system of production.

Pastoralists in northern Senegal have been faced with climatic variability as well as the threat of agricultural encroachment on their grazing lands. Nonetheless, their creativity and innovative spirit have enabled them to overcome the hazards of the drought, and even to take advantage of the new opportunities provided by the changed situation. As a result, FuutankoBe herders have become richer than they were before the drought forced them to migrate, a trend also found among a number of the 'first-comer' herders. The result is a paradoxical situation in which, although there are now more people and more livestock in a smaller area than before the drought, herd productivity and prosperity are steadily increasing among both first-comers and newcomers. This has also led to a political strengthening of the herders in the face of the powerful groups of cultivators who have tried to encroach on pastoral lands.

In a number of cases, this successful adaptation to a post-drought situation has implied re-interpretations and social manoeuvrings which have transgressed existing moral standards and codes of proper conduct. The most prominent examples to be evoked have been where 'indigenous' herders have denied access to herders who are drought victims, where rural councillors have charged herders for settling on the range or when part of the range has been subjected to private expropriation by individual herders through the establishment of a privately owned well. Obviously, processes tending towards increasing exclusivity, commodification and even privatisation were in train even before the droughts. However, as I have shown here, on several occasions the perception of crisis, in terms of deficient precipitation or situations of scarcity, has provided the necessary licence for actors to extend these processes to previously unacceptable levels. The period of post-drought rehabilitation must therefore be analysed as a series of events in the course of which people have actively contested and revised key notions and representations. These events are part of a practical political struggle in which different groups of people defend their interests and claims. In this struggle a vast range of direct and indirect strategies are employed, demonstrating the adroitness of both elites and subordinate groups in identifying sources of power and leverage.

This material from Senegal may represent a special case, which does not lend itself readily to generalisations. Nonetheless it clearly runs contrary to mainstream thinking on post-drought rehabilitation and indicates the need, expressed by Salzman (1995: 163), to adopt a pluralist perspective. Such a perspective stresses multi-causality and focuses upon the interaction of many different factors in the processes that generate the patterns of human custom and action that we wish to understand. Although human adaptation to an area takes account of the area's environmental conditions, it is important to stress that there are many different kinds of adaptation and many likely outcomes.

References

Agrawal, Arun 1998. *Greener Pastures: Politics, Markets and Community among a Migrant Pastoral People*. Durham and London: Duke University Press.

Ba, Cheick 1986. *Les Peul du Senegal : Etude Géographique*. Dakar: Les nouvelles Editions Africaines.

Baxter, P.W.T. 1993. "The 'New' East African Pastoralist: An Overview" in J. Markakis (ed.), *Conflict and Decline of Pastoralism in the Horn of Africa*. London: Macmillan Press.

Blundo, Giorgio 1998. "Decentralisation, Participation and Corruption in Senegal". Paper presented at the 14th International Congress of Anthropology and Ethnological Science, Williamsburg, Virginia.

Berry, Sara 1989. "Social Institutions and Access to Resources" in *Africa* 59 (1): 41–56

Berry, Sara 1993. *No Condition is Permanent: The Social Dynamics of Agrarian Change in Sub-Saharan Africa*. Madison: University of Wisconsin Press.

de Bruijn, Miriam and Han van Dijk 1995. *Arid Ways: Cultural Understandings of Insecurity in FulBe Society, Central Mali*. Amsterdam: Thela Publishers.

Dietz, Ton 1993. "The State, the Market, and the Decline of Pastoralism: Challenging Some Myths, With Evidence from Western Pokot in Kenya/Uganda" in J. Markakis (ed.), *Conflict and Decline of Pastoralism in the Horn of Africa*. London: Macmillan Press.

Ferguson, James, 1990. *The Anti-politics Machine: Development, Depolitisation and Bureaucratic State Power in Lesotho*. Cambridge: Cambridge University Press.

Juul, K., 1999. *Tubes, Tenure and Turbulence: The Effects of Drought Related Migration on Tenure Issues and Resource Management in Northern Senegal*. Ph.D. Dissertation, Roskilde: Roskilde University Centre.

Markakis, J. 1993. "Introduction" in J. Markakis (ed.), *Conflict and Decline of Pastoralism in the Horn of Africa*. London: Macmillan Press.

Moore, Sally Falk 1994. "The Ethnography of the Present and the Analysis of Process" in R. Borofsky (ed.), *Assessing Cultural Anthropology*, New York: McGraw-Hill

Morton, J. 1994. *The Poverty of Nations: The Aid Dilemma in the Heart of Africa*. London and New York: British Academy Press.

Nielsen, Henrik 1999. "Diguettes in Burkina Faso: Sustainable Development or Stones for Bread" in *Geografisk Tidskrift Danish Journal of Geography*, Special Issue, 2.

Peters, Pauline 1992. "Manoeuvres and Debates in the Interpretation of Land Rights in Botswana" in *Africa* 62 (3). 413–434

Peters, Pauline 1994. *Dividing the Commons: Politics, Policy and Culture in Botswana*. Charlottesville: University Press of Virginia.

Sahlins, Marshall 1972. *Stone Age Economics*. Chicago, New York: Aldine/Atherton Inc.

Salzman, P.C. 1995. "Studying Nomads: An Autobiographical Reflection" in *Nomadic Peoples* no. 36/37: 1995. pp. 157–167.

Santoir, C. 1982. *Contribution à l'étude de l'exploitation du cheptel : Region du Ferlo-Senegal*. Dakar: ORSTOM.

Santoir, C., 1994. "Decadence et résistance du pastoralisme: Les peuls de la vallée du fleuve Senegal" in *Cahiers d'Etudes Africaines* 133–5, XXXIV-1-3, pp. 231–63.

Solway, Jacqueline S. 1994. "Drought as a Revelatory Crisis: An Exploration of Shifting Entitlements and Hierarchies in the Kalahari, Botswana" in *Development and Change*, vol. 25, pp. 471–95.

Thébaud, Brigitte 1994. *Projet 'Exploitation agro-sylvo-pastoral des sols dans le Nord du Sénégal : Bilan et identification d'un nouveau projet*. Rapport de mission 28 mars au 5 mai 1994. Saint Louis, Sénégal: Mission Forestière Allemande, GTZ.

Tluczykont, Siegfried 1991. "Le modèle de pâturage contrôlé" in Kasberger-Sanftl, G. et al (eds), *Le pâturage controlé: un système d'exploitation sylvo-pastorale comme modèle pour la sauvegarde des ressources naturelles*. Saint Louis, Sénégal: Mission Forestière Allemande, GTZ.

Touré, O. 1990. *Les societés peuls du Ferlo: continuité, changements et menaces*. Dakar: Publication du Centre de Suivi Ecologique.

Tourrand, J.F. 1989. *Un pasteur devient agro-pasteur: une étude de cas dans le Delta du fleuve Sénégal*. Accra : Seminaire RESPAO.

Understanding Resource Management in the Western Sudan

A Critical Look at New Institutional Economics

Leif Manger

Introduction

The management of natural resources in Third-World countries arguably represents one of the major challenges to contemporary social science research. Through the many contributions to this debate we know now that human resource utilisation systems are far more complex than earlier anticipated, and also that such management exists in cases where Western onlookers had concluded that it did not. Policy-makers and planners alike must struggle to find policy options for a situation that is characterised by various types of problem related to the working of production systems. Ideally such policy options should be based on realistic assumptions about the driving forces behind existing patterns of utilization. But what does this realism consist of? Is it characterised by the over-utilization of a finite set of resources, requiring a focus on *resource management*? And is such over-utilization, if it exists at all, caused by population increase or by the introduction of more intensive technologies: that is, is it population-driven or investment-driven? Or are we dealing with situations of conflict that are not necessarily related to any absolute over-use of resources but that have to do with other factors that are rather social and cultural in nature, thus requiring a focus on *conflict management*?

My focus in this chapter is on the second type of problems. Drawing on the empirical situation in the western Sudan, I would like to raise some issues of relevance to the problem of resource management and resource conflicts. As many causes of conflict in the region are related to natural resources, both land and water, this requires an understanding of the way people deal with access to and the use and management of natural resources at the local level and the social structures in which they are embedded. However, this also requires a broader focus within which wider economic, administrative and political contexts are made relevant. What such a broad presentation shows is that not all resource conflicts are based on a situation of resource scarcity; rather, they are political in nature and have to do with the workings of the Sudanese state. But once conflicts erupt they tend also to be interpreted in tribal and ethnic terms and can be linked to other types of conflicts, leading to their escalation. Hence, an increase in levels of conflict, which we see in the western Sudan, cannot automatically be interpreted as another example of the many gloomy accounts of the 'degradation' of African environments or that all conflicts are environmental in nature, thus requiring resource management solutions. The way in which conflicts evolve in the western Sudan seems to require, rather, a focus on the state and on the concept of 'governance', in this case 'bad governance', i.e. the reproduction of autocratic leadership, corruption and the collapse of states into warring factions. This suggests a need to look at people's use of, and control over, resources at many different levels, thus permitting a consideration of processes of power and authority.

This leads to the conceptual discussion I wish to pursue in this chapter. I shall try to relate this broader thinking to one particular type of theorizing, that of the so-called 'New Economic Institutionalism' (NIE), and discuss to what extent this type of theorizing is helpful in our attempts to explain current resource use and conflicts. The NIE belongs to a type of theorizing which deals with institutions and resource management. One particularly influential branch is the 'transaction and information cost theories' of Douglass North and Elinor Ostrom. Along with Garrett Hardin's 'tragedy of the commons', this type of thinking is inspired by the assumptions of game theory in that it deals with the tension between individual, rational self-interest and group interests, in particular the likelihood of and conditions for 'collective action'. The general basis for this type of thinking is based on methodological individualism, which assumes that individuals behave rationally, weighting strategies and likely outcomes, based on the various contexts within which they find themselves, the main goal being to minimize risk. Hardin's particular contribution and general point is that if indivdual users of the commons, that is, of a limited common resource, are not controlled, their aggregate exploitation of the commons will lead to over-exploitation. There are two alternatives in dealing with this problem, namely privatisation, or political control through an outside force like a government. Elinor Ostrom's contribution relates directly to Hardin's argument, as she is concerned with how one may create institutions that can deal with this problem, that is, institutions that allow for 'rational management'. Ostrom states (1990: 13–14):

> Analysts who find an empirical situation with a structure presumed to be a commons dilemma often call for the imposition of a solution by an external actor: The 'only way' to solve the commons dilemma is by doing X.... But the content of X could hardly be more variable. One set of advocates presumes that a central authority must assume continuing responsibility to make unitary decisions.... Others presume that a central authority should parcel out ownership rights.... Both centralization advocates and privatisation advocates accept a central tenet that institutional change must come from outside and be imposed on the individuals affected.

Opposed to this is the position that the pastoralists themselves are the carriers of a resource management culture, and that this culture, if left to operate on its own, can solve the problem. Although some of the arguments in this direction border on romanticism, it is true that there is a need to learn from what people themselves are doing. In Ostrom's comparative study of situations that work and those that do not, she concluded that the following factors are particularly important in defining the efficiency of resource management groups: the total number of decision makers; the number of participants minimally required to achieve the collective benefit; the discount rate in use; similarities of interests; and the presence of participants with substantial leadership or other assets (1990: 188). This Institutional Rational Choice Theory argues that it is possible to create a situation in which such institutions may emerge and that they may lead to optimal resource use. The present case study from the western Sudan shows that at its best this entails an uphill struggle. In trying to understand why NIE thinking runs into problems, my problem is not so much with game theory thinking as such or the focus on rational actors, but rather with how such rational actors are assumed to act according to simple incentive models. We need to spend more time trying to understand the complexity of the structures of incentives within which people act. Management is not a simple relationship between actors' preferences and immediate incentives affecting the choices they make, but a complex relationship in which the narrow process of management must be understood also against a background of broader social and political relations, relations that are defined by power inequalities. In this I find myself in agreement with Pauline Peters, who states: 'The main points of disagreement are the reduction of agency to individual choice, the privileging of property rights, the assumption that conflict or contestation is antipathetic to a functioning institution, an exclusive focus on interests that ignore meaning, and the failure to theorize power' (Peters 2000:10).

I shall have more to say on this towards the end of the chapter, but let me start at the empirical end.

The Western Sudan: Production Systems in Transformation

The Western Sudan includes the two regions of Kordofan and Darfur, of which North Kordofan and North Darfur States are part. The great majority of population is classified as rural and derives its livelihoods from agriculture and pastoral production (see Haaland 1980, 1990). Generally, the population is concentrated in a belt between 11 and 14 degrees N. North of this belt, towards 16 degrees N, the decreasing annual rainfall reduces the importance of agricultural activities, and nomadic pastoralism based on camels, goats and sheep become the dominant subsistence activity. South of the belt, the heavy, cracking clay soil was hardly used by cultivators before the introduction of mechanised equipment. Migratory cattle nomads, the Baggara Arabs, travelled quickly through these areas, moving between dry season pastures at Bahr el Arab and the rainy season pastures in the middle belt. This general situation has constituted a planning dilemma in the Sudan: should priority be given to the zone of dense population, the sandy soils (*qoz* and *qardud*) mainly being cultivated by household-based farming units, or should it be placed on the potentially very productive clay soils (*tin*), which require capitalised enterprises. Hence, a history of development reporting has moved between focusing on the agricultural potential of the regions as a food supplier of the country as a whole, as well as the Middle East (the 'bread-basket strategy'), and a focus on household-based agro-pastoral and pastoral production on the *qoz*, with its inherent problems of accelerating environmental deterioration. In both scenarios conflicts arise, but for different reasons and between different types of economic unit. Thus it is important to understand these units, as many types of conflicts derive from what they are and how they are constituted.

The first observation is that the population is made up of a multitude of different ethnic groups, often associated with different economic activities and integrated in different ways into wider systems of exchange. Some groups in the middle zone on the *qoz*, around Jebel Marra and the Nuba Mountains, specialised in cultivation, whereas others, the Baggara, Fulani Umbororo etc. specialise in cattle-rearing, while yet others are camel-herders, such as the Kababish and Zaghawa. Today, however, this classification is far from clear. Among the pastoralist groups only a small percentage are actually involved in animal-rearing: many combine it with cultivation, while others have taken up urban-based occupations, without cutting their links with their home areas. The same is the case for cultivators, some of whom (for instance, in eastern Darfur) have gone into sheep farming, raising sheep for export using hired herders.

This general situation has produced several types of conflict. The expansion of mechanised farming on the clay plains has affected the southern migration routes of the Baggara in Kordofan. The expansion of cultivation on the *qoz*, together with an accumulation of animals in the same area, has produced over-cultivation, over-grazing and deforestation. However, the situation is also affected by other factors. The various periods of drought have affected the areas of the north badly, pushing people towards the towns, and also southwards into the *qoz* and *gardud* belts that are already under pressure. The civil war in the country creates pressure from the south, blocking the dry-season migrations of the Baggara in the Bahr el Arab and the Nuba Mountains areas, and making them stay longer in the *qoz* and *gardud* areas (e.g. Manger 1994).

In the political field, various land-use policies have also had their implications. The customary laws were set aside by legislation in 1970, under which all land was made government land, to which people could obtain access through lease arrangements. Local customary rights continued to exist and were acknowledged in principle, but the way the system was managed soon produced negative consequences. The lease system was undermined by corrupt political practices through which politicians, leading bureaucrats, army officers and traders obtained access to land resources and schemes and could operate without applying existing regulations of rotation etc. Hence, in addition to an unbalanced division of resources, this also created negative environmental consequences over vast areas (environmental 'mining'). Arguably, it also blocked the development in the lighter, non-cracking clay areas of intermediate technology through which family farms could also exploit the clay plains, thereby relieving pressure on the over-populated sandy zone. As the time of cultivation is different in the two sectors, the end result has been that people join the schemes as cheap labour, thus becoming one additional factor in the commercialisation of small-scale family-farmer.

The dominant economic unit involved in agriculture is the family farm, consisting of husband, wife and children. Millet grown on *qoz* soil and sorghum grown on the alluvial soils were and still are staple crops. However, the risk of crop failure is always present, due to drought, locusts and other pests. Therefore alternative income possibilities are important, primarily livestock, but also other agricultural crops as well as gathering fruits, seeds and roots from wild plants. The rotation of cultivated plots was an important characteristic as no chemical fertiliser was available, but due to population increase people are forced to stay longer on the land, thus creating processes of degradation. Time studies have shown that about half of a man's labour and most of a woman's labour is taken up with millet (*dukhn*) and sorghum (*dura*) in the rainy season, which then is a major constraint on which other crops can be cultivated and which other activities engaged in. In those areas where irrigation is possible, labour input is balanced out on more crops. For the individual unit access to land was, and still is, primarily through descent, and the land was allocated by the sheikh. Although the rotation of land was common in earlier times, increasing pressure through general population increase and expansionist commercialisation processes have led to a situation in which people cultivate their plots more or less continuously.

Usufruct rights in land and one's own capacity to work it are thus the two factors that are under the control of the units themselves. But as already mentioned, land management is not only dependent on those factors, it is also interrelated with a host of other factors. Market ties have allowed for a certain regional division of labour, in which different economic units have been able to exploit the most favourable environments, and then obtain access to other crops through the market. Exchanges of crops, live animals, meat and milk between cultivators and pastoralists is one example (Manger, ed. 1984). When it comes to labour, the existence of the famous *nafir* (see Barth 1967, Manger ed. 1987) allows farmers to solve bottlenecks in the production, particularly weeding. However, this system also carries constraints, as it was not possible traditionally to buy in labour for weeding, a fact that worked as a check on differentiation, but at the same time also limited capital accumulation. In the traditional system, animals constituted the main investment link. It is documented for the Fur, for instance, that people accumulated animals locally and thus had a buffer against crop failures. However, if they acquired so many animals that this created problems for local production, certain units would opt for a strategy of nomadisation, joining a Baggara group and migrating with them (Haaland 1972).

Apart from cultivation, an important source of income in these areas has been the collection of gum arabic from the *hashab* trees (*Acacia senegal*), which provided people with a traditional cash crop in the areas. The right to tap such trees was granted by the sheikhs and *omda*s of the tribe if the trees were on virgin land. Alternatively the right to trees on fallow land (*gineina*) followed cultivation rights. *Hashab* trees yield after about five years (1–5 lb. per tree) and remain productive for fifteen to twenty years. Then they are cut and the land cultivated for four to five years. Traditionally gum arabic was sold through the Gum Arabic Corporation. This system of inter-cropping also provided browse for animals, wood for houses and eventually charcoal incomes when finally cut. Thus, the agricultural cultivation of millet and groundnuts, animal husbandry and gum-tapping constitute the basic locally available resoures for the farmers' strategy of survival. Additional to this are labour migration to the towns and commercial schemes for wage labour.

The pastoral units can be divided into two categories, camel nomads of the north, and cattle nomads in the south. The camel-herders of the north subsist by raising camels, cattle, sheep and goats. Individuals and family units own animals, and extended families may co-operate in herding. The migration routes run north-south, with southward movements (*dammer*) in the dry season and northward movements (*nishuq*) in the rainy season. A major problem for these groups has been the recurrent droughts in the area, the Sahel drought in the early seventies and the drought of the eighties being major occurrences, but on the whole the last thirty years have seen a long dry period that has forced the camel people into the towns, where they have ended up as paupers, and also led them to become involved in cultivation to add to their income. This has been achieved by acquiring access to cultivation land in areas controlled by other tribes. The marginalization of pasture areas has made pastoralists stay longer in the southern part of this region, thus meeting the other groups, a situation that has led to conflicts. Baggara cattle nomads move seasonally between the good *toich* grasses of Bahr el Arab in the south and the *qardud* areas in the rainy season, where they also engage in cultivation in their home *dar*. At the height of the rainy season the cattle are moved further north, where they stay until the shortage of pasture and water at the beginning of the dry season stimulate movement back to the *dar*.

Both camel nomads and cattle nomad management units are based on family units (nuclear or extended), which ideally should be able to satisfy their consumption needs from the herds, but cultivation, as well as other activities such as labour migration (service as soldiers in the army, moving to urban labour markets in Sudan or travelling to Saudi Arabia and the Gulf) have also been important. The number of purely pastoral units is decreasing, and over the decades the system has been transformed, with women keeping milking animals in and around settlements and towns in order to sell the milk, whereas the young men move with the herds themselves. Keeping livestock has also been commericalised. Those who are no longer viable as herders and lose their herds can join others as herders on a wage basis, thus producing new patterns of differentiation. Moreover, the rich herd owners can buy fodder and water, thus being less dependent on the natural environment than other herders. In periods of drought the rich can buy animals from the poor, thus exploiting falling prices during such periods to enrich themselves and add further to the differentiation in pastoral communities. The pastoralists have also adopted cultivation, the Baggara of grain and groundnuts in southern Darfur using Dinka labour, and grain and cotton in the Nuba Mountains using Nuer, Shilluk and Nuba as labourers. Some rich Baggara have also invested in mechanised farming. The camel nomads have cultivated grain and groundnuts using labour from among themselves, as well as available labour from Arab and Fellata groups in the area.

The situation outlined above can be addressed with different foci in mind. One might focus on the actual resource management issues involved, and to what extent there is a situation of the over-use of natural resources amounting to Hardin's 'tragedy of the commons'. One might also debate to what extent such a 'tragedy', if it exists, derives from population pressure in the way that Hardin predicted, or whether it is a result of increased investments in more intensive technology. One might also discuss the situation as one of complementary production systems, that is, as a case of agro-pastoral integration, looking for regional exchange links, and discussing whether animals benefit by grazing fields after cultivation, or whether draught linkages have developed between cultivators and pastoralists.

I have touched on such issues in earlier publications, but in this chapter I would like to focus on the *conflict linkage*. Conflicts appear, generated by localised pressure points in the systems, for instance, through some people's efforts to privatise areas that are regarded as being part of a commons, by creating enclosures or by monopolizing water points. But because the conflicts also tend to be tribal and ethnic, not to mention political in nature, they easily escalate and get out of control. One context for such developments is the ways in which various types of land-tenure policy have evolved in the Sudan.

Land Tenure in the Western Sudan

Let us shift our focus now, from the context of productive activities to that of understanding what tenure arrangements we find in the western Sudan. The situation in Sudan is not unlike that which obtains generally in Africa (Bruce 1996), in which indigenous land-tenure systems are specific to particular ethnic groups, having evolved in the interaction between culture and the environment over the centuries. They have been defined by factors discussed above: local climate and ecology, the quality of land resources, population density, the level of agricultural technology, crops, markets, kinship organisation, inheritance patterns, settlement patterns, political organisation, the religious significance of land, and patterns of ethnic conquest, dominance and rivalry. Tenures are often 'communal', but this does not mean that everyone has equal access. Rather, there is a hierarchy of rights, which are available to members of the group at different levels, from rights to individual plots at a local level, rights that may vary with the type of land use (cultivation versus pasture, irrigated land, land with trees etc.), to rights within a general territory (*dar*) at the tribal level. There are also rights within traditional political units originating in pre-colonial states, such as the *hakura* system in Darfur or *wathiga* in Funj. The different levels are tied together by rules of descent or ethnicity, with insiders and outsiders. But there are also secondary tenures, so-called derived rights, such as share-cropping arrangements, rights of way and water, and the rights of wives in their husbands' land. Many conflicts occur as a result of outsiders' infringements of insiders' rights, but conflicts may also arise as a result of tensions within the group itself. Such internal conflicts of interests are based on the different types of positioning and different types of interest that occur among the units and individual actors themselves. Young men may want to work as hired labourers to earn money for bridewealth rather than to work for their fathers, as the fathers obviously would like. Young, unmarried women may want to work in the market selling tea etc., while married women may want to allocate time for their own fields, rather than work the joint household fields.

The various local developments have also produced new local tenure situations, primarily due to external interventions. Colonial rule and the subsequent independent regimes in Sudan have intervened in local production systems in ways that have produced profound changes in them. A commercial sector was developed with tenure arrangements inspired by western examples, co-existing with traditional forms that remained under subsistence agriculture. One problem with this development was that the outsiders saw traditional tenure, being based on kinship rules, as being 'private', and did not recognise the ways in which the kinship and descent systems were interwoven with larger systems that defined political units. Western-inspired systems were seen as coming under public law, thus producing a basic inequality in systems within the emerging nation states. With the arrival of colonialism and native administration, the higher levels of this tribally based system were given status as 'native elites', thus making tribal leaders part of the public system, whereas other, lower level parts remained 'private' and received little attention. This also created a situation in which leaders in the native administration could acquire more power to interfere in the system than what was traditionally was available to them. We see this clearly in the Nile Valley, where the British registered agricultural land, and where the traditional elites of the day could acquire estates. In the Central Rangelands the British introduced 'grazing lines' to divide pasture land from land for cultivation, and local orders stipulated the rules of the game. Special *dar* areas were designed with specific rights for those who belonged there, as well as for those who were passing by. The system was controlled by the native administration leaders, the *nazir*, *omda* and sheikhs. Water points were also opened and closed in order to regulate movement. This period represents a flourishing of pastoral development in the central rangelands of the Sudan.

The period of independent regimes saw a lot of land tenure legislation, as well as reform. Various patterns were chosen in different countries, individualisation of tenure (Kenya), co-operativization of production (Tanzania), re-institutionalisation of indigenous land tenure (pre-revolutionary Ethiopia), reform of inheritance law, nationalization and the bureaucratization of land administration. This last type of legislation is characteristic of the Sudan, with its declaration of the state ownership of nearly all land through the 1970 Unregistered Land Act, an act which also instituted a leasehold tenure system. In the Sudan case traditional tenure continued, but the state used its powers to acquire land for the development of modern schemes. The choice of models was related to the basic ideological outlook, the Sudanese law that introduced this coming in the early, socialist-oriented years of the Nimeyri regime (1970). The argument was that a leasehold system was more consistent with the traditional situation in which the state was supposed to operate as a 'super-tribe' playing the same role as the tribal leaders had done. However, the state did not develop as a neutral factor, but rather became an operator in its own right, using the laws and the system to establish enterprises that benefited its supporters. The Mechanised Farming Coorperation (1968) was one mechanism that was used to achieve this. Other parastatals were created to deal with other sectors. In spite of the Islamization efforts of the 1980s, leasehold remains the tenure on which the government makes land available for development projects, both in irrigated and rainfed areas. Rents are nominal, and the lack of political will to deal with slack conservation and husbandry requirements or to prevent mechanised cultivation outside scheme areas has added to the problem in the traditional sector, particularly for the pastoralist using the areas. This has also fuelled conflict. Rather than providing order, the policy has facilitated further land-grabbing by the elites. These various policies marginalised pastoralists through the introduction of schemes. With the abolition of native administration in the 1970s the various grazing policies disappeared, adding further problems.

Various reorganisations of government institutions also took place, with SCLUWPA (Soil Conservation, Land Use and Water Programming) being divided into two, the Range Management Administration, and the Rural Water Development Corporation. The effect was of course to create a bureaucratic barrier between the co-ordination of policies relating to range and to water respectively. In 1980 the tribal homelands were also abolished, making it difficult for people to keep outsiders out. This happened at a time in which the need for movement into certain areas became more important as a result of drought and war. The Range and Pasture Management Administration was also progressively marginalised within the government system, losing out in many cases to the Forestry Department, which prioritised tree protection over the needs of pastoralism. It should also be noted that this development also relates to strong lobbying by the international community through the various desertification initiatives. With the current regime and its policies of decentralisation and federalisation (spelled out in the National Comprehensive Strategy, 1992–2002), there is pretty much complete institutional chaos as far as dealing with the pastoralists is concerned. Schemes have blocked pastoralists, grazing corridors do not function and the legal system does not protect the rights of pastoralists. Policies of privatisation have led to a situation in which people do not obtain services unless they can pay for them themselves. And the land-grabbing goes on through the now dominant privatisation policies. Rich farmers and pastoralists can develop strategies with scheme owners for their own benefit, but the ordinary pastoralist is losing out. At the national level, the federalisation of the regional system has areas further divided into smaller administrative units. Hence, the logic of a local administrator, being concerned with his small, administrative unit, is not paralleled by the logic of local people, particularly pastoralists, who base their thoughts on the totality of their adaptive systems.

Back to the New Institutional Economics

In dealing with this dilemma, we should consider the New Institutional Economics, a school of thought that systematically tries to exploit the approaches of game theory. The argument is that the reliable functioning of markets and of land tenure systems depends on institutions whose significance lies above all in their reduction of the cost of transacting. Douglass North defines institutions as 'the rules of the game in a society or, more formally, the humanly devised constraints that shape human interaction…they structure incentives in human exchange, whether political, social or economic' (1990: 3–4). Of course one problem here is the assumption that 'humanly devised constraints' can find a ready translation into game theory terms, which can easily amount to the assumption that social actors are atomized and homogeneous. Game theory formulations of institutional theory regard institutions as mechanisms sustaining one of multiple possible equilibria in some 'underlying game', as exemplified, for instance, by the Prisoner's Dilemma type of game, in which each player has the choice of cooperating with or deceiving others. The problem is that the underlying rules of the game are represented as being outside human control. But whereas the underlying game is characterised by an exhaustive list of possibilities, namely to cooperate or to deceive, humanly devised institutions are open ended.

This is the problem in the case of land tenure. It is difficult to translate humanly created institutions into an underlying game in accordance with game theory. This is so for a number of reasons. Humanly devised rules are selectively implemented to serve tactical aims, and they are ignored when they become inconvenient. They are also non-exhaustive, meaning that they do not specify a full and complete set of possible actions. Moreover, human creativity can always create situations that the drafters of rules did not envisage. Resources themselves are carriers of meaning, which relates them not to the narrow 'rules' only, but also to wider arenas of social and political relations. Game theory arguments state that actors' expectations govern their adherence to the rules, and this is followed by assumptions of social homogeneity and standardization. Hence there is an assumption that the actor somehow sees himself as belonging to an *abstract* category of people subject to a rule, and that violation of the rule brings identical sanctions. But this is not the case. People are very different in their ability to escape sanctions through mechanisms such as bribery, family relationships etc. Thus the abstraction that might be theorised before the act is not there after the act. Then people experience difference, and they will, of course, learn from this.

Game theory as used in the New Institutional Economic type of thinking obscures this asymmetry between applying rules to abstract potential acts and applying them to completed acts. Hence the models represent rather flat social topographies. The model does not start out from the assumption reflected in the empirical material, namely that rights are understood as being very concrete and located in time and space, having to do with a person's chances of survival. In this type of situation we can obtain access to people's thinking about tenure only through concrete cases, in which we see the specific ways in which any person acquires rights. Questions such as what is one's first farming experience (on one's parents' land), what is the first land that a person possess in his or her own right (at marriage), what is the basis of current rights, of plans for the future – these are questions that take us into this concrete world of the user. This requires a time dimension that shows how units are established and how rights are acquired over the generations.

One likely outcome of this is a situation full of local compromises, of situational give and take, rather than strict rule enforcement. This personal aspect is also important because locally engineered changes in land tenure often start as individual deviance from the norms, as we see in the early establishment of gardens on communal lands, introducing elements of private ownership rights that can be developed later. Such systems have been dynamic and have changed with use and time. An understanding of how people act within a particular context at a particular moment in time does not explain how that context came to develop in that way. This is crucial, as the history of rules and of how rules have been understood at different times is very often an important part of discussions between people who are in conflict.

Such debates are moral in character and relate to notions of what is right and wrong. The fact that many of the types of conflict we see today also have historical links with earlier conflicts between the same groups illustrates this point. Earlier solutions to conflicts become reference points for how people understand contemporary conflicts and affect how conflicts are played out. Rather than rational egoists who always put narrow self-interest first, we are looking at people who reflect on the history of their relationships with other groups, making decisions based on such broader reflections as much as on the immediate, context-specific structure of incentives. But such reflections are not homogeneous and do not turn the members of a community into a bounded, homogeneous entity. Differentiating dimensions such as wealth, political authority, ethnicity or gender affect the positioning of people and decide their participation. As a consequence of this, various romantic calls to refer all conflicts to the 'local level' and the level of the 'community' are as far-fetched as governments' attempts to enforce their solutions more or less coercively. Both perspectives overlook the crucial importance of conflicts as *contestations of meaning*, that is, as definitions and interpretations. The various ways in which resource-related conflicts are related to general issues of social identities in the Sudan, in which such conflicts are understood as being related to processes pitching 'Arab Muslims' against 'African Christians', is a case in point. In certain areas, local conflicts are thus interpreted as part of the national crisis in Sudan, as represented by the ongoing civil war. We have indeed moved a long way from an understanding of conflict based on narrowly defined resource-management problems.

This is not to say, however, that game theory is never relevant to human affairs. My point in this discussion has been to indicate the limits to game theory's empirical applicability in the ongoing discussion of African resource management. The NIE type of thinking seems to assume that land tenure relationships derive from nature and that they represent contexts for rational actors. But we have seen that land tenure rules do not derive from nature but are wholly sociological in nature, requiring a different type of analysis than that offered by NIE. Transaction technologies cannot be understood independently of social relations, but are in themselves forms of organizing social relations. And it is not unproblematic to model such social relations within a game theory framework. Theoretically, of course, this is being done again and again, but in the real world it is difficult to make such models predictive of human behaviour. Failed attempts to regulate access to resources in the western Sudan are as examples of this difficulty.

Moreover, the present case also demonstrates the contradiction between locally evolved systems and those imposed by the state. The new models of land tenure introduced by the latter also come combined with assumptions about the effectiveness of state sovereignty and the nature of the legal order. The groups involved are not abstract groups sharing a joint, abstract characteristic, but individualised, concrete groups. Moreover, people join others in informal and highly personalised decision-making processes that relate to their self-interests, not with reference to laws alone. Hence land tenure laws are adhered to only to the extent they do not threaten the interests of the players. 'Politics' in the system is not the collision of preconstituted interests, but rather the mutual interaction of interests and politics influenced by the institutional order.

Thus we need to look at particular developmental sequences and the particular institutions that transmit and organize the process. In generalizing about this we need to examine the level of specific actors acting according to the rules that apply in specific situations. In the Sudan that the state's attempt to introduce land tenure regulations based on rationalized forms of tenure have had little success. Indeed, the pursuit of universality in tenure laws is bringing the state into much deeper confrontation with existing patterns of social interaction. This interaction is one basic dynamic in the working of the state itself, its end result being the crisis we are witnessing. People are being squeezed by drought or war. The overall political development is unfavourable to nomads and is increasing problems between local people. However, others are benefiting from these developments, namely civil servants, the military, politicians and big traders, who are in the political game and who can exploit relations within the privatised state. So-called development inputs are not based on proper planning procedures, but rather on the private interests of individual actors. Political representation is only to a limited degree based on elections. Increasingly key officers are being appointed on the basis of loyalties to the state rather than legitimacy from the people. Although these developments still have an ethnic dimension to some extent, the general development is towards a group of winners who are close to the state apparatus and an increasing group of losers who are not. Winners and losers are represented in most groups in the Sudan.

This vicious circle is not adequately understood by interpretations of market imperfections or analyses of transaction costs and institutions as 'collective goods' within a well-structured and homogeneous setting. We need perspectives that regard institutions as the consequences of much more complex processes. Several options exist, and I shall not deal with them in any detail here. Some see institutional development as a struggle between conflicting interests, where the oucome is determined by the relative power of different groups. Others tend to problematize the defining and delimiting of social entities. People identify and consider themselves as part of many 'communities' based on identities informed by gender, age, caste and ethnic affiliations, as well as by economic positions. Institutional development must therefore be analysed from the perspective of the strategies and actions of specific social categories towards a multiplicity of institutions which derive their origins and logics from very different economic, political and cultural contexts, thus making it impossible to say anything a priori about the functionality of institutional develoment. Feminist scholars, for example, challenge the notion of efficient and rational distribution systems by pointing at the various ways in which they are biased by gender and age differentials.

Our case studies also show that the political field and the state are important. The involvement of the state in land tenure systems in Sudan is based on the idea that the state is the best implementer of resource management regimes. In the past decade this has been challenged by 'community-based' and 'co-management' regimes, leading to a reduced belief in 'statism', but not in any reduction in the state itself. These tendencies are connected with how contemporary international society is relating to the nation state, as well as with the types of development that are currently considered legitimate and thus are backed up by funding, and which ones are 'out'. Since the international order these days is itself dominated by a kind of thinking that is close to the game theory thinking described in this paper, the conflict between local realities and outside interventions is further accentuated.

Bibliography

Barth, F. 1967. "Economic Spheres in Darfur" in R. Firth (ed.) *Themes in Economic Anthropology.* London: Tavistock.

Bruce, J. 1996. "Country Profiles of Land Tenure: Africa". Research Paper, Madison: Land Tenure Center, University of Wisconsin.

Haaland, G. 1972. "Nomadization as an Economic Career Among Sedentaries in the Sudan Savanna Belt" in I. Cunnison and W. James (eds), *Essays in Sudan Ethnography.* London: Hurst.

Haaland, G. (ed.) 1980. *Problems of Savanna Development.* Bergen Studies in Social Anthropology, No. 19. Bergen.

Haaland, G. 1990. "Systems of Agricultural Production in Western Sudan" in G.M. Craig (ed.) *The Agriculture of the Sudan.* Oxford: Oxford University Press.

Hardin, G., 1968. "The Tragedy of the Commons" in *Science*, 162: 1243–48

Manger, L. 1981. *The Sand Swallows Our Land. Overexploitation of Productive resources and the Problem of Household Viabililty in the Kheiran – a Sudanese oasis.* Bergen Studies in Social Anthropology, No. 24. Bergen.

Manger, L. (ed.) 1984. *Trade and Traders in the Sudan.* Bergen Studies in Social Anthropology, No. 32. Bergen.

Manger, L. (ed.) 1987. *Communal Labour in the Sudan.* Bergen Studies in Social Anthropology, No. 41. Bergen.

Manger, L. 1994. *From the Mountains to the Plains: The Integration of the Lafofa Nuba into Sudanese Society.* Uppsala: Nordic Africa Institute.

North, D. 1990. *Institutions, Institutional Change and Economic Performance.* Cambridge: Cambridge University Press.

Ostrom, E. 1990. *Governing the Commons: The Evolution of Institutions for Collective Action.* New York: Cambridge University Press.

Peters, P. 2000. "Grounding Governance: Power and Meaning in Natural Resource Management". Keynote Address to *International Symposium on Contested Resources: Challenges to Hovernance of Natural Resource in Southern Africa.* Cape Town.

Within, and Beyond, Territories

A Comparison of Village Land Use Management and Livelihood Diversification in Burkina Faso and Southwest Niger[1]

Simon Batterbury

Introduction

A common response to scarcity among the peoples of dryland West Africa is to diversify their livelihoods by responding to, and exploiting, new opportunities for income generation. This is achieved economically, socially and politically, and requires great flexibility (Batterbury and Baro 2005). The arrival of significant international development finance in the dryland Sahel region following the major drought emergencies of the 1970s and the funding of projects initiated by states and international donors offered new opportunities to rural people. But these opportunities were far from straightforward. Development aid, like Sahelian rainfall, can be fickle. It can dry up, becoming desiccated by disputes with donors, changing aid priorities in the donor countries, local conflicts or economic collapse and instability. Some development interventions were short lived, while others have endured as long-term programmes.

Sahelian people are opportunists. They have become skilled at using development interventions as part of the pool of assets and opportunities upon which they can draw. This chapter contrasts two cases in which the 'presence' and 'loss' of international development project assistance in the rural Sahel has had impacts on livelihood strategies. On the Central Plateau of Burkina Faso a range of initiatives termed 'village land-use management' have been taking place since the 1980s, offering sometimes lucrative assistance for 'territorial' land improvement at the scale of villages and communities. By contrast, in southwest Niger, Zarma farmers responded to that country's national political and economic crises and 'loss' of different varieties of rural development funding in the 1980s and 1990s by redoubling their efforts at livelihood diversification (for locations, see Map). Close analysis of these two cases using a political ecology framework reveals that development-induced community resource management in Burkina Faso and di-

---

1. I would like to thank the organizers of the 'Beyond Scarcity' conference in 2002, IDS at Roskilde University, the SSRC in New York for supporting the Burkina Faso study with an African Agriculture and Health fellowship 1991–4, the LSE for supporting fieldwork in 2001, and the British ESRC's Global Environmental Change Programme for funding the work in Niger from 1996 to 1999. The latter was a collaborative effort involving many individuals, in particular Professor Andrew Warren.

versification 'away' from territories and across different livelihood possibilities in Niger are actually two sides of the same coin. Underlying both scenarios, we find innovative responses to scarcity by local people, and the incorporation of new assets and opportunities in livelihood decisions.

Map 1: Fieldwork locations (drawn by Fatima Basic)

2. The Political Ecology of Scarcity

Farming systems and pastoralism in Africa have often been the focus of neo-Malthusian arguments that highlight population growth and land shortages as the driving forces behind scarcity (Jones 1999). The Danish economist Esther Boserup's famous retort to neo-Malthusianism was to demonstrate how population pressure, far from creating scarcity and human misery, actually seeds human innovation, hard work and technological change (Boserup 1965). Some empirical studies support her general proposition (Tiffen et al. 1994), although its applicability to more marginal and resource-poor regions has been questioned, and the treatment of social issues and the political economy of agriculture in her formulation was superficial at best (Stone 2001). A more nuanced and realistic picture of population-resource relationships in the African drylands goes well beyond Boserup and Malthus by accepting the contingency of the relationship and the influence of other important variables upon it (Stone 2001, Mortimore this volume). These include the extent to which markets act as 'benign' sources of rural transformation that are capable of mediating resources and population through the purchase and sale of productive assets and technologies (Mortimore and Adams 2001: 51), and recognizing the vital role played by spatial strategies, like the temporary migration of household members to accumulate capital or for settlement, in order to help sustain individuals and the communities to which they belong (Rain 1999, Raynaut 2001). People and goods travel across porous territorial boundaries, and neither Malthus nor Boserup devoted sufficient attention to the scale of these flows. In addition, more radical interpretations of the plight of African rural people and their environments privilege the role of external political and economic agents in determining the population–resource relationship, for example by introducing locally disadvantageous terms of trade for commodity production, or creating conditions of instability or violence in which local resource-management systems break down or are destroyed completely. Clearly, examples of land-grabs by urban elites or the deliberate and cynical perpetuation of instability for political reasons (Keen 1998; Manger, this volume) take us well beyond the rather simplistic and universalistic claims made by both neo-Malthusian arguments and their cornucopian antidotes.

These different analytical perspectives inform many studies of the political ecology of land use and livelihood systems in Africa. Twenty years ago, building on a rich tradition of agrarian studies, Piers Blaikie recognized that struggles over natural resources at the local level need to be analyzed as part of a nested 'chain' of processes at different scales, rather than in isolation (Blaikie 1985). Field-level soil erosion might have its roots in agrarian social relations, national agricultural policy, and even the workings of international commodity markets. While 'political ecology' initially suggests that this scaled analysis attends to a binary set of explanatory variables — politics *and* ecology[1] — in my view, a threefold framework offers greater explanatory power. If we conceive of the drivers of change in any locality as being some combination of biophysical, social/political and 'socially constructed' (in simple terms, what people believe about a phenomenon, and how they act on that belief), and if we then add scale and time dimensions to all three, the political ecology framework becomes a useful starting point for discus-

---

1. Since its early roots were in political economy, political ecology had an understandable emphasis on political processes and power dynamics in some of its early variants, with less of a focus on environmental forces. Bryant (1997) still argues for such an approach.

sions of land-based livelihood systems (Figure 1). Political ecology has an intellectual and an analytical appeal because there is an explicit recognition of factors that are external to territory or communities, as well as significant attention to local environments and human agency, in the three domains. Less interdisciplinary approaches to rural systems, like agricultural economics, have not examined their subject matter in such a 'rich' fashion as this.

Figure 1. A three-fold approach to political ecology

Processes act upon a place in three realms:
• Environmental process
• Social and political relations
• Social construction and meaning

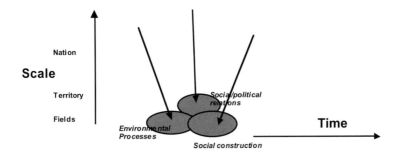

Although there is much more to political ecology than this brief sketch suggests, it too has its limitations. The approach may be used to explain everything from field-level soil erosion to international conservation policies (see Robbins 2004, Zimmerer and Bassett, 2003, Paulson et al. 2003, Peet and Watts 2004). But most of the authors that advocate it are concerned with the transformation of nature into some type of productive asset, such as food, timber or forage grasses, or the ways in which these are conserved by a variety of actors and institutions. Political ecologists can be rather poor at explaining some of the cultural variables alluded to in the introduction to this book. Ethnographic accounts demonstrate very clearly that struggles for land and other material resources may not be driven by instrumental/material concerns and that they cannot be analytically reduced to material necessity or greed alone. Religious ideologies or disputes, kinship feuds, ethnic tensions and culturally significant differences in 'world-views' also play a role. Christian Lund's work in Bawku, Ghana (2003) shows this clearly. A variety of recent conflicts in the town, including several over land, have been sparked by minor incidents or casual insults, before escalating into ethnic contests and even serious violence. These conflicts are actually about deep seated ethnic tensions between rival ethnic groups going back decades, and do not originate in resource scarcity. Michael Watts's work in the oil production region of the Niger

Delta in Nigeria (2001) shows how corporations and the Nigerian state stand to benefit from oil production, while the local Ogoni people protest against their marginalization from the benefits of 'black gold' and the destruction of local habitats in its extraction. But their struggle is as much about ethnic *identity* as it is about oil wealth, and these identities are themselves diverse. A simplistic analysis that pits locals against the predatory state misses the complex political allegiances and identities of the region. The lesson here is that grievance as well as greed – terms usually restricted to the analysis of complex emergencies and warfare (Keen 1998) – may also underlie more mundane struggles over access to resources.

In the rural Sahel everyday resource struggles are common, but the region (luckily, perhaps!) lacks the lucrative and abundant high-value resources present in regions like eastern Congo and southern Sudan (Fairhead, this volume; Manger, this volume). Thus in the Sahel, it is the scarcity of productive resources, as well as great environmental risks, that provide the context for the entry of development aid. Any external actors in the rural Sahel, such as government agents and development projects, are 'enlisted' in the livelihoods of rural land managers and become part of the set of assets upon which local people may draw (Raynaut 2001). Socially constructed notions of risk and opportunity and material or financial gains from everyday livelihood strategies are nested within the cultural and social frameworks of agrarian society, community norms and ethnic allegiances.

Making a living in the rural Sahel can be a tough business. Since the great droughts the 1970s, which generated substantial international aid and many urgent efforts to make Sahelian systems less vulnerable to climatic perturbations, local livelihood systems have featured strongly in the language and programmes of development agencies. Not all the region has been touched by their activities of course: northern Nigeria and Chad have seen little development project aid, and many agencies withdrew temporarily from Burkina Faso in the 1980s and from Niger in the 1990s. Aid tended to be guided by analytical frameworks that were alien to the local region. In the language of neoclassical economics associated with Robert Solow and others (Neumayer 1999), for example, a local production system practising 'strong sustainability' meets many of its food requirements from the immediate territory, and resource depletion can be avoided through careful land management. Some policy-makers, especially those with a scientific training, do believe that this is the aim of sustainable Sahelian development, namely that spatially fixed communities should preserve their 'natural capital' for future generations (Moore 2001, Warren, Batterbury & Osbahr 2001b). Yet this is very unrealistic in the region, given the pattern of movement and exchange that Sahelian people have enjoyed for centuries and the paucity of local resources (Raynaut 1997).

A more realistic way of viewing Sahelian livelihoods is to see them as 'weakly' sustainable, acknowledging that communities have labour power, skills and social networks to diversify away from reliance on local natural capital (Warren, Batterbury and Osbahr, 2001a). The livelihoods framework, developed as an analytical device for rural development interventions, including those of CARE (a large international NGO) and the British aid agency, DfID, is one analytical approach to research and policy that follows this logic. The trick for policymakers becomes how best to support the different components of a livelihood system such that natural, human or 'social' capital is not exhausted beyond repair (Carney 1998, Bryceson 1999). This livelihoods approach has proved a useful, if sometimes frustrating tool for agencies that now look well beyond agriculture alone when offering support to Sahelian peoples. It is recognized that people migrate; that soil may occasionally be left to erode when there are labour shortages; and that households must make complex decisions that may not always accord with a western notion of 'environmental sustainability'.

This shift in development thinking is welcome. Even ten years ago, many development interventions in dryland Africa were, and in some cases still are, driven by scarcity arguments (Gausset and Whyte, this volume). For example, innumerable project documents in Burkina Faso produced by the international agencies in the 1980s talked of worsening land-degradation problems, frequently arguing that 'the poor' degraded their own resources (Moore 2001).

The analytical gaze of political ecology, focused on the different components of livelihoods, leads us towards the identification of processes that may lead to resource degradation or significant resource conflicts at different scales. This could direct us towards regional climatic changes, to the actions of a national environmental ministry, a World Bank office, or a less-than-efficient and honest local government department. How do such decisions impact upon particular places? Carefully practised, political ecology presents an explanatory 'chain', with a historical and a spatial reach. What such 'nested' stories tell us is important. In the Sahel, we know that, despite the incipient globalization of production and consumption, local rural territories matter, especially as places where people obtain as least part of their living, make their homes and originate their beliefs. I shall now explore two cases where such local territories still figure strongly in more diverse livelihood systems, despite the linkages of these places to other scales and places.

3. Development on the Central Plateau, Burkina Faso

The *gestion des terroirs villageois* (GTV, or village land-use management) approach to natural resource management emerged in the late 1980s, in the francophone countries of West Africa, including Burkina Faso and Mali (Batterbury 1998, Engberg-Pedersen 2002). This approach had its roots in numerous community forestry initiatives and local soil conservation projects in the region (see Atampugre 1993, 1997, Toulmin 1994) and was developed and tested by agencies including UNDP, Plan International, CARE and GTZ (German bilateral aid). Its more distant academic origins may be found in the work of francophone geographers working to define and categorize rural *systèmes agraires* back in the 1960s. In Burkina Faso, the individuals who were important in its elaboration and implementation included several expatriate researchers with a long record of residence and service in the region, as well as young Burkinabe government *functionnaires*, several of them with a training in geography in France or at the University of Ouagadougou. The aim of GTV is to assist local communities to delimit, and then assume greater responsibility for, the fate of bounded units (*terroirs*), over which they hold land rights, and to manage their own natural resources in these *terroirs*. The first step is to for villagers and extension agents to delimit and map village lands, soil quality, land uses, water bodies etc., using aerial photographs and sketch-maps. This is generally done in participatory meetings with the members of a single community. A committee formed by the village will then propose and implement a plan for the rehabilitation of eroded pastures and fields, using cheap and appropriate conservation measures. The development project supplies the necessary technical assistance and transport to enable soil conservation, tree planting and so on to progress, while the village committee organizes labour for these activities and draws up a programme of works. Eventually, the project is no longer needed, and responsibility passes to the village to maintain its natural resources in this way.

This strategy, of which I have given a simplified description here, has evolved over almost twenty years to become an established sub-component of the Burkinabe Ministry of Agriculture, with a national programme and multi-million dollar funding from the World Bank (the PNGT, now in its second phase). The early days of GTV programmes generated considerable excitement in Burkina Faso, which welcomed the arrival of a participatory, locally based approach to environmental management. It was in marked contrast to the hierarchically organized world of francophone West African development and government bureaucracies, and GTV was popular in rural areas and achieved results. It made perfect sense in the post-drought Sahel of the late 1980s to turn over land management to local people, after decades of authoritarian regimes and a dysfunctional state bureaucracy. The prevailing discourse in rural development circles was all about 'local sustainability' and 'self-help'.

I worked with one of the largest GTV projects on the Central Plateau of Burkina Faso, PATECORE, from 1992–3, and I also revisited the region in 2001. By the late 1990s this project was operating in 240 communities, and the German project officers were working with local government in several of the provinces that make up the Central Plateau, applying the *terroirs* approach to conserve soils through *diguettes* (low contour stone lines), small dams and other methods, and the afforestation of degraded common areas. Participation in many communities was high. People turned out in large numbers to load up Mercedes trucks with stones and to transport them to their *terroirs* to construct *diguettes* to slow the run-off from the heavy summer rains (Figure 2).

Figure 2. Participation in the construction of *diguettes* in the village of Ibi Palaga, Bam Province, Burkina Faso, 1992. Photo: author.

In the late 1990s concerns were addressed, by myself among others, that the GTV approach had become a 'second best' form of community development and therefore needed some additional thought (Batterbury 1998; cf. Nielsen 1999). The gender dimensions of conservation were certainly overlooked in the early days. Mossi women did most of the backbreaking work of hauling rocks and constructing *diguettes*, often for less reward than men, since they lacked formal land rights and thus could not harvest their crops on the land they were rehabilitating. This, and the tendency to treat target villages and communities as 'black boxes' for the GTV interventions, thus ignoring social issues, has been noted (Kahrmann 1997; Nielsen 1999; Engberg-Pedersen 2002). Commentators agreed that some projects gave insufficient attention to social complexities. For example, the fact that the 'participants' in conservation were not necessarily the same as the 'beneficiaries' was overlooked, as was the fact that Mossi peoples operate hetereogeneous livelihood systems on multiple farm plots on different soil types and with significant incomes from non-agricultural activities. This meant that some were not aided by the project at all (Mazzucato and Niemeijer 2000). Most importantly, could such an approach be draped over a complex system of existing land-tenure rights, and would pastoral peoples, who had no such stake in local territories and usually lacked such rights, be disadvantaged thereby (Painter et al. 1994)?

Over the last ten years, the approach has changed and morphed to accommodate some of these concerns. It works quite well in settled agricultural communities with relatively secure land rights and few power struggles, and PATECORE, although it is faced with the possibility of closure in 2004, has notched up an impressive fifteen years of continued operation, still maintaining a largely Burkinabe staff, with support from GTZ and a small number of German expatriates and volunteers. Its work has been given renewed credibility by Chris Reij, the Dutch doyen of the *diguette* in Burkina Faso, in a recent study of the changes in land use resulting from conservation efforts. The landscape of Bam Province and surrounding areas has been re-vegetated and 'greened', partly as a result of project *diguettes* that have rehabilitated large areas and brought them back into productive use (Reij et al. 2004).

However, this type of localized, populist, but ultimately rather flawed development intervention had a 'hidden transcript' (Scott 1985). Internal village disputes were set aside when German film crews came to in town. Visitors were presented with a united front, with serious conflicts tucked away from view (Batterbury 1997; Kahrmann 1997). The visible, tangible image of *diguettes* was persuasive: the dominant 'social construction' was that they increased millet productivity and were willingly built by cooperative groups of Mossi farmers. These images were widely aired (Nielsen 1999). However, researcher were more sceptical than the film crews and reporters. Assessing the veracity of these images required a political ecology investigation. In accordance with my threefold framework, a trilogy of concerns needed to be addressed, as follows:

a) *Do diguettes really conserve soils, and really augment crop yields?*
It was found that they did conserve soil against heavy summer run-off, and did augment yields for several years, but that the results depended on soil type and rainfall.

b) *How do labour, decision-making, and gender politics play out in this interesting form of agricultural intensification?*
As already noted, what emerged was that women worked more in building *diguettes* (Batterbury 1998). Whether an individual benefited from a *diguette* built with group labour depended on whose fields it passed through. Many men were absent from the village when the structures were completed in the dry season. Existing disputes over chieftaincy arrangements and land access continued during communal conservation work, which might aggravate them.

c) *How did the hermeneutics of soil conservation circulate and have real effects on project activities, and on the landscape? With so many 'actors' now involved in rural communities, including project workers and extension agents, how was development actually achieved across the 'actor interfaces' between these human agents (Long 1992)? What were they all thinking?*
It was found that technical knowledge and discourses flowed between villages, and project and government offices, in interesting ways. For example, some of the less experienced expatriates and project staff were keen to conserve natural resources, buying into the scarcity discourse, but nonetheless realizing there were other stories that they were never going to know about, particularly those con-

cerning local conflict and inequality. The Burkinabe counterparts in the project and the ministries understood more about local politics and had less interest in tackling land degradation in conflictual situations, and they sometimes demonstrated less faith in Burkinabe 'people power' to get things done against the odds. Villagers had the most interesting approach to conservation, frequently viewing it as a way to obtain other benefits, unrelated to resource management. I shall address the last point in a little more detail.

The PATECORE project has had a very real effect on many aspects of village life: new management committees had to be formed, people were summoned to frequent meetings, there were new communal activities to be undertaken, and new agricultural techniques were developed in association with the village conservation plans. People learned to identify degradation patterns and their own plots on aerial photographs and to develop their own village maps and diagramming techniques. These seemed to work remarkably well, and in the two communities in which I conducted ethnographic research and surveys (near Rollo in Bam Province), land was actually conserved in a broadly consensual way. There were also major problems where pastoralists, who lacked land rights or much social status, co-existed close to the settled Mossi landowners. There was, in addition, a culture of dependence on foreign aid that had been created among the local government cadres with which PATECORE worked. This issue persists to the present day.

Yet this was not a case of wholly inappropriate, western-dominated development. On the Central Plateau, the 'scarcity narrative' did not reach the draconian heights noted by the famous study of deforestation conducted in Guinea by James Fairhead and Melissa Leach (Fairhead and Leach 1996). After a few years of pilot operations, by the mid 1990s PATECORE had a team of intelligent and thoughtful development expatriates who worked well with equally professional government officers, several from the local area who were trained in techniques like aerial photograph analysis, project logistics, soil science, and so forth (Batterbury 1998). *Diguettes* grew in scale and length, and the staff learned much about their environmental and social impacts. Had the anti-development critic James Ferguson (1990) visited the project at its height, he might have been just a little less cynical about western-led development! The respected anthropologist Sally Falk Moore actually did visit several times in the mid 1990s, and offered critical assessments of PATECORE's work, but I think she ignores some of the local success stories I witnessed (Moore 2001).

There is an important twist to the standard arguments of both the neo-Malthusians and their critics. Both groups tend towards a 'productivist' or materialist analysis, and they make a deterministic link between demographic change, livelihood systems, and natural resources. What I discovered, however, was that participation in natural resource management had major *symbolic* value, creating 'symbolic capital' for a community, to use Bourdieu's terms (1977). Mossi villagers were not duped into contributing their labour to project activities unwittingly, simply because they were told to do so by the village chief or his elders. Nor were they entirely convinced by the productivist argument that *diguettes* improved crop yields, until they could experience this themselves. In the village of Toessin, 'participation' in resource conservation was put on display to the local state, visiting officials, the extension service and other donors. This reaped other material rewards for the community.

This last point is the crux of my argument. Having observed the vigorous participation of this community in project activities in the early 1990s, I returned there eight years later in 2001. The village was still, by and large, poor. Many males still migrated for work to Côte d'Ivoire or to the cities. An extensive network of *diguettes*, built with project assistance, criss-crossed the agricultural land over which villagers held long-term rights. Most importantly, though, the village had a new primary school. Nearby, in the small hamlet of Ibi Palaga, a poor community that had also worked with PATECORE for a number of years, I found a new well, costing thousands of dollars. These were just two of the material gains from the socially constructed vision of harmony, participation and hard work that the villagers had been able to maintain in earlier years. Symbolic capital was, literally, transformed into concrete. Toessin villagers had successfully created the image of a hard-working and unified village, ready and willing to work with outside agencies and projects (Batterbury 1998). Primary schools cost more than *diguettes* and they need staff, who need houses and food. Because Toessin was very widely praised for its natural resource management work, this image stood the village in good stead when it came to convincing the local government that it, not neighbouring communities, should receive a new school.

Yet Toessin is rife with conflicts and consuming jealousies, linked in part to a longstanding dispute with a neighbouring community, Kiella, over land rights and previous perceived injustices. The point is that Toessin obtained the school, while nearby villages, which built no *diguettes* and had few links to external projects, did not. Development requires a sales job (Biershenk et al. 2000; Laurent 1996). When one talks of supporting livelihood security and locally appropriate forms of development, the appropriation of such benefits should form part of our analytical and practical interest in how rural communities 'get by' and 'get on' (Ellis 2000). They are also part of the population–environment relationship that Malthus and Boserup addressed, yet they go unnoticed in that literature. Symbolic capital leads to material outcomes. And the material outcome – the *diguettes* – also allow symbolic capital to grow.

A new phase of ill-conceived and much-debated territorial development is starting in Burkina Faso, which makes these local stories relevant to current policymaking. This is the creation over the next few years of rural municipalities that will probably amalgamate together groups of at least 5000 citizens, usually spread among several villages, to act as fiscal and political units. Decentralization is following the Senegalese and Malian model and is likely to lead to the same problems of scale and governance as in those countries (Ribot 2002). If village communities have difficulties reaching consensus over the management of common resources like wells, lakes and forest groves at the present time, and are busy seeking new development benefits, then the problems will be magnified when their grievances have to be taken to an elected council representing several communities. Creating new local decentralized councils and municipalities will potentially create an absence of downward accountability to villages and their members (Ribot 2002).[1]

Development Marches Out: Farmers Diversify in Southwest Niger

> Deteriorating economic conditions require households to construct livelihoods from a medley of different resources and activities, throwing into question the material basis of household construction and maintenance, as well as power relations within households. Liz Francis (2000)

My second example, in southwest Niger, traces a very different socioeconomic trajectory. Political security, economic prosperity and international development donors have at certain times been absent from parts of the Sahel. Such was the fate of parts of Niger in the late 1980s and 1990s. Niger shares a border with Burkina Faso, but while the latter was courting international donors, privatizing state assets and attracting large World Bank loans, Niger was experiencing two military coups, the loss of several important aid donors, the almost complete shutdown of the rural education and extension systems, the continuing effects of the loss of uranium revenues due to falling demand and foreign competition from Australia, a falling GDP, and great uncertainty over land rights, health provision, taxation and other issues. These processes were very evident in the village of Fandou Béri in southwest Niger, which is in the hinterland of Niamey, the capital city. Since 1989, rural 'development' had truly become to be a matter of self-help rather than assistance from external agencies or the state. The last international project to have a real impact in the village and many of those surrounding it, a seed-supply scheme, folded at that time when the economic downturn kicked in. The regional matrix of supporting institutions, like the extension service and the village school, also ceased to function.

The story here is complex and has been set out in several papers (Batterbury 2001; Osbahr and Allen 2003; Warren et al. 2001 a, b; Warren et al. 2002). It begins in pre-colonial times, with the establishment of agrarian communities like Fandou Béri on a region called the Zarma Plateau in the 1800s. By the 1980s Zarma farmers were making a continuous series of efforts to ensure basic subsistence and household needs, both symbolic and material. The region has a lower population density, less investment and poorer soil fertility than the Central Pla-

---

1. In Toessin, the village fears it will lose the small revenue it obtains from charging Fulani herders to water their animals at a lake that the villagers maintain if that money is now passed upwards to a newly established municipality.

teau of Burkina Faso (Osbahr and Allen 2003). Modern-day livelihood strategies consisted of an increase in male out-migration to northern Côte d'Ivoire (where men work selling cloth), increased livestock ownership by agriculturalists and business activities like trading in the local region, selling firewood for consumption in Niamey, labouring for cash, and so on.

By combining social and environmental data in a 'local political ecology' project, our research team was able to claim that household livelihood decisions actually have visible landscape effects (i.e. on biodiversity and erosion levels), and that these were very different from those described above for Burkina Faso. Households whose male members migrated to find work rather than remaining during the farming season tended to downplay agricultural sustainability, since labour became unavailable on the fields in the very season when wind erosion on exposed soils was at it strongest. We were able quantify erosion trends over thirty years using CS^{137} measurements, and to link this to basic variables describing the household livelihood system and its evolution over the same period. Figure 3 gives data for just two households out of sixteen that were analyzed over a one-year period, showing the difference in net productive assets and the extent of livelihood activities for them. Both produced less grain than they needed from eroded fields, but both made up for this through other livelihood activities.

Figure 3. Diverse income sources in two households, Fandou Béri, Niger, 1997

House-hold number	Millet Harvest (bottes, a local grain measure)	Annual grain requirements (bottes)	Soil loss measured using caesium 137 analysis for main field (t ha-1 yr-1)	Annual house-hold income (CFA)	Annual house-hold expenditure (CFA)	Balance of previous two columns (CFA)	Animal owner-ship (TLUs)	No. of long-term migrants in house-hold	Total house-hold size	Local trading?	House-hold status
6	178	250	37.66	375,875	246,700	+129,175	13	1	8	N (but income includes private firewood sales)	Wife is a prominent entrepreneur
1	146	300	41.09	179,425	188,650	+9,225	2	0	12	son	Some political influence

Source: Batterbury 2001. In 1997, US$1= 625 CFA (approx).

Reading a range of 'signals' in the landscape and soils, we discovered that this village has far higher rates of net erosion on its agricultural lands than the scientific literature on the Sahel predicted. We also noted a trend towards the household atomization of production units and cross-community institutions over a thirty-year period, which had accompanied population growth to about 20 persons/km². Mechanical soil conservation techniques, like the *diguettes* of Burkina Faso, were absent. The presence of sandy soils, together with the economic choices made by farmers to diversify production, meant that economic sustainability rose *above* environmental sustainability in everyday decision-making and time horizons. Figure 4 shows land-use change in the village territory and highlights the aggregate loss of non-cultivated land since the 1950s (scrub/bush land reduced as farmed or fallow land grew in extent). Households without much labour to invest in agriculture were busy elsewhere and thus suffered more erosion on their primary fields. We argue, therefore, that 'erosion is the consequence of decisions to invest or re-invest in the management of particular fields at particular times' (Warren et al. 2001b: 89). Erosion is not just a function of net population density, or of population growth. Density and growth were relatively low, yet erosion was visible and sometimes severe.

Figure 4. Land use and cover change of village terroir, Fandou Béri, 1950–1992

Land use category	% of the 35 km² Fandou Béri *terroir*	
	1950	1992
Scrub/bush	76.3	34.1
Tiger bush*	4.7	4.1
Current fields	11.3	23.4
Recent fallows	4.1	27.4
Older, detectable fallows	3,5	10.9
Settlement	0.1	0.1
Total	100.0	100.0

Source: Aerial photograph interpretation and ground-truthing, 1996
* Characteristic linear vegetation bands, found on plateaux.

In Fandou Béri, then, a form of 'sensible' or 'weak' sustainability seemed to offer the best option to the local community (Warren et al. 2001). Out-migration and non-agricultural activity offers essential income and livelihood possibilities in communities like this that are distant from economic opportunity. This finding is shared by other studies in West Africa, particularly in Mike Mortimore's extensive investigations in dryland Nigeria (Mortimore and Adams 1999; Mortimore, this volume). Regions like the Zarma Plateau have a median population density and few opportunities to intensify agricultural production for profit, and do not show the positive relationship between land use intensification and soil quality that is emerging in the Burkina Faso case discussed above. The Boserup hypothesis is not rejected just because population growth has created livelihood diversification rather than in-situ intensification of production, but our study did reinforce the notion that intensification is not always the norm. Intensification of production can be hastened by development project activity (as in Burkina), but this is unusual in some Sahelian contexts.

With no effective local government presence and no development projects or NGOs working in the community any more, the type of performativity and generation of 'symbolic capital' that I witnessed in Burkina Faso had a much smaller audience in Fandou Béri (except, perhaps, our small research team for a couple of years!). Given the nature of its livelihood system, the village has less need for communal activity and labour-sharing arrangements, and it did not need to conceal inter-household differences and disputes from outsiders somehow in quite the same way (see Kelley 2002, who worked in the same village). The lack of external agencies operating in the region meant that Zarma farmers have fewer 'symbolic' reasons to nurture their cross-community institutions in order to attract future benefits. In Burkina Faso, by contrast, the decision to participate in conservation was effectively subsidized by PATECORE, and it took on greater meaning and importance there. Fandou Béri did, however, construct one project together as a village: it built a relatively costly mosque out of bricks and concrete in 1997–8, using migrant and extended household remittances. But this was not accomplished with development project assistance.

Village territory in Fandou Béri is quite well defined except at the margins of the village lands, and much land is loaned out or in temporary use, which blurs its territorial boundaries (Kelley 2002). But as I have noted above – and just as in Burkina Faso – it is possible to read the effects of livelihood activities in the landscape: for example all households farmed or raised livestock that were entrusted to and grazed in this territory and further afield. Some of the village territory had prohibitions on grazing. There were established areas of protected bush, high on the plateaux. 'Grievance' could be read in the landscape too, for example, in the exaggeration of field boundaries in areas of disputed tenure, or the spatial disposition of different sub-groups in village *quartiers*. Fulani, the resident agro-pastoralists, had extremely high manure inputs on the small amount of land they were permitted to use, but this was of necessity – they were denied land rights by the Zarma, and had to intensify production on their loaned plots. 'Greed' was visible in the activities of a recalcitrant and opportunistic chief, although in this case Islamic codes diluted the effects of his attachment to rent-seeking and land control (Batterbury 2001).

The point here is that in this case in Niger, the locality, land, and the finitude of local resources all mattered hugely to village residents. While diversification of household activities was pronounced, as might be expected in this post-development economy with so few choices available to rural residents, everybody farmed when they were at home, while simultaneously having household members earning cash 'outside' the village. The community should be seen as an extended network of social relationships, but one that is firmly anchored to the village territory. Territories still matter, even when migration is extensive.

5. Conclusion: Tracing Impacts and Analyzing Scarcity Arguments

There are commonalities and differences between these two cases, which the threefold political ecology model helps to illuminate.

Empirical assessment in these two studies was carried out in three broad realms: accounting for the role of biophysical change, particularly the quality of land-based resources, the effects of *diguettes* and soil erosion; understanding the social and economic context in which everyday activities are carried out and the networks in which such activities are embedded; and tracing through the real impacts of ideas, 'symbolic capital' and narratives developed at different scales. This threefold approach is able to explain, for example, whether the faith that development projects have in the intensification of production via *diguettes* is justified by their effects on crop yields; why it is that Zarma farmers allow their fields to degrade as they depart for dry-season economic migration; and the nature of livelihood systems where capital and resources are scarce.

The main difference uncovered between the two cases had to do with the positive investment, and symbolic benefit, of participation in formal natural resource management activities in Burkina Faso, contrasted with the livelihood options pursued in Niger, where economic considerations outweighed a concern for local environmental sustainability in the minds of most Zarma farmers. Where they are present, international projects clearly have an influence on the range of choices that people can make. In Burkina Faso, project assistance leaves visible signs in social networks, village institutions, the new 'landscapes of conservation' and material gains. In particular, some village committees, and the pattern of *diguettes* in villages like Toessin, are a direct outcome of project intervention. *Diguettes* are interesting because they are hybrid structures reflecting both indigenous and external processes of experimentation and inputs of labour and time. They suggest a Boserupian rather than Malthusian response to scarcity. And yet the driving forces behind their construction have less to do with population growth than with the desire of external actors to do something about extensive land degradation and 'desertification' on the Central Plateau. Projects implementing these ideas were developed in Europe and Ouagadougou, sometimes in a politically loaded climate, and this is where discourses about them have circulated. Yet their impacts are transferred to farmer's fields and are visible there. Given the region's previous experimentation with unsuccessful top-down conservation techniques (Atampugre 1993), it is fortuitous that *diguettes* are of benefit to crops and farms, at least for a number of years.

Both studies identified a similar range of options for livelihood diversification. It was clear that 'territories' still matter to local people, even if the spatial reach of Sahelian farmers is now very great. In other contexts, Sahelians' migration routes have extended as far as Japan, Europe and North America. Mossi and Zarma farmers are adept at making what money they can in Côte d'Ivoire, albeit in different ways. Both groups were heavily affected by the rising tide of xenophobia that affected that country in 2000 and its recent civil war. The range and the richness of options pursued in both case studies again suggest an anti-Malthusian conclusion. Faced with the loss of project and state support in Niger, farmers did not quit farming through economic bankruptcy; rather, they found a new mix of activities to keep their communities in business.

In sum, 'development' and 'diversification' exemplify common phenomena in conditions of scarcity in rural Africa, and indeed in other rural areas. Hybrid productive practices and cultural identities are forged both under economic diversification, and through the presence of 'development assistance'. In arguing the case for a post-Malthusian or anti-Malthusian view of agrarian change in Africa, we need to recognize both scenarios and to see them as mediators in the population–environment relationship. Both form part of the everyday range of pressures and opportunities that characterize livelihoods in the rural Sahel. Although the region is suffering from rising populations and chronic poverty, the acceptance of Malthus' position is unacceptable: we need to add a detailed understanding of the 'symbolic', the economic and the political to this 'productivist' and limited analysis of agrarian change. It is this detailed, interdisciplinary analytical work that the three-fold model of political ecology seeks to elaborate. Understanding the actions and logics of the 'moving targets' that are innovative and mobile people and institutions in diverse ecologies and under different economic development paths surely cannot occur without such an analysis.

References

Atampugre N. 1993. *Behind the Lines of Stone: The Social Impact of a Soil and Water Conservation Project in the Sahel.* Oxford: Oxfam Publications.

Atampugre N. 1997. "Aid, NGOs and Grassroots Development: Northern Burkina Faso" in *Review of African Political Economy* 71: 57–73.

Batterbury S.P.J. 1997. *The Political Ecology of Environmental Management in West Africa: Case Studies from the Central Plateau, Burkina Faso.* PhD Thesis, Graduate School of Geography, Clark University, USA. Michigan: University Microfilms.

Batterbury, S.P.J. 1998. "Local Environmental Management, Land Degradation and the 'Gestion des Terroirs' Approach in West Africa: Policies and Pitfalls" in *Journal of International Development* 10: 871–98.

Batterbury, S.P.J. 2001. "Landscapes of Diversity: A Local Political Ecology of Livelihood Diversification in South-western Niger" in *Ecumene* 8 (4): 437–64.

Batterbury, S.P.J. and M. Baro 2005. "Continuity and Change in West African Rural Livelihoods" in C. Toulmin and B. Wisner (eds), *Towards a New Map of Africa.* London: Earthscan.

Batterbury, S.P.J and A.Warren (eds) 2001. "The African Sahel 25 Years after the Great Drought" *Global Environmental Change* (special issue) 11 (1): 1–96.

Bierschenk T. et al. (eds) 2000. *Courtiers en développement: les villages africains en quête de projets.* Paris: Editions Karthala.

Blaikie, P.M. 1985. *The Political Economy of Soil Erosion in Africa.* London: Methuen.

Boserup, E. 1965. *The Conditions of Agricultural Growth: The Economics of Agrarian Change under Population Pressure.* London: Allen & Unwin.

Bourdieu, P. 1977. *Outline of a Theory of Practice.* Cambridge: Cambridge University Press.

Bryant, R.L. 1997. "Beyond the Impasse: The Power of Political Ecology in Third World Environmental Research" in *Area* 29: 1–15.

Bryceson, D.H. 1999. "African Rural Labour, Income Diversification and Livelihood Approaches: A Long Term Development Perspective" in *Review of African Political Economy* 80: 171–89.

Carney, J. (ed.) 1998. *Sustainable Rural Livelihoods: What Contribution can we Make?* London: UK Department for International Development.

Ellis, F. 2000. *Rural Livelihoods and Diversity in Developing Countries.* Oxford: Oxford University Press.

Engberg-Pedersen, L. 2002. *Endangering Development: Politics, Projects, and Environment in Burkina Faso.* Westport, CT: Praeger.

Fairhead J. and M. Leach 1996. *Misreading the African Landscape: Society and Ecology in a Forest-Savanna Mosaic*. Cambridge: Cambridge University Press.

Ferguson, J. 1990. *The Anti-politics Machine: 'Development', Depoliticization, and Bureaucratic Power in Lesotho*. Cambridge: Cambridge University Press.

Francis, E. 2000. *Making a Living: Rural Livelihoods in Africa*. London: Routledge.

Jones, S.J. 1999. "From Meta-narratives to Flexible Frameworks: An Actor Level Analysis of Land Degradation in Highland Tanzania" in *Global Environmental Change* 9: 211–19.

Kahrmann, C. 1997. "Survival in the Sahel: Problems with Applying Participatory Methods" in *D+C - Development and Cooperation* 5: 22–4.

Keen, D. 1998. *The Economic Functions of Violence in Civil Wars*. Adelphi Paper 320. Oxford: Oxford University Press/IISS.

Kelley, T. 2002. "Squeezing Parakeets into Pigeon Holes: The Effects of Globalization and State Legal Reform in Niger on Indigenous Zarma Law" in *New York University Journal of International Law and Politics*. 34(3) 635–710.

Laurent P-J. 1996. *Le don comme ruse: Anthropologie de la coopération au développement chez les Mossi du Burkina Faso*. Paris: Karthala.

Long, N. and Long, A., ed. 1992. *Battlefields of Knowledge: The Interlocking of Theory and Practice in Social Development*. London: Routledge.

Lund, C. 2003. "Bawku is still Volatile: Ethno-political Conflict and State Recognition in Northern Ghana" *Journal of Modern African Studies* 41(4): 587–610.

Mazzucato, V. and D. Niemeijer 2000. "The Cultural Economy of Soil and Water Conservation: Market Principles and Social Networks in Eastern Burkina Faso" in *Development and Change* 31(3): 831–55.

Moore, S.F. 2001. "The International Production of Authoritative Knowledge: The Case of Drought-stricken West Africa" in *Ethnography* 2(2): 161–90.

Mortimore, M.J., and W.M. Adams 1999. *Working the Sahel: Environment and Society in Northern Nigeria*. London: Routledge.

Mortimore M.J. and W.M. Adams 2001. "Farmer Adaptation, 'Change' and Crisis in the Sahel" in *Global Environmental Change* 11 (1): 49–58.

Nielsen, H. 1999. "Diguettes in Burkina Faso: Sustainable Development or Stones for Bread?" in *Danish Journal of Geography* 2: 105–112.

Neumayer, E. 1999. *Weak versus Strong Sustainability*. London: Edward Elgar.

Osbahr, H. and C. Allan 2003. "Indigenous Knowledge of Soil Fertility Management in Southwest Niger" in *Geoderma* 111 (3–4): 457–79.

Paulson S. et al. 2003. "Locating the Political in Political Ecology: An Introduction" in *Human Organization* 62 (3): 205–17.

Painter, T.M. et al. 1994. "Your Terroir and my 'Action Space': Implications of Differentiation, Mobility and Diversification for the Approche Terroir in Sahelian West Africa" in *Africa* 60 (4): 447–63.

Peet, R. and M.J. Watts (eds) 2004. *Liberation Ecologies: Environment, Development, Social Movements* (second edition). London: Routledge.

Rain, D. 1999. *Eaters of the Dry Season: Circular Labor Migration in the West African Sahel*. Boulder: Westview Press.

Raynaut, C., ed. 1997. *Societies and Nature in the Sahel*. London: Routledge.

Raynaut, C. 2001. "Societies and Nature in the Sahel: Ecological Diversity and Social Dynamics" in *Global Environmental Change* 11 (1): 9–18.

Reij, C. et al. 2004. "Changing Land Management Practices and Vegetation on the Central Plateau of Burkina Faso (1968–2002)" in *Journal of Arid Environments*, forthcoming.

Ribot, J. 2002. *Democratic Decentralization of Natural Resources: Institutionalizing Popular Participation*. Washington DC: World Resources Institute.

Robbins, P. 2004. *Political Ecology: A Critical Introduction*. Oxford: Blackwell.

Scott, J.C. 1985. *Weapons of the Weak: Everyday Forms of Peasant Resistance*. New Haven: Yale University Press.

Stone, G.D. 2001. "Theory of the Square Chicken: Advances in Agricultural Intensification Theory" in *Asia Pacific Viewpoint* 42 (2/3): 163–80.

Tiffen, M. et al. 1994. *More People, Less Erosion? Environmental Recovery in Kenya*. Chichester: John Wiley.

Toulmin, C. 1994. *Gestion de terroir: Concept and Development*. Discussion paper. Nairobi: UN Sahelian Office (UNSO).

Warren, A. et al. 2001a. "Sustainability and Sahelian Soils: Evidence from Niger" *The Geographical Journal* 167 (4): 324–41.

Warren A. et al. 2001b. "Soil Erosion in the West African Sahel: A Review and an Application of a 'Local Political Ecology' Approach in South West Niger" in *Global Environmental Change* 11 (1): 79–96.

Warren, A. et al. 2002. "Indigenous Views of Soil Erosion at Fandou Béri, Southwestern Niger" in *Geoderma* 111 (3–4): 439–56.

Watts, M.J. 2001. "Petro-violence: Community, Extraction and Political Ecology of a Mythic Community" in N. Peluso and M.J. Watts (eds.) *Violent Environments*. Ithaca: Cornell University Press.

Zimmerer, K. and Bassett T.J., eds. 2003. *Political Ecology: An Integrative Approach to Geography and Environment-Development Studies*. New York: Guilford Publications.

Moving the Boundaries of Forest and Land Use history

The Case of Upper East Region in Northern Ghana

D. Andrew Wardell

1. Introduction

Tropical dry woodland ecosystems provide a broad range of goods and services at the local, national and regional levels in West Africa. The woodlands often form part of a complex mosaic of different land uses in a landscape characterised by a large number of resource users. Vegetation patterns are the unique outcomes of particular bio-physical endowments and social histories.

Several recent surveys of tropical deforestation have concluded that there is no conclusive evidence linking population increases, poverty or access and rates of deforestation (Intergovernmental Panel on Forests, 1996; Angelsen and Kaimowitz, 1999; Mather and Needle, 2000; Geist and Lambin, 2001). These studies do not exclude population as a possible driver of deforestation, but they highlight the need to consider variables such as population or access in a broader agricultural landscape (Reenberg, 1996) or wider developmental context (Bernstam, 1991). Tropical deforestation is increasingly recognised as being driven by changing economic opportunities. These opportunities are, in turn, influenced by the changing socio-political, institutional and infrastructural endowments of particular localities.

This chapter explores changing land cover, land use and settlement patterns in a densely populated region of northern Ghana during the period 1901–2001. The chapter argues that the biological and socio-political endowments of this region, reinforced by colonial labour and forest reservation policies, have determined contemporary patterns of land cover, land use and settlement. The estimated rate of deforestation in Upper East Region differs significantly from recent FAO estimates aggregated at the national level. Although population densities remain high in the region, livelihood diversification encompassing male labour migration has constituted an integral part of local strategies to retain access to or control over land. The recent control of river blindness in northern Ghana and trade liberalisation policies may alter these historically embedded patterns, as forest reserves and peripheral village lands are increasingly occupied by migrant artisanal ('*galamsey*') gold miners. The paper questions the notion of a bounded and isolated rural territory and reaffirms the importance of biophysical parameters, historical context, social determinants and changing economic opportunities in shaping contemporary land cover patterns. This suggests a need to move beyond both established deforestation myths and the more recent social constructions of nature if we are to challenge neo-Malthusian discourses.

The chapter is divided into eight sections. Following the present introduction (Section 1), additional information regarding deforestation 'myths' is provided in Section 2. A brief description of the methods and materials used is presented in Section 3. The key characteristics of the case study area are provided in Section 4. Section 5 provides an overview of the development of forest policy and approaches to forest reservation in the Northern Territories of the Gold Coast Colony prior to independence in 1957.[1] Section 6 presents the results of empirical mapping of land cover changes in Upper East Region, based on satellite imagery analysis for the period 1968–2001. Section 7 presents archival evidence of changes in settlement patterns in, and labour migration from, Upper East Region during the last century. Some concluding remarks are presented in Section 8.

2. Moving beyond Deforestation Myths

Population growth and human access have consistently been assumed to be drivers of land use and land cover change in general, and of deforestation in particular. These assumptions have been reinforced and perpetuated by widely cited works (Ehrlich and Holdren, 1971; Myers, 1984; Allen and Barnes, 1985; Harrison, 1992), even though the theoretical and empirical underpinnings of the relationships between population, access and environmental resources have been contested over the same period (Harvey, 1976; Brown and Pearce, 1994 and Lambin et al., 2001). Recent studies continue to affirm that population pressure is one of the universal underlying causes of pan-tropical deforestation (Palo and Lehto, 1996) or that population growth is the most important explanatory variable (Lambin, 1997). The persistence of the population myth in explaining deforestation can be partially understood in terms of the historical influence of established ecological and social 'equilibrium' theories (Mazzucato and Niemeijer, 2000), the attractive simplicity and political expediency of (neo-) Malthusian crisis narratives (Malthus, 1803; Holdren and Ehrlich, 1974) and the comparative ease of using demographic parameters as a basis for modelling forest trends (Meyer and Turner II, 1992). The last of these has tended to create a self-perpetuating loop which over-emphasises negative forest trends at the expense of determining the positive relationships between population and forest expansion through, for example, natural regeneration, the abandonment of agricultural land, afforestation and reforestation (Mather and Needle, 2000). The accuracy of data on forest resources and the methodological weaknesses associated with the use of different demographic variables and different measures of deforestation have also clouded the evidence (Palo, 1994; Bilsborrow and Geores, 1994; Grainger, 1996; Lambin, 1999; Tucker and Townshend, 2000 and Matthews, 2001).

---

1. Further details are presented in Wardell, 2002.

The theoretical underpinnings of the deforestation discourse remained essentially a-political, a-historical and a-cultural until well after independence in many developing countries. Many challenges to the over-emphasis on population as a key determinant of deforestation have subsequently come from historical and local-level studies. As Jack Westoby remarked back in 1985 during a lecture at the Berkeley School of Forestry and Conservation, 'once we start to examine history closely, we find that very rarely has deforestation, even of the temperate forests, been a simple matter of numbers outstripping environment – of population increase bringing with it the need to clear more land to grow food' (1987: 312). Researchers from a broad range of disciplines have increasingly focused on identifying the underlying causes of 'forest degradation' and 'deforestation' by trying to understand the socio-political, economic, institutional and historical settings of developing countries. No interdisciplinary consensus has yet been reached. However, global, regional and local-level studies have repeatedly revealed that the relationships between population dynamics and resource degradation are much too complex to support reductionist generalizations about cause and effect (Barraclough and Ghimire, 1996; Rudel and Roper, 1996; Fairhead and Leach, 1996). In some cases positive relationships between population growth and tree resources have been documented (Tiffen et al., 1994).

Several counter-narratives to that of constant forest and ecological decline have also developed as more social-anthropological, agricultural and ecological information has emerged and new practice discourses have become established (Sprugel, 1991; Sullivan, 1996; Ribot, 1999; Campbell et al., 2000). Other scholars have used historical data to question forest conservation orthodoxies which have failed to recognise the important roles played by local custodians and the extent to which they have been influential in managing and/or enriching agricultural landscapes (Fairhead and Leach, 1995; 1996 and 1998). The use of archival information can complement 'memory and land management practices of current land users…to help understand past land use' (Fairhead and Leach, 2001: 12). Other scholars have shown that the 'general cropping systems pattern and its adapatation to local ecological conditions can be modified by social factors and hsitorical events' (Vierich and Stoop, 1990: 122).

3. Methods and Materials

Two main approaches were used to acquire information on land use and land cover dynamics in the savannah woodlands: mapping based on satellite images, and studies of archival materials. Satellite images were selected as the main source of information in order to create a contemporary land cover map and statistics, as well as to monitor major directions of change within the last 35 years. The archival sources were triangulated by oral histories of the forest reserves, developed using semi-structured interviewing techniques with chiefs, *tendanas* (earth priests) and village elders in selected villages (Sekoti and Biung) bordering the Red Volta

West Forest Reserve and other key informants in Upper East and Northern Regions and in Accra. The fieldwork, conducted in February–March 2002 and November–December 2002, encompassed a review of archives in, *inter alia*, Upper East Region, the Public Records and Archives Administration Division (PRAAD) in Tamale and Ghana National Archives in Accra (Table 1), and ground-truthing of Landsat TM and ETM imagery for 1986 and 2001 (Table 2).

Table 1: Sources of archival material for the Northern Territories of the Gold Coast Colony

1	District Forestry Offices, Bolgatanga, Bawku and Navrongo Districts, Upper East Region
2	Regional Forest Office, Bolgatanga, Upper East Region
3	Catholic Mission Diaries, Navrongo and Bolgatanga
4	Public Records Administration and Archives Department, Tamale
5	Resource Management Support Centre, Forestry Commission, Kumasi
6	Forestry Commission, Accra
7	Ghana National Archives, Accra
8	Balme Library, University of Ghana-Legon
9	Oxford Forestry Institute Library, University of Oxford, Oxford
10	Special Collections, Edinburgh University Library, Edinburgh
11	Public Records Office, London
12	Records and Historical Department, Foreign and Commonwealth Office, London

Table 2: Satellite data used to study land use and land cover changes in Upper East Region

Sensor	Path/row	Date	Country/Village coverage
Landsat ETM+	194/52	12-01-2001	Ghana/Burkina Faso
Landsat ETM+	194/53	12-01-2001	Ghana
Landsat TM	194/52-53*	27-01-1986	Ghana/Burkina Faso
CORONA	752.000; 1.179.000	28-01-1968	Biung (10*10 km)
CORONA	757.000; 1.200.000	28-01-1968	Sekoti (10*10 km)

*Shifted 50 per cent southwards

4. The Case Study Area

The forest resources of Ghana are broadly divided into two distinct ecological zones: the moist tropical high forests of southern Ghana, and the savannah woodlands of northern Ghana. Formal 'forestry' in Ghana has largely been concerned with the High Forest Zone (HFZ), on which many studies of forestry in Ghana continue to be focused, with negligible reference to dry forests (Gillis, 1988; Hawthorne and Abu Juam, 1995; Mayers and Kotey, 1996). This has resulted in 'the relative paucity of information on forest resource condition and use in northern Ghana' (Kotey et al., 1998: 21).

Upper East Region (UER) is located in the northeastern part of Ghana and forms part of the Volta River basin (See Figure 1). UER is one of Ghana's poorest regions (Republic of Ghana, 1999). Hydrologically the region is drained by the Red and White Volta and Nasia Rivers. The climate is semi-arid, distinguished by the alternation of distinct wet (May–October) and dry (November–April) Seasons. Mean annual rainfall for the period 1931–1990 was approximately 1,000 mm. Lithosols are found on dispersed laterite and granite hills and hydromorphic soils occur in the lowest parts of broad valleys, which are subject to ephemeral drainage. Large areas on the floodplains have traditionally not been utilized due to water logging and the incidence of sleeping sickness and river blindness.

Three main land cover classes can be distinguished in the study region:
i) 'fringing' or gallery forest, which forms a narrow (20–100 m) vegetative strip along the permanent and seasonal watercourses of the Volta River system;
ii) Guinea/Sudan savannah woodlands, which occupy the sparsely populated valleys and protected forest reserve areas; and
iii) densely populated savannah 'parklands' associated with compound farming systems in the upland areas.

UER is a densely populated, ethnically hetereogeneous and predominantly rural region. In 2001 it was estimated that 80% of the population depended on subsistence farming as the mainstay of their livelihoods (Ofori-Sarpong, 2001).[1] Demographic trends vary at national, regional, district and village levels (Table 3). The estimated population density (based on net land areas, i.e. excluding uninhabited protected areas) in Bolgatanga District in 2000 was 144 inhabitants per km^2 (cf. averages of 126 inhabitants per km^2 in Upper East Region and 87 inhabitants per km^2 in Ghana). Ethnic groups belonging to the Frafra community in the region, such as the Tallensi and Nabdam (who inhabit Biung and Sekoti villages respectively), are politically organised as acephalous segmentary societies.

The predominant land use systems can be characterised as rain-fed subsistence arable farming on compound and bush farms (Benneh, 1973), irrigated dry-season 'market gardening' on small protected plots and extensive livestock grazing based on crop residues, bush farm fallows and dry-season transhumance along the river valleys and within forest reserves. Farmers in Upper East Region have developed distinctive land use patterns broadly distinguished by the intensive "ring' pattern, developed on the basis of traditional land tenure arrangements and on the increase of soil fertility around compounds, (Webber, 1996) and the "toposequential' pattern, developed on the basis of differential fertility of soils located along the toposequence.

The major food crops grown include millet, red and white sorghum, maize, rice, groundnuts, sesame and bambara nuts. In addition to agriculture, the local inhabitants collect a broad range of Non-Timber Forest Products (NTFPs) from the savannah woodlands and gallery forests for subsistence use and/or for sale in local markets. These include inter alia wood-fuels, thatching materials, building

---

1. The 1960 Census estimated that between 91–96% of men were engaged in agriculture (*1960 Population Census of Ghana*, Volume IV, 1964).

Figure 1: Location of the study area – the Volta River Basin.

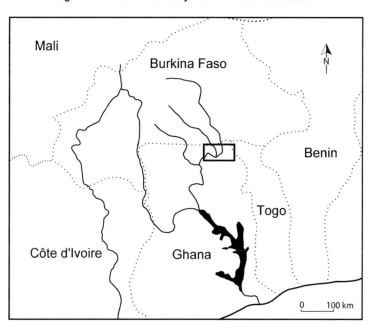

poles, medicinal plants for human and livestock disorders and bush meat (Blench, 1999). Cotton, tobacco, shea nut kernels and shea butter, dry-season vegetable gardening, traditional handicrafts and, more recently, artisanal gold-mining provide complementary sources of household income within Upper East Region.

Table 3:Demographic trends at national, regional, district and village levels, 1891–2000

Territory	Census year									
	1891	1901	1911	1921	1931	1948	1960	1970	1984	2000[1]
Gold Coast/ Ghana	764,185	895,330	1,502,286	2,296,400	3,160,386	4,118,450	6,726,815	8,559,313	12,296,081	18,912,079
Northern Territories	-	307,724	361,806	530,355	717,275	1,039,283	1,292,209	1,590,341	2,375,335	3,317,478
Upper East Region	-	-	-	257,949	365,465	453,188	470,453	542,858	772,744	920,089
Bolgatanga District	-	-	-	-	133,981	163,474	150,028	172,202	241,921	228,815
Bolgatanga Town[2]	-	-	-	-	-	3,645	5,515	18,896	32,495	49,162
Sekoti Ben-zure	-	-	-	-	-	1,569	798	276	634	1,081
Biung	-	-	-	551	363	214	87	70	87	159

1. The preliminary results of the 2000 Population and Housing Census were published in March 2002. These include a summary report of Final Results, a Special Report on 20 Largest Localities and a Special Report on Urban Localities. The provisional estimates for village localities are presented in Ghana Statistical Service, 2004. *2000 Population and Housing Census: Gazeteer – Upper East Region. Alphabetical Listing of Localities*, Ghana Statistical Service, Accra, March 2004.

2. Bolgatanga, the capital of present-day Upper East Region, emerged as an important commercial and later administrative centre after the commissioning of the bridge at Pwalugu in 1937 that crosses the White Volta River.

5. Development of Forest Policy in the Northern Territories of the Gold Coast Colony

The distinctive demographic characteristics of Upper East Region were already noted in 1935, when two members of the Forestry Department in Accra were instructed to make tours to look at the 'forestry problems'[1] and 'forestry requirements'[2] of the Northern Territories of the Gold Coast Colony. 'The very densely inhabited areas in the Bawku, Zuarungu, Navrongo Districts point a warning as to the result of uncontrolled development. The population of the Northern Territories is increasing very rapidly and steps should be taken to prevent a repetition of this wholesale deforestation'. Moreover, 'Over a large part of the area, where the population is scanty, as in the Gonja Districts, this work is not urgent, the heavily populated areas should be tackled first, also those areas where immigrants are forming new settlements' (Vigne, 1935).[3]

Forest policy and practice in the NTs were also significantly influenced by the 'empire forestry mix' (Barton, 2001). The three main preoccupations – the establishment of a Forestry Department to oversee the introduction of a 'scientific forestry', the development of a network of forest reserves and the control of bush fires (Wardell et al., 2004) – were introduced initially in the southern HFZ in the 1920s, using institutional and jurisprudential models first developed in India and Burma.[4] The Gold Coast Government's subsequent efforts to develop a forest policy in the NTs only began in earnest after the Second World War (Wardell, 2002).

Institutional and Legislative Precedents in Southern Ghana

Early efforts to enact legislation in the Gold Coast Colony[5] to give powers to either traditional councils or the colonial administration to establish forest reserves and to control the activities of mining and timber firms met with sustained resist-

---

1. *Forest requirements of the Northern Territories* (Moor, H.W., May 1935).

2. *Forestry problems in the Northern Territories* (Vigne, C., June 1935).

3. It should also be recognised that the NTs, and in particular the densely-populated regions, ultimately served as a labour reserve for the maintenance of law and order, the development of infrastructure and to service an alliance between southern indigenous political interest groups and metropolitan capital investments in the agricultural, mining and timber sectors in Ashanti and the Gold Coast Colony (Bening, 1975; Ladoucer, 1979 and Saaka, 2001).

4. By 1939 the Forestry Department in southern Ghana had established a total of 214 forest reserves in the High Forest Zone, covering ca. 15.000 km [2] of forest to meet local needs for forest products, to create a suitable local climate for agriculture especially cocoa production and to safeguard water supplies. In contrast, only 160 km^2 of forest reserve had been constituted in the Northern Territories by the end of 1939.

5. These included the Native Jurisdiction Ordinance, 1883; Public Lands Bill of 1897; Forest Reservation and Water Courses Protection Bill of 1899; Concessions Ordinance No. 14, 1900; Timber Protection Ordinance No. 20 of 1907 and Forest Bill of 1911.

ance from European merchants and their native middle-class intermediaries during the first three decades of the twentieth century (Agbosu, 1983 and Grove and Falola, 1996).[1] The introduction of formalised legal mechanisms associated with forest reservation and the application of forest reserve settlement procedures in southern Ghana only occurred after the promulgation of the Forests Ordinance in 1927.[2] Nevertheless this provided a useful testing ground, which permitted further refinement prior to their eventual application in the NTs.

Efforts to Incorporate the Northern Territories into the Global Economy

The first extensive forestry tour of the Northern Territories was undertaken in 1922, with the dual purpose of evaluating the potential for the government to exploit teak plantations at Yendi and Tamale and the feasibility of developing an export industry based on shea nut, shea butter and silk cotton (Mcleod, 1922). Other attempts to support economic development focused on the improvement of agriculture, including cotton for export and food crops, for the 'southern colonies' and cattle-raising. Most of these efforts were abandoned, as the commodities could not be produced cheaply enough for export due to the inadequacies of the transport system. Hence, road building became one of the earliest priorities of the colonial administration in the NTs (Bourret, 1949), which for many years were dependent on government grants, the deficit between revenue and expenditure continuing to exist until after the outbreak of the Second World War.[3]

Indirect Rule and Native Authority Forestry

Early forestry initiatives in the NTs were influenced by both the first tour reports of forestry 'technicians' (Mcleod, 1922; Moor, 1935 and Vigne, 1935) and political officers under the leadership of the Chief Commissioner of the Northern Territories (CCNT). This was after agreement had been reached with the CCNT that 'all forestry work should be carried out through the Native Authorities (NAs)...'

---

1. The draft Forest Bill and rules which aimed to give the government powers to establish forest reserves were read twice in Legislative Council in October 1910 and May 1911. This engendered fierce resistance from local chiefs, timber merchants and intelligentsia in the metropolis led by the Gold Coast Aborigines' Protection Society. The Forestry Bill was deemed 'unconstitutional', with opposition primarily being directed against interference by the government in native rights over land. This was the second unsuccessful attempt by the colonial administration to pass land-related legislation: in 1897 an earlier Land Bill was also opposed because of the fear of an official seizure of tribal lands.

2. Forests Ordinance No. 13, Cap. 157 was passed by the Legislative Council in March 1927 and amended by Ordinances No. 16 of 1928, No. 31 of 1928, No. 38 of 1929 and No. 10 of 1932. The Forests Ordinance, No. 4 of 1929 applied to the Northern Territories.

3. The ratio of Native Authority expenditure: revenue in Mamprusi District was almost 50:1 in 1946–1947 (see letter from CCNT to the Conservator of Forests (CF), Navrongo Ref: 0052/24 dated 1 July 1947 *Native Authority Revenue and Expenditure*, NRG 8/6/104. PRAAD, Tamale).

(Marshall, 1945: 5).[1] The overriding concern, that of facilitating 'indirect rule', was put to the test and eventually enabled the colonial forestry department in the Protectorate to assist in drawing up sets of rules for NAs[2] to enact concerning the protection of trees of economic value (1932), control of bush fires over a total area of more than 25.900 km[2] (after 1936), forest reservation to protect the headwaters of the Volta River (after 1940) and the training of NA Forest Rangers (after 1949).

In many cases the chiefs and *tendanas* believed that forest reservation would cause hardships to their people. The Forestry Department developed a number of strategies to allay such fears. These included the exclusion of all existing farms from the proposed reserve area, verbal assurances that exploitation would be permitted after a Working Plan had been drawn up, the provision of revenue and certain powers to the Nas, and educating NAs on the importance of forestry. In practice, however, shortages of staff,[3] limited capital investment and operational funds and the transformation of the Forestry Department into a timber supply organisation after the outbreak of the Second World War (Brooks, 1947) severely hampered efforts to develop NA forestry in northern Ghana.

'Scientific Forestry' and the Formalisation of Forest Policy

The appointment of Senior Assistant Conservator of Forests Cox in 1943 to continue defining forest policy and its particular application to Navrongo, Zuarungu and Kusasi Districts was instrumental in raising concerns about the efficacy of NA forestry and in advocating a more direct and active future role for the Forestry Department. By 1944 the CCNT had informed the NA that the Government had decided to take over the maintenance and patrolling of reserves. NA forestry was increasingly to be superseded by 'scientific forestry' managed by a strengthened Forestry Department.

Another forest officer, concerned about Malthusian threats in the north-east corner of the NTs, proposed removing and resettling the local population in order to implement the future forest reservation policy in Upper East Region:

1. Two 'tour' reports (Moor, 1935 and Vigne, 1935) influenced the Forestry Department's perception that one of the primary aims of protecting the savannah woodlands was to safeguard supplies of forest products for local communities. The Upper East Region was selected as the priority area in the Northern Territories, due to its high population density.

2. Section 17 (1) of the Native Authorities (Northern Territories) Ordinance (Cap. 84) enabled the Native Authorities – with the approval of the CCNT– to establish *Forest Reserve Rules*. The first rules were drafted between 1939–1940 by forester Vigne in consultation with Captain Mothersill, while brief Working Plans were being prepared for Builsa, Kassena-Nankani, Kusasi and Zuarungu Districts (Letter CCF to CCNT, ref. 175/21/32.S.6, 16 September 1940 (NRG 8/11/7, PRAAD, Tamale).

3. Three forest officers were posted to Navrongo, Bawku and Lawra between February and August 1938. However, by the end of September 1939 all European forestry staff stationed in the Northern Territories had been withdrawn to join the army or undertake other war work for the Forestry Department in Accra.

[Forest] reservation is, unfortunately, in many cases now a matter of considerable difficulty, largely owing to the density of population and the extent of their farms. This is particularly the case in the north-east where the areas which should be permanently under protective forest are the most heavily farmed. In these localities the only satisfactory solution may prove to be the removal and resettlement elsewhere of part of the population, followed by the necessary reafforestation, either by direct planting or by ecological means. (Logan, 1943: 6.)

However, the resolutions emanating from the North Mamprusi Forestry Conference held at Navrongo in 1947[1] proved to be a decisive 'check and balance' on the ambitious plans of both the Gold Coast Colony and the Forestry Department (Wardell, 2003). This was particularly in terms of i) the rejection of any plans to evict and resettle local communities on the grounds of impracticability; ii) the lack of evidence of the beneficial effects of watershed protection as claimed by the Conservator of Forests; and iii) the substitution of a sectoral approach to forest reservation by a broader land planning approach which aimed to conserve soils and to protect forests and water supplies.[2]

Land Planning Areas

Forest reservation in Ghana's densely populated Sudano-Sahelian zone was eventually completed as an integral part of Land Planning Areas (LPAs) established during the period 1948–1957. The Forestry Department's role in the LPAs was essentially limited to the establishment of i) forest reserves to protect the headwaters of rivers and their catchment area in order to maintain and improve the natural vegetation and thus minimise erosion; ii) plantations to provide adequate supplies of wood-fuel and building poles to the local communities; and iii) plantations to protect river and stream banks. The greatest hindrance to progress in the LPAs was deemed to be the 'extreme shortage of staff' (Ramsay, 1957: 26). In addition, collaboration between the different government departments proved problematic. After LPA surveys had been completed, each department was responsible for its own plan of work, which further limited the scope for continued cooperation. This, in effect, gave the Forestry Department every opportunity to

---

1. The conference was chaired by the Mamprusi Senior District Commissioner and attended by the District Commissioners for Navrongo and Zuarungu, two forest officers, an agricultural and a veterinary officer and two medical entomologists. See *Minutes and Resolutions of the North Mamprusi Forestry Conference*, Navrongo 12–14 November 1947 (NRG 8/6/104. PRAAD, Tamale).

2. Earlier plans to evict and resettle up to 70,000 people from the densely populated north-east to facilitate the establishment of headwaters protection forest reserves (with the concomitant intention of providing labour for groundnut production under the auspices of the ill-fated Gonja Development Corporation) were formally rejected at the North Mamprusi Forestry Conference in 1947 (Resolutions 1, 3 and 5). Mrs Morris, the Assistant Medical Entomologist from Lawra, was instrumental in questioning the assumed benefits of headwaters reserves. The Agricultural Officer also suggested that 'it was not much good conserving the soil and moving the people' (*Minutes and Resolutions of the North Mamprusi Forestry Conference*: 5–6).

implement its own *Ten Year Plan for the Northern Territories*.[1] A total of 66 forest reserves were established throughout the NTs, using both Native Authority Rules and the Forest Ordinance (Wardell, 2002). This included 28 forest reserves covering a total of 153.587 hectares in Upper East Region, 65% of which were established along the Red and White Volta Rivers (Table 4).

The Red Volta West Forest Reserve (RVWFR) was formally gazetted in November 1956,[2] using the provisions of the Forest (Amendment) Ordinance of 1949.[3] This constituted the culmination of a protracted reservation process first initiated by forest officer Vigne in 1939.[4] Although the original demarcation of the proposed RVWFR was undertaken in 1941, a formal Demarcation and Selection Report was not prepared until May 1950.[5] The objectives of reservation were specified as: 'To preserve the little remaining woodland in Zuarungu District and to insure a permanent supply of forest produce including poles, fuel, fruits and grasses for the Sub Native Authority areas of Zuarungu'.[6]

Table 4:Forest Reserves established along the Red and White Volta Rivers

Forest Reserve	Gazetted area (ha)
Gambaga Scarp East	12,573
Gambaga Scarp West I	11,500
Gambaga Scarp West II	22,222
Red Volta West	26,159
Morago West	3,976
Morago East	881
Red Volta East	21,760
Total area gazetted	99,071

Upper East Region was selected as the initial and primary focus for the development of the forest reservation policy in northern Ghana, due to both the colonial forest officers' perceptions of population pressure and associated land degradation proc-

1. The *Ten Year Plan for the Northern Territories* was drawn up in 1946 and approved by the Chief Conservator of Forests in Accra in early 1947. At this stage there were only two Forest Officers in the Northern Territories stationed at Navrongo and Bawku. It was hoped that work would commence in Zuarungu District in 1948, but additional senior staff were not expected before 1950.

2. The Forests (Red Volta West Forest Reserve) Order, 1956 was published as L.N. 282, Subsidiary Legislation Supplement No. 53, in the *Gold Coast Gazette* No. 76 on 24 November 1956.

3. For example, it had already been agreed that 'production reserves on the Red and White Volta Rivers could be most satisfactorily constituted in the Reserve Settlement Commissioner's Court' (*Minutes and Resolutions of theNorth Mamprusi Forestry Conference* 1947: 3, NRG 8/6/104. PRAAD, Tamale).

4. *Zuarungu District Working Plan Part I (Chapters I and II)*, including sketch maps produced on 8 March 1939 and 15 March 1940 (Vigne, 1940).

5. Wheelan, 1950 *Red Volta West Forest Reserve Demarcation and Selection Report* (PRAAD, NRG8/11/49).

6. As specified under Reasons for Reservation for the Proposed Red Volta West Forest Reserve. Notice under Section 7 of Ordinance No. 122 of 1936, 18 July 1953.

esses, *and* the influence of the dominant environmental narratives of the era (Stebbing, 1937 and Anglo-French Forestry Commission, 1973). Other sparsely populated regions were essentially ignored,[1] but at a later stage they provided the 'spaces' for the colonial administration to implement its resettlement schemes (Wardell, 2003).

6. Land Cover Trajectories in Upper East Region since 1968

Colonial forestry policy in the NTs ultimately resulted in up to a quarter of contemporary district land areas being formally excluded from customary agricultural production systems in Upper East Region. Limiting access to cultivable lands was exacerbated in post-independence Ghana, since forest policy was characterized by centralization, exclusion and restrictive legislation that ignored people's property and use rights (Wardell and Lund, 2004 a and b). Recognising that 'forest histories have important implications for how one understands both forest ecology and people's social and political relationships with *currently* forested land' (Fairhead and Leach, 1995: 2), remotely-sensed data was used to create contemporary land cover maps and statistics, as well as to monitor major directions of change within the last 35 years in a (still) densely populated rural region in northern Ghana.

Mapping and Monitoring Land Cover

Landsat satellite images provide different options for land cover monitoring, and the spatial resolution is well suited to detecting changes between major classes of land cover, such as cultivated parkland and savannah woodland (Francklin, 1991 and Bobbe et al., 2001). CORONA satellite photography was used for the longer term land cover change assessment (Tappan et al., 2000).

A land cover classification was carried out for Upper East Region. Four classes were defined as relevant for the study (Table 5). Training areas for the respective land cover classes were delineated by using an on-screen interpretation of the satellite image supported by ground control points verified in the field and positioned by use of a global positioning system (56 training areas). Classification accuracy was evaluated by standard procedures using independent data collected in the field (further details are presented in Wardell, Reenberg and Tøttrup, 2003).

---

1. The census conducted in 1931 revealed the large variation in population densities between 2.52 people per square mile in Western Gonja compared with 171.55 people per square mile in Zuarungu. See also Cardinall (1931).

Table 5: Major land cover classes considered in the satellite-based classification

Class	Description
Parkland	Cultivated savanna. Refer to intensively cultivated areas, with limited fallowing. The major crops are millet and sorghum. Trees may be present, but tree cover is typically less than 5 per cent. The predominant tree species are *Vitellaria paradoxa* (Shea butter), *Parkia biglobosa* (Locust bean), *Andansonia digitata* (Baobab), *Azadirachta indica* (Neem), *Faidherbia albida*, *Bombax costatum* and *Lannea* sp. The parkland class also includes rural settlements and urban areas.
Savannah Woodland	Dry tropical woodlands. Refer to areas of intermediate to dense woody cover with an understorey of shrubs and grasses. The predominant ligneous species include *Combretum sp.*, *Vitellaria paradoxa*, *Detarium microcarpum*, *Acacia* sp., *Pterocarpus erinaceus*, *Crossopteryx fabrifuga*, *Terminalia sp.*, *Sterculia sp.*, and *Burkea africana*. The class also includes plantations of *Tectona grandis*, *Cassia siamea*, *Anogeissus leiocarpus* and *Eucalyptus sp.* Principal grass species include *Loudetia togoensis*, *Andropogon* sp. and *Setaria pallidefusca*.
Gallery forest	Mixed vegetation formation along seasonal watercourses and around the main rivers draining the Volta River basin. More flourishing than the surrounding vegetation. The major species are *Mitragyna inermis*, *Pterocarpus santalinoides*, *Acacia seyal*, *Ficus sp.*, *Daniellia oliveri*, *Anogeissus leiocarpus*, *Vetiveria nigritana* etc. Permanently cropped areas based on various levels of water control are also included in this class.
Water	The main water bodies.

Land Use and Land Cover Dynamics

The satellite-based analysis of land use and land cover dynamics in the savannah woodlands in Upper East Region reveals some interesting trends as regards land cover development in the last 35 years. Considerable change from savannah woodland into parkland (i.e. cultivated land) has occurred, as well as considerable natural regeneration of savannah woodland on, *inter alia*, abandoned farmland, long-term fallows and fire-damaged and river blindness-affected areas. The relative change expressed as net deforestation (Table 6) differs significantly from aggregated national rates of deforestation for Ghana presented in the FAO's most recent Forest Resource Assessment (FAO, 2001).[1] A smaller estimate of the *regional* net rate of deforestation of savannah woodlands when compared with aggregated *national* deforestation estimates parallels the significant exaggeration of early forest cover and subsequent estimates of deforestation which have characterised the High Forest Zones and Guinea Transition Zone forests in many West African countries, including Ghana (Fairhead and Leach, 1998).

The exaggeration of net rates of deforestation is significant for researchers and planners who use inflated statistics to model, *inter alia*, the region's climate, greenhouse gas emissions, carbon sequestration potentials and biodiversity. The use of incorrect data may ultimately mislead national, regional and district-level forestry and land use policy and planning and cross-country analyses which aim to identify the underlying causes of deforestation. This issue is of particular concern given the current interest in strengthening the conservation of biological diversity in Upper East Region, Ghana (World Bank, 2001).

---

1. In the African region, increases or decreases in tropical forest cover resulting from changes in assessment methodology adopted during forest resource assessments undertaken in 1980, 1990, 1997 and 2000 have been shown to be greater than the changes estimated to have taken place on the ground (Matthews, 2001:7).

Deforestation 1986 to 2001	20,404 hectare
Regeneration 1986 to 2001	11,361 hectare
Forest cover 1986	292,178 hectare
Gross-deforestation (Overall)	6,98 %
Net-deforestation (Overall)	3,09 %
Annual rate of Gross-deforestation	0.44 % year^{-1}
Annual rate of Net-deforestation	0.19 % year^{-1}

Figure 2 provides a picture of the significant spatial dynamics of land use and forest cover changes in Upper East Region, which is normally characterized as having a relatively permanent field pattern (Webber, 1996). Deforestation and regeneration are both scattered throughout the region. However, the distribution of the 'no change' areas is largely confined to the uninhabited belts along the seasonal water courses of the Red and White Volta Rivers. These are essentially the same areas that were gazetted as Forest Reserves during the 1940s and 1950s by the colonial administrations. The agrarian population has remained spatially concentrated on the upland compound farming areas in the region for at least seventy years, in spite of population densities of up to 150 persons/km^2 (Nabila, 1997). This is confirmed by the spatial distribution of population presented in Figure 3, using census data from 1948. Archival records indicate, however, that the concentration of population in the riverine areas has changed during the last century due to famine, drought and the occurrence of vectors of livestock and human diseases. This is discussed further in Section 7.

Population development trends vary at the national, regional, district and village levels (cf. Table 3). At the national level, the population has increased by a factor of approximately 4.5 since 1948, in the UER by a factor of 2 and in Bolgatanga District by a factor of 1.3, whereas both study villages have experienced significant downward trends in population. Changes in forest cover during the period 1968–2001 at the village scale are shown for two selected villages (Biung and Sekoti) in Figures 4 and 5 respectively. What is specifically worth noting is that the rate of change is closely related neither to areas characterised by heavier population pressure (Sekoti) nor to those characterised by poor access to infrastructure (Biung).

The relative change in forest cover during the period 1968–2001 in UER was more significant in Biung, an inaccessible village with less population pressure, than in Sekoti, which is located on all-weather roads with access to markets in both Pelungu and Bolgatanga. The broad-scale determinants of contemporary land use patterns – vectors of sleeping sickness and river blindness, and colonial forest reservation policy – have resulted in a distinctive settlement pattern in Sekoti in accordance with a cyclical theory of advance and retreat first proposed in the 1960s (Hunter, 1966 and 1967; Hilton, 1966). In contrast, the more recent changes in forest cover in Biung village have largely been driven by an influx of galamsey (gold) miners since 1995, following the successful control of river blindness (Boatin et al., 1997) and the liberalisation of the mining investment code in

Ghana (Awudi, 2001). Tens of thousands of prospectors have now occupied temporary settlements in areas south of Datoko Village (between Sekoti and Biung) on the western boundary of the Red Volta West Forest Reserve. Formal demographic data does not capture this transient population.

The forest reservation policy was shaped by colonial perceptions of 'over-population' and resource degradation, particularly in the north-east corner of the NTs. Similar concerns continue to be raised by some contemporary scholars in Ghana – for example, 'Forest reserves meant to protect watershed and prevent soil erosion are all under serious threat from population pressure' (Nabila, 1997: 78) – and their neo-Malthusian arguments stress (again) 'the need for designing effective resettlement schemes for people from these areas which have far exceeded their carrying capacities' (ibid.: 85).

Figure 2: Grey scale representation (Landsat ETM + band 3) of the study region in Upper East Region, Ghana (above) and corresponding mapping of areas with deforestation and regeneration between 1986 and 2001 (below)

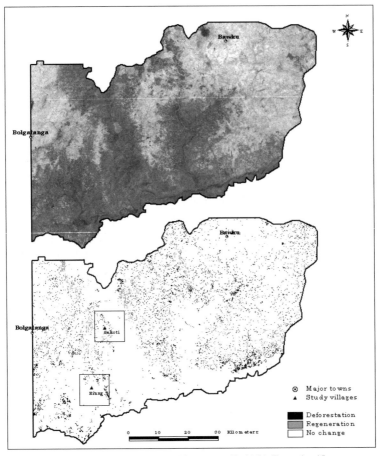

The two frames give the location of study villages which are mapped in detail in Figures 4 and 5.

Figure 3: Population distribution in part of the Northern Territories of Gold Coast Colony, 1948

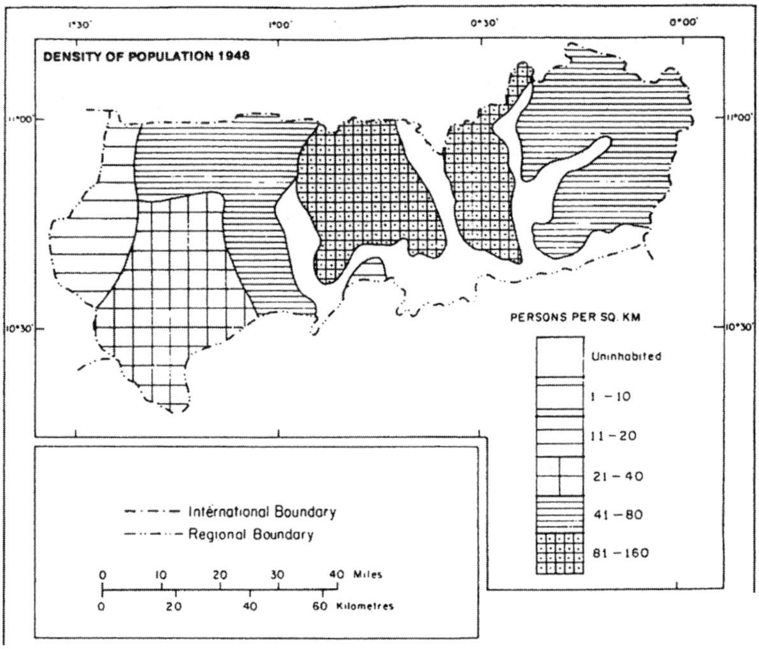

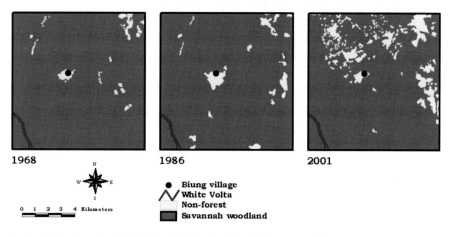

Source: Benneh, 1985.

Figure 4: Change in forest cover 1968–2001 around Biung Village in Ghana

1968

1986

2001

- ● Biung village
- ∧ White Volta
- ☐ Non-forest
- ■ Savannah woodland

N
W—E
S

0 1 2 3 4 Kilometers

Maps from 1968 are based on CORONA data; 1986 on Landsat TM and 2001 on Landsat ETM+.

Figure 5: Change in forest cover 1968–2001 around Sekoti village in Ghana

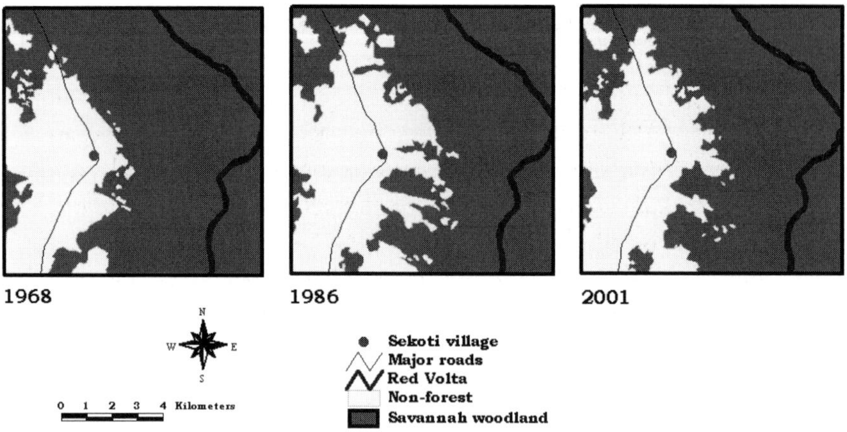

1968   1986   2001

- Sekoti village
- Major roads
- Red Volta
- Non-forest
- Savannah woodland

0 1 2 3 4 Kilometers

Maps from 1968 are based on CORONA data; 1986 on Landsat TM and 2001 on Landsat ETM+.

6. Biological Constraints within, and Economic Opportunities within and beyond Upper East Region

The colonial footprint influenced present-day land cover patterns in Upper East Region. However, many of the gazetted forest reserve areas in the region were superimposed on areas where the spatial distribution of the Guinea savannah woodlands and fringing (riparian) forests had been determined by the occurrence of the *Glossina* (sleeping sickness) and the *Simulium damnosum* (river blindness) blackfly complexes, customary land and resource use systems, and earlier settlement (and depopulation) patterns. I suggest that the colonial heritage was in turn shaped by the pre-colonial impacts of human and livestock diseases on forest policy and practice. Furthermore, significant increases and decreases in population have occurred in the region during the last century. Structural changes in long-established patterns of labour migration have influenced the availability of male labour, and hence the amount of land cultivated (or abandoned).

The Impacts of Human and Livestock Diseases on Forest Policy and Practice

Historical patterns of the colonization and depopulation of riverine areas in Upper East Region were influenced by the occurrence of human and livestock diseases, and they ultimately shaped the establishment of forest reserves by the colonial administration. However, the links between onchocerciasis, blindness and river valley abandonment were not well understood during the colonial era, and several different explanations were put forward for the perceived 'anomalous' distribution of the population.[1]

Oral data indicate that famine and drought forced migrants to start colonizing the banks of the Red Volta already during the period 1890–1895 (Hunter, 1966: 414–15). The well-watered and fertile land along the river continued to be occupied until 1915–1918, when, due to river blindness, the population began to retreat (Hunter, 1966: 409, 414–15).[2] Hunter proposed a cyclical pattern of colonization of vacant land near streams, a gradual increase in river blindness, and the eventual demise of the afflicted population or its withdrawal to higher ground, out of the flight range of the vector. He estimated that land was abandoned at the rate of one mile every 7–14 years between 1915 and 1965 (Hunter, 1966: 415–416). Hunter's cyclic theory *may* be valid for the west side of the Red Volta River and villages such as Nangodi, Sekoti and Datoko. (However, this theory may be questioned on the basis of the first detailed map of north-west Gold Coast, which shows extensive uninhabited strips along both the Kulpawn and Sissili (onchocerciasis-affected) rivers (M.P. 412, 1905. NAG, Map Collection, Accra)). Oral data collected in 1935 suggests that Sekoti was settled in the 1880s and that the newcomers found only empty bush to greet them (Ghana National Archives (GNA), 1935). In 1908 the compounds of Sekoti extended to the river (GNA, 1908), and by 1917 land along the river in the Nangodi-Sekoti area had been thickly settled (GNA, 1917). Similarly, 'Land in Detokko was also being rapidly occupied and compounds were scattered almost as far as the river' (GNA, 1919). By 1949 aerial photography (cited in Hunter, 1966: 409) revealed a total absence of settlement near the Red Volta River. As habitations were abandoned

---

1. These included raids by Samori and Babatu (Holden, 1965); smallpox and cerebrospinal meningitis (Hunter, 1966: 411); land exhaustion (Hunter, 1966: 410–411); sleeping sickness (Hunter, 1966: 410) and depradations by elephants, roan antelope and monkeys (Hilton, 1968: 283). Hyperendemic onchocerciasis was recognized as an important cause of skin and eye disease in francophone West Africa by 1938 (Richet, 1939).

2. Symptoms of river blindness infection were first reported by colonial officials in the Northern Territories of the Gold Coast from as early as 1907 (Anon, 1907 and Hilton, 1959). Colonial preoccupation with vectors of livestock disease (livestock constituted an important source of tax revenue for the CCNT after 1926) delayed attempts to address the problem of river blindness. The occurrence of the *Simulium damnosum* blackfly complex, the vector of river blindness along the White, Red and Black Volta River basins in northern Ghana, was re-discovered in the late 1940s but only formally recognised at a later stage (World Health Organisation, 1966). An Onchocerciasis Control Programme in West Africa was initiated in 1974, based initially on the chemical control of the black fly vectors and, after 1987, by chemotherapy, when ivermectin was licenced for the treatment of river blindness in humans. Initial ground application of DDT was replaced by the aerial spraying of temephos and subsequently the rotational use of insecticides, including *Bacillus thuringiensis*, permethrin and carbosulfan. In spite of the setbacks due to reinvasion and insecticide resistance (Davies, 1994), onchocerciasis as a disease of public health and an obstacle to development has to a large extent been successfully controlled in northern Ghana (Boatin et al., 1997).

and farming declined, savannah scrub and woodlands regenerated to re-colonise the abandoned areas.

These historical patterns of the colonization and depopulation of riverine areas in Upper East Region ultimately shaped the establishment of forest reserves by the colonial administration. Part of the Red Volta West Forest Reserve bordering the chiefdoms and sections of Nangodi was demarcated in 1941[1] to include an already abandoned area (Hunter, 1966: 404): 'Although the order establishing the reserve was not promulgated until 1956, it was demarcated as early as 1941. At that time there were no settlements within the proposed reserve. Indeed, the boundary was deliberately drawn to exclude all habitations, and it therefore gives a good idea of the frontier of settlement in 1941. A Forestry Department Selection Report of 1950 refers to abandoned and derelict compounds and rubbish mounds throughout the reserve.' (Hunter, 1966: 408).

The Impacts of Labour Migration on the Use of Land and Woodland Resources

Evidence from early colonial reports suggests that present-day Upper East Region was already densely-populated and distinguished by its compound farming system more than a century ago, ' the whole of the country north of the White Volta River is thick [*sic*] populated, and closely cultivated. The density of population denies to the inhabitants the opportunity of shifting their patches of cultivation to fresh ground every two years, and there was abundant evidence of the universal use of manures.'[2] Settlement and cultivation patterns in Upper East Region have been influenced by migration into and out of the region throughout the past century. The first significant increase in population in the region probably occurred after 1901, when migrants from neighbouring French and German territories, reluctant to penetrate the country, established themselves close to the frontiers throughout the region (Cardinall, 1931). The exodus from, for example, the (then) Haut-Sénégal-Niger was attributed to a number of different factors, for example, 'The French tax, their forced labour and the extortion alleged to be practised by their Chiefs and public officers of the lower ranks are given by the people

---

1. Forest Officer Vigne prepared the original *Zuarungu District Working Plan Part I (Chapters I and II)*, includingsketch maps of the forest reserve boundaries produced on 8 March 1939 and 15 March 1940 (Vigne, 1940).

2. Lt. Col. H.P. Northcott headed a British military detachment stationed in Gambaga in the late 1890s at the peak of the territorial 'Scramble for West Africa' between the British, French and German colonialists. He subsequently became the first Chief Commissioner of the Northern Territories of the Gold Coast Colony (Enc. 1 in No. 34, p. 61.African (West) No. 564, PRO/CO 879/54, PRO, London).

as their reasons for preferring British Territory.'[1] In contrast, a significant decline in population occurred in parts of Upper East Region during 1948–1960 (Nabila, 1975).

The *seasonal* migration of male labour from Upper East Region has long been associated with pre-colonial trade between Ashanti, Accra and the Sudano-Sahelian hinterland.[2] Patterns of labour migration were reinforced and altered by British colonial policies; forced labour was required for railway, bridge and road construction, cotton cultivation, and the maintenance of law and order, as well as for the mining, timber and cocoa sectors in southern Ghana (Ladoucer, 1979; Sutton, 1983 and Bening, 1975). Similarly, the changing fortunes of northern agricultural production, 'entrepot' trading and administrative centres in northern Ghana influenced patterns of migration and settlement within the region (Bening, 1974). The publication of Marshall's *Forestry in the Northern Territories of the Gold Coast* in 1945 recognised that 'A considerable amount of labour from the Northern Territories is absorbed in the Colony and Ashanti and a proportion of their earnings goes back…for the support of their families' (Marshall, 1945: 2). These changes resulted in a more permanent pattern of migration, which cumulatively limited the availability of male labour to cultivate compound and bush farms in the region (Hart, 1974). This contributed to the re-growth of areas of woodland on abandoned farmland.[3]

Seasonal labour migration has nevertheless continued to influence land use and settlement patterns to the present day, as young males (particularly 15–45 years old) avail themselves of the changing economic opportunities *within* Upper East Region. The collection and marketing of Non-Timber Forest Products, the

---

1. *Census Report on the Mandated Area of Togoland which is incorporated in the Kusasi District*. District Commissioner's Office, Kusasi 6 June 1931: 2 (NRG 8/34/1. PRAAD, Tamale). In contrast, Cardinall, a former Provincial Commissioner in the NTs, attributed the movement to an ecological *malaise* in West Africa, referring to 'the essential driving force…forcing the population southward from the French Sudan…. This movement has been attributed to political and administrative causes, but it is far more likely that behind the human movement southward there is the same unknown force which is visibly compelling the fauna of the French Sudan into the protectorate and adjacent areas. Possibly the rate of dessication is progressing or owing to the intensive attacks of the dry winds from the Sahara the soil is becoming less productive. Both factors are of importance.' (Cardinall, 1931: 152).

2. Historically, economic development in southern Ghana depended on seasonal and permanent migrant labour from northern Ghana and neighbouring Burkina Faso to support, *inter alia*, the international and national slave trade, the internal regional trade in kola nuts and salt with the Sahelian countries (Sutton, 1983 and Lovejoy, 1985), the expansion of the external trade in African mahoganies after the mid-1800s (Parren, 1994), the introduction and expansion of cocoa cultivation in the Gold Coast Colony after 1874 (Acquaah, 1999), the rise and fall of the wild rubber trade between the 1880s and the 1920s (Brooks, 1947 and Bourret, 1949), and the staffing and active service of the West African Frontier Force during both World Wars (Bourret, 1949: 152–3).

3. Similar patterns were observed following the creation of a national park in Malawi in 1922. See McCracken, 1987.

development of rice irrigation schemes in the 1960s and 1970s (Shepherd, 1981), the construction of a tomato-canning and a meat-processing factory in the 1970s and 1980s and the resurgence of interest in gold mining (*galamsey*) in the mid-1990s (notably the spontaneous settlements south of Datoko, such as 'Takwa', 'Accra', 'Kumasi' and 'South Africa', along the western boundary of the Red Volta West Forest Reserve) have all provided opportunities to supplement the meagre incomes of rural communities once the subsistence farming season is over. In some years, the scarcity of wage opportunities may encourage some households to increase their production of cash crops while maintaining levels of food crop production, thus expanding, for example, tobacco cultivation along the banks of the Red Volta River within forest reserves (Wardell and Lund, 2004 a and b).

8. Conclusions

The colonial inheritance has been a significant determinant of present-day land cover and land use patterns in Ghana's biogeographically and demographically distinct Upper East Region. The forest and land use history of the region is clearly a product of British colonial policies, but one which was superimposed upon customary agricultural land use and settlement patterns. The latter, in turn, had been shaped by the biogeographical endowments of this location. I suggest that the forest reservation policy was less controversial in Upper East Region than it had been earlier on in the Gold Coast and Nigeria (Grove and Falola, 1996), precisely because many of the gazetted reserve areas occupied former farmlands and localised settlements abandoned between the 1920s and the1940s, where savannah woodlands had regenerated.

Contemporary land use and land cover patterns are commonly explained in terms of population parameters and current natural resource management strategies. They are frequently framed in a Malthusian perspective often suggesting shifting cultivation, over-grazing and bush-fires as the prime underlying causes of deforestation, and they are commonly couched in a-political, a-historical and a-cultural terms. The evidence of this case study suggests that the continuing transformation of wooded agricultural landscapes in the Sudano-Sahelian region is the outcome of historically and culturally embedded interactions between complex social, economic and ecological processes which operate at widely varying scales and change over time. Many finer-scale processes interact with the broad-scale trends driven by colonial forest policies, changing population pressures linked to migratory patterns, and the waxing and waning of economic opportunities within and outside the region. The case study of Upper East Region does not exclude population as a possible driver of deforestation, but it reaffirms the need to consider variables such as population or access in a broader agricultural landscape or wider developmental context.

The persistence of interest in tropical 'deforestation' nevertheless generates, and continues to perpetuate, 'myths' which represent over-simplifications of cause-consequence relationships, which have increasingly become embedded in broader land and environmental degradation narratives and continue to shape environment and development policies, even though they are difficult to support empirically. The importance of local-level studies is that they tend to highlight the complexity of specific geographical and historical situations, demonstrating the uniqueness of particular causes of land use change. The immense diversity in settings, the scale-specific nature of the relations and the frequent lack of quantitative information make it difficult to use such locally founded relations for regional or global assessments. This highlights the need to integrate the results from different disciplines and to identify the need for new fields of research to develop a better understanding of land use change and its drivers.

The case study of Upper East Region highlights the spatial and temporal complexity of the relationship between land use and land cover and changing economic opportunity structures, both within and outside the region. The patterns in Upper East Region suggest that, as a mechanism to diversify rural incomes while retaining access to or control over clan and lineage lands, labour migration has constituted an integral part of local livelihood strategies for at least a century. This contrasts with suggestions that the current 'scramble in Africa' is a recent sponsored process driven by structural adjustment and market liberalization policies (Bryceson, 2002).

References

Acquaah, B.1999. *Cocoa Development in West Africa: The Early Period with Particular Reference to Ghana*. Accra: Ghana Universities Press.

Agbosu, L.K. 1983. The Origins of Forest Law and Policy in Ghana during the Colonial Period. *Journal of African Law* 27 (2): 169–87.

Allen, J.C. and B.F. Barnes 1985. The Causes of Deforestation in Developing Countries. *Annals of the Association of American Geographers* 75 (2): 163–84.

Angelsen, A. and D. Kaimowitz 1999. "Rethinking the Causes of Deforestation: Lessons from Economic Models" in *The World Bank Research Observer* 14 (1): 73–98.

Anglo-French Forestry Commission 1973. "Rapport de la mission forestière Anglo-Francaise Nigeria-Niger (décembre 1936–février 1937)" in *Revue Bois et Forêts des Tropiques* 148: 3–26.

Anon. 1907. "Medical Report for the Northern Territories" in *Annual Report on the Northern Territories of the Gold Coast, 1907*: 21. Accra: Ghana National Archives.

Awudi, G.B.K. 2001. "The Role of Foreign Direct Investment in the Mining Sector in Ghana and the Environment". Paper presented to the OECD Conference on Foreign Direct Investment and the Environment, 7–8 February 2002 in Paris.

Barraclough, S.L. and K.B. Ghimire 1996. "Deforestation in Tanzania: Beyond Simplistic Generalizations" *The Ecologist* 26 (3): 104–7.

Barton, G. 2001. "Empire Forestry and the Origins of Environmentalism" in *Journal of Historical Geography* 27 (4): 529–52.

Bening, R.B. 1974. "Location of Regional and Provincial Capitals in Northern Ghana 1897–1960" in *Bulletin of the Ghana Geographical Association* 16: 54–66.

Bening, R.B. 1975. "Colonial Development Policy in Northern Ghana, 1898–1950" *Bulletin of the Ghana Geographical Association* 17: 65–79.

Benneh, G. 1973. "Small-scale Farming Systems in Ghana" in *Africa* XLIII (2): 134–46.

Benneh, G. 1985. NPopulation, Disease and Rural Development Programmes in the Upper East Region of Ghana" in J.I. Clarke et al. (ed)., *Population and Development Projects in Africa*. Pp. 206–18. Cambridge: Cambridge University Press .

Bernstam, M.S. 1991. "The Wealth of Nations and the Environment" in K. Davis and M.S. Bernstam (eds), *Resources, Environment and Population*. Pp. 333–73. Oxford: Oxford University Press.

Bilsborrow, R.E. and M. Geores 1994. "Population, Land Use and the Environment: What can we learn from Cross-national Data?" in K. Brownand D.W. Pearce (eds), *The Causes of Tropical Deforestation*. Pp. 106–33. London: UCL Press.

Blench, R. 1999. *Natural Resource Management in Ghana and its Socio-economic Context*. London: Overseas Development Institute.

Boatin, B. et al. 1997. "Patterns of Epidemiology and Control of Onchocerciasis" in *Journal of Helminthology* 71: 91–101.

Bourret, F.M. 1949. *The Gold Coast: A Survey of the Gold Coast and British Togoland 1919–1946*. The Hoover Library on War, Revolution and Peace Publication No. 23. Stanford: Stanford University Press.

Bobbe, T. et al. 2001. "A Primer on Mapping Vegetation using Remote Sensing" in *International Journal of Wildland Fire* 10: 277–87.

Brooks, R.L., 1947. *Empire Forests and the War*. Accra: Government Printer, Gold Coast Colony.

Brown, K. and D.W. Pearce (eds), 1994. *The Causes of Tropical Deforestation*. London: UCL Press.

Bryceson, D.F. 2002. "The Scramble in Africa: Reorienting Rural Livelihoods" in *World Development* 30 (5): 725–39.

Campbell, B.M. et al. 2000. "Special Section: Land Use Options in Dry Tropical Woodland Ecosystems in Zimbabwe" in *Ecological Economics* 33: 341–51.

Cardinall, A.W. 1931. *The Gold Coast*. Accra: Government Printer, Gold Coast Colony.

Davies, J.B. 1994. "Sixty Years of Onchocerciasis Vector Control: A Chronological Summary with Comments on Eradication, Reinvasion, and Insecticide Resistance" in *Annual Review of Entomology* 39: 23–45.

Ehrlich, P.R. and J.P. Holdren 1971. "Impact of Population Growth" in *Science* 171: 1212–17.

Fairhead, J. and M. Leach 1995. "False Forest History, Complicit Social Analysis: Rethinking some West African Environmental Narratives" in *World Development* 23 (6): 1023–35.

Fairhead, J. and M. Leach 1996. *Misreading the African Landscape: Society and Ecology in a Forest-Savanna Mosaic*. Cambridge: Cambridge University Press.

Fairhead, J. and M. Leach 1998. *Reframing Deforestation: Global Analysis and Local Realities: Studies in West Africa*. London and New York: Routledge.

Fairhead, J. and M. Leach2001. "History, Memory and the Social Shaping of Forests in West Africa and Trinidad". Paper presented to the workshop *Changing Perspectives on Forests: Ecology, People and Science/policy Processes in West Africa and the Caribbean*, 26–27 March 2002, Institute of Development Studies, University of Sussex.

FAO 2001. *Forest Resources Assessment 2000*. Rome: FAO. Available online at: http://www.fao.org/forestry/fo/fra/index.jsp

Francklin, J. 1991. "Land Cover Stratification using Landsat TM data in Sahelian and Sudanian Woodland and Wooded Grassland" in *Journal of Arid Environments* 20 (2): 141–63.

Geist, H.J. and E.F. Lambin 2001. *What Drives Tropical Deforestation? A Meta-analysis of Proximate and Underlying Causes of Deforestation based on Subnational Scale Case Study Evidence*. Report Series No. 4. Louvain-la-Neuve: University of Louvain, LUCC .

Gillis, M. 1988. "West Africa: Resource Management Policies and the Tropical Forest" in R. Repetto and M. Gillis (eds), *Public Policies and the Misuse of Forest Resources.* Pp. 299–351. Cambridge: Cambridge University Press.

Grainger, A. 1996. "An Evaluation of the FAO Tropical Forest Resource Assessment 1990" in *Geographical Journal* 162: 73–9.

Grove, R. and T. Falola 1996. "Chiefs, Boundaries and Sacred Woodlands: Early Nationalism and the Defeat of Colonial Conservationism in the Gold Coast and Nigeria, 1870–1916" in *African Economic History* 24: 1–23.

Harrison, P. 1992. *The Third Revolution: Population, Environment and a Sustainable World.* Harmondsworth: Penguin Books.

Hart, J.K. 1974. "Migration and the Opportunity Structure: A Ghanaian Case Study" in S. Amin, (ed.), *Modern Migrations in West Africa.* Pp. 321–42. Oxford: Oxford University Press.

Harvey, D. 1976. "Population, Resources and the Ideology of Science" in *Economic Geography* 50: 256–77.

Hawthorne, W. and M. Abu Juam 1995. *Forest Protection in Ghana with Particular Reference to Vegetation and Plant Species.* Gland: The World Conservation Union (IUCN).

Hilton, T.E. 1959. "Land Planning and Resettlement in Northern Ghana" *Geography* XLIV (4): 227–40.

Hilton, T.E. 1966. "Depopulation and Population Movement in the Upper Region of Ghana" in *Bulletin of the Ghana Geographical Association* 11 (1): 27–47.

Hilton, T.E. 1968. "Population Growth and Distribution in the Upper Region of Ghana" In J. C. Caldwell and C. Okonjo (eds.) *The Population of Tropical Africa.* Pp. 278–90. London, Longmans.

Holden, J.J. 1965. "The Zabarima Conquest of North-West Ghana" in *Transactions of the Historical Society of Ghana* VIII: 60–86.

Holdren, J.P. and P.R. Ehrlich 1974. "Human Population and the Global Environment" in *American Scientist* 62: 282–92.

Hunter, J.M. 1966. "River Blindness in Nangodi, Northern Ghana: A Hypothesis of Cyclical Advance and Retreat" in *Geographical Review* 56: 398–416.

Hunter, J.M. 1967. "Population Pressure in a Part of the West African Savanna" in *Annals of the Association of American Geographers* 57: 101–14.

Intergovernmental Panel on Forests 1996. *The Causes and Possible Solutions to Deforestation and Forest Degradation.* Ad Hoc Intergovernmental Panel on Forests, United Nations Commission on Sustainable Development. New York.

Kotey, N.A. et al. 1998. *Falling into Place: Policy that Works for Forests and People.* Ghana Country Study (No. 4). London: International Institute for Environment and Development.

Ladoucer, P. A. 1979. *Chiefs and Politicians: The Politics of Regionalism in Northern Ghana.* London: Longman.

Lambin, E.F. 1997. "Modelling and Monitoring Land-cover Change Processes in Tropical Regions" in *Progress in Physical Geography* 21: 375–93.

Lambin, E.F. 1999. "Monitoring Forest Degradation in Tropical Regions by Remote Sensing: Some Methodological Issues" in *Global Ecology and Biogeography* 8: 191–8.

Lambin, E.F. et al. 2001. "The Causes of Land-use and Land-cover Change: Moving beyond the Myths" in *Global Environmental Change* 11: 261–9.

Logan, W.E.M. 1943. "Forestry in Relation to Soil and Water Conservation in the Gold Coast" Unpub. manus. Accra: Forestry Department.

Lovejoy, P.E. 1985. "The Internal Trade of West Africa before 1800" In Ajayi, J.F.A. and M. Crowder (eds.) *History of West Africa, Volume 1,* 3rd edition, pp 648–90. Harlow: Longman.

Malthus, T.R. 1803. *An Essay on Population.* London: J.M. Dent.

Marshall, R.C. 1945. *Forestry in the Northern Territories of the Gold Coast.* Accra: Government Printing Department, Gold Coast Colony.

Mather, A.S. and C.L. Needle 2000. The Relationships of Population and Forest Trends. *The Geographical Journal* 166 (1): 2–13.

Matthews, E. 2001. *Understanding the Forest Resources Assessment 2000.* Forest Briefing No. 1, Washington: World Resources Institute. Available online at: http://www.wri.org/pdf/fra2000.pdf.

Mayers, J. and E. Nii Ashie Kotey 1996. *Local Institutions and Adaptive Forest Management in Ghana.* Forestry and Land Use Series No. 7. London: International Institute for Environment and Development.

Mazzucato, V. and D. Niemeijer 2000. *Rethinking Soil and Water Conservation in a Changing Society: A Case Study in Eastern Burkina Faso.* Tropical Resource Management Papers 32. Wageningen: Wageningen University and Research Centre.

McCracken, J. 1987. "Colonialism, Capitalism and the Ecological Crisis in Malawi: A Reassessment" in D. Anderson and R. Grove (eds), *Conservation in Africa: People, Policies, and Practice.* Pp. 63–77. Cambridge: Cambridge University Press.

McLeod, N.C. 1922. "Report on a Tour of Inspection in the Northern Territories" in *General Tour and Inspection Reports by Local Officers on the Northern Territories.* Case No. 01611. Kumasi: Gold Coast Colony Forest Department.

Meyer, W.B. and B.L. Turner 1992. "Human Population Growth and Global Land use/Cover Change" in *Annual Review of Ecological Systems* 23, 39–61.

Moor, H.W. 1935. "Preliminary Report on the Forest Requirements of the Northern Territories" in *General Tour and Inspection Reports by Local Officers on the Northern Territories.* Case No. 01611. Kumasi: Gold Coast Colony Forest Department.

Myers, N. 1984. *The Primary Source: Tropical Forests and Our Future.* New York: Norton.

Nabila, J. 1975. "Depopulation in Northern Ghana: Migration of the Frafra People" In A.S. Davida et al, (eds) *Interdisciplinary Approaches to Population Studies.* University of Ghana Population Studies No. 4. Legon: University of Ghana.

Nabila, J.S. 1997. NPopulation and Land Degradation in the Upper East Region of Ghana" in *Bulletin of the Ghana Geographical Association* 20: 74–86.

Ofori-Sarpong, E. 2001. "Impacts of Climate Change on Agriculture and Farmers Coping Strategies in the Upper East Region of Ghana" in *West African Journal of Applied Ecology* 2: 21–35.

Palo, M. 1994. "Population and Deforestation" in K. Brown and D.W. Pearce (eds), *The Causes of Tropical Deforestation.* Pp. 42–56.London: UCL Press.

Palo, M. and E. Lehto 1996. "Modelling Underlying Causes of Pantropical Deforestation" in M. Palo and G. Mery (eds), *Sustainable Forestry Challenges for Developing Countries.* Pp. 27–62. Dordrecht: Kluwer.

Parren, M.P.E. 1994. *French and British Colonial Forest Policies: Past and Present Implications for Côte d'Ivoire and Ghana.* Working Papers in African Studies No. 188. Boston University: African Studies Centre.

Ramsay, J.M. 1957. "Land Planning in the Northern Territories" in *The Gold Coast Teacher's Journal*: 20–6.

Reenberg, A. 1996. "A Hierarchical Approach to Land Use and Sustainable Agriculture Systems in the Sahel" in *Quarterly Journal of International Agriculture* 35 (1): 63–77.

Republic of Ghana 1999. *Ghana Living Standards Survey, 1992 and 1999.* Accra: Ghana Statistical Service.

Ribot, J.C. 1999. "A History of Fear: Imagining Deforestation in the West African Dryland Forests" in *Global Ecology and Biogeography Letters* 8: 291–300.

Richet, P. 1939. "La Volvulose dans un cercle de la Haute Côte d'Ivoire. Ses manifestations cutanées et oculaires" in *Bulletin de la Société de Pathologie Exotique* XXXII: 341–55.

Rudel, T.K. and J. Roper 1996. "Regional Patterns and Historical Trends in Tropical Deforestation 1976–1990: A Qualitative Comparative Analysis" in *Ambio* 25: 160–6.

Saaka, Y. (ed.) 2001. *Regionalism and Public Policy in Northern Ghana.* New York: Peter Lang.

Shepherd, A. 1981. "Agrarian Change in Northern Ghana: Public Investment, Capitalist Farming and Famine" in J. Heyer et al. (eds), *Rural Development in Tropical Africa*. London: Macmillan.

Sprugel, D.G. 1991. "Disturbance, Equilibrium and Environmental Variability: What is 'Natural' in a Changing Environment?" in *Biological Conservation* 58: 1–18.

Stebbing, E.P. 1937. *The Forests of West Africa and the Sahara: A Study of Modern Conditions*. London and Edinburgh: W. & R. Chambers.

Sullivan, S. 1996. "Towards a Non-equilibrium Ecology: Perspectives from an Arid Land" in *Journal of Biogeography* 23: 1–5.

Sutton, I. 1983. "Labour in Commercial Agriculture in Ghana in Late Nineteenth and Early Twentieth Centuries" in *Journal of African History* 24: 461–83.

Tappan, G.G. et al. 2000. "Use of Argon, Corona and Landsat imagery to access 30 years of land resources changes in West-Central Senegal" in *Photogrammetric Engineering & Remote Sensing* 66 (6), 727–735.

Thomson, H.N. 1910. *Report on Forests. Gold Coast*. Cd. 4993. London: HMSO: 185–192.

Tiffin, M., Mortimore, M. and Gichuki, F. 1994. *More People, Less Erosion: Environmental Recovery in Kenya*. New York, John Wiley and Sons.

Tucker, C.J. and J.R.G.Townshend 2000. "Strategies for Monitoring Tropical Deforestation using Satellite Data" in *International Journal of Remote Sensing* 21 (6 & 7): 1461–71.

Vierich, H.I.D. and W.A. Stoop 1990. "Changes in West African Savanna Agriculture in Response to Growing Population and Continuing Low Rainfall" in *Agriculture, Ecosystems and Environment* 31: 115–32.

Vigne, C. 1935. "Forestry Problems in the Northern Territories" in *General Tour and Inspection Reports by Local Officers on the Northern Territories*. Case No. 01611. Kumasi: Gold Coast Colony Forest Department.

Vigne, C. 1940. *Zuarungu District Working Plan Part I*. NRG 8/11/4. PRAAD, Tamale.

Wardell, D.A. 2002. "Historical Review of the Development of Forest Policy in the Northern Territories of the Gold Coast Colony 1901–1957" in Reenberg, A. et al., *SEREIN Working Paper* No. 41, pp. 102–61. Copenhagen: Institute of Geography, University of Copenhagen.

Wardell, D.A. 2003. "Groundnuts and Headwaters Protection Reserves: Tensions in Colonial Forest Policy in the Northern Territories of the Gold Coast Colony, 1901–1957". Paper presented at t*he International Conference on Forest and Environmental History in the British Empire and Commonwealth*, 19–21 March 2003. Brighton: University of Sussex.

Wardell, D.A. and C. Lund 2004a. "Governing Access to Forests in Northern Ghana: Micro-politics and the Rents of Non-enforcement" in *World Development* (in press).

Wardell, D.A. and Lund, C. 2004b. "En marge de la loi et au coeur de la politique locale : colonisation agraire des forêts classées au nord Ghana" in *Autrepart* 30 : 117–37

Wardell, D.A. et al. 2003. "Historical Footprints in Contemporary Land Use Systems: Forest Cover Changes in Savannah Woodlands in the Sudano-Sahelian Zone" in *Global Environmental Change* 13 (4): 235–54. (also selected to appear in the *Virtual Journal of Environmental Sustainability* 2 (1), January 2004, available online: http://www.elsevier.com/vj/sustainability)

Wardell, D.A. et al. 2004. "Fire History, Fire Regimes and Fire Management in West Africa: An Overview" in Goldammer, J.G. and C. de Ronde (eds.) *Wildland Fire Management Handbook for Sub-Saharan Africa*. Pp. 350–81. Freiburg University: Global Fire Management Centre and Oneworldbooks.

Webber, P. 1996. "Agrarian Change in Ghana" in *Geography Review* 9 (3): 25–30.

Westoby, J. 1987. *The Purpose of Forests: Follies of Development*. Oxford: Basil Blackwell.

World Bank 2001. *Northern Savanna Biodiversity Conservation Project, Ghana. Project Appraisal Document on a Proposed Grant from the Global Environment Facility Trust Fund*. Report No: 21847-GH. 14 May 2001. Washington: The World Bank.

World Health Organisation 1966. *WHO Expert Committee on Onchocerciasis: Second Report*. Technical Report Series, No. 335. Geneva: World Health Organisation.

Ghana National Archives: references cited

Year	Source	Reference
1908	Biu. Navrongo District Record Book, 1909–1918: 247 (Biu).	NAG ADM 63/5/2
1917	Zuarungu District Office Records. Informal Diary (Nash, 16 June 1917).	NAG ADM 68/5/1
1919	Zuarungu District Office Records. Informal Diary (Nash, 17 June 1919).	NAG ADM 68/5/1
1931	Census Report on the Mandated Area of Togoland which is incorporated in the Kusasi District (District Commissioner's Office, Kusasi 6 June 1931: 2).	NRG 8/34/1
1935	Zuarungu District Record Book II, 1935–1952: 79 (Sekoti)	NAG ADM 68/5/5

NAG: Ghana National Archives, Accra

NRG: Public Records, Administration and Archives Department, Tamale

Transnational Dimensions
to Environmental Resource Dynamics
Modes of Governance and Local Resource Management in Eastern DRC

James Fairhead

The British in 1940 'agreed on the necessity of preventing the territories' [Congo's] raw materials from falling into the hands of the Germans (Fetter 1988: 382).

It was said [during the Cold War] that the West would go to war to keep Zaire within the western orbit (Mazrui and Ajayi 1993: 651).

We must also find effective ways to secure Africa's vast natural resources – its diamonds, cobalt, uranium, oil, timber, coltan, its gold – so they do not provide currency for the world's terrorists (Rice 2001: 12).

We think the West has used Uganda and Rwanda to invade our country so they can mine our riches without paying (Pole Institute 2001).

The number of excess deaths directly attributable to Rwandan and Ugandan occupation can be estimated at between 3 million and 3.5 million (UN 2002).

A great deal of transnational policy and associated research concerning African natural resource use has explored opportunities for reshaping patterns of governance to influence and improve the management of environmental resources. However, such aspirations must contend with an inverse process: how transnational engagement with environmental resources is influencing patterns of governance and local resource management.

Nowhere has this been clearer than in the Democratic Republic of the Congo, whose rubber supported the car revolution, whose uranium supported the nuclear revolution, and whose cobalt and tantalum now support the technological revolution. Alongside these strategic minerals, it has massive reserves of diamonds, gold and now oil. These resources have been financing conflicts since 1996, which best estimates suggest have cost three million Congolese lives. This chapter will state what has become so obvious during the recent civil wars: that it is impossible to consider politics and governance anywhere in the DRC without considering the country's wider engagement with the industrialised world. Yet how does this influence local resource use? In beginning to address this question, I shall consider how the modes of resource governance associated with these current conflicts long precede them, and thus why, as Keen puts it (1998), 'war can usefully be seen as a deepening of exploitative processes already existing in "normal" times'. The present chapter shows how current modes of resource extraction that we can associate with the conflict have been shaped in a similar fashion for a century.

A linked statement of the obvious is that international interest in some of the DRC's resources will shape modes of governance and thus the management of others. Viewed in this way, it becomes inappropriate to differentiate environmental resources in the conventional way between 'renewable' and 'non-renewable', or between agro-ecological/living resources (such as forest, cocaine, coffee, conservation and rubber), and minerals (such as oil, cobalt, coltan[1], uranium, diamonds and gold). Arguably, making a strong distinction between these and treating them as if they were radically separate has long enabled the transnational configuration of resource governance, use and sustainability to be downplayed. The focus on renewables and land, as well as on their scarcity, always seems to lead analysts to explore the causes of resource conflicts in a localised way. For example, 'population increase' on location has been considered to increase demand for renewable resources and their value, or poverty or social transformation on location to undermine long-term sustainable management. The way that *international and global political and economic forces affect wider governance and thus local environmental practices is eclipsed.* We lose sight of how mining, timber, agri-business and conservation business affect governance (and conflicts) and through this, affect located social, political and economic orders, environmental practices and their sustainability. The wider links are often marginal in works relating territory, demography and scarcity together as the main explanation for conflicts over natural resource management. My intention here is to demonstrate that they need to be analytically centred by tracing how profoundly they shape the social relations of everyday resource management.

I shall consider these links in the Kivu region of the DRC, and more particularly through the lens of the province of Bwisha, and of a small village there where I conducted fieldwork some time ago, for two years between 1986 and 1989. The province has since attracted considerable attention, if not detailed fieldwork, that enables me to contextualise the current war economy within a deeper economic history. Bwisha is a Rwandan (Kinyarwanda)-speaking province extending north of the town of Goma, and filling out a triangle where the DRC borders on both Uganda and Rwanda. Following the Rwandan genocide in 1994, it hosted hundreds of thousands of Hutu refugees fleeing the post-genocide regime in Rwanda. Then in 1996, Rwandan and Ugandan troops occupied the province and forcibly emptied these camps. These troops then supported the major rebellion that went on to topple the DRC's notorious kleptocratic president, Mobutu Sese Seko – a

---

1. Coltan is the ore from which tantalum is derived. The tensile, heat and electrical properties of tantalum make it a crucial ingredient in armour penetration and missile technology, housing radioactive elements, including in nuclear reactors, manufacturing capacitors for third-generation computer technology (e.g. in mobile phones), rocket motors and radiation shielding

rebellion of allied oppositions led by Laurent Kabila. After two years, however, Laurent Kabila fell out with his Ugandan and Rwandan backers, and the latter gave their support to a second rebellion, this time against Kabila that continued until 2003. At the time of writing, Bwisha is currently under the control of Rwanda and Rwandan-backed rebels. To its north, the Nande-speaking region of the DRC is controlled by Uganda and Ugandan-backed rebels. There have also been clashes between these rebel groupings, and indeed, between different factions within each of them, linked to competition over mining areas. Whilst the occupation by Rwanda and Uganda had its origins in their need to protect their borders from hostile forces based in the DRC, a sequence of UN reports documents how this logic has mutated into, or been a cover for, 'the Illegal Exploitation of Natural Resources and Other Forms of Wealth of DR Congo' (e.g. UN 2001 2002).

Looting Kivu: A History of Practice

Kivu was looted before by Rwanda, during in the nineteenth century. While this Rwandan presence protected the province from being looted by Tippu Tip's interior slave- and ivory-trading empire, which was based near modern Kisangani, its own occupation was not itself benign. Kivu was then looted by the Belgian colonial administration, which established a mode of land, labour and resource expropriation that has lasted up until the present day. Understanding this mode is important in order to consider its local manifestations in lived experience – how it plays out in one village and its resource management.

Bwisha was relatively independent of Rwandan rule until the mid-nineteenth century. Until then there had been a gradual influx of pastoralists (Batutsi), but they recognised the authority of the more or less confederated principalities that they encountered (Vunabandi 1979: 11). How and when the Rwandan state first came to rule over Bwisha is not certain, but three phases in the development of Rwandan rule can be distinguished: the conquering of Bwisha (on and off from the fifteenth century): the imposition of Rwandan delegate rulers (late eighteenth century), and the systematic taxation of the province from the late nineteenth century.

During the eighteenth century, the Rwandan monarchy acquired sufficient power to appoint chiefs to rule over Bwisha's principalities. In some of them the existing lineage rulers were chosen as the vehicle for indirect rule, but in others direct rule was imposed. In all, a hierarchical administrative structure was created in which the province *(ikihugu)* was ruled by a provincial delegate. The province was subdivided into districts ruled by local district chiefs, and this was itself divided into administrative hills, each with their own chief (Kashori 1983).

Bwisha was first taxed systematically during the rule of the expansionist Rwandan monarch, Rwabugiri in the late 19th century. He extended Rwanda's borders far into what is now the Kivu region of the DRC. By the time of his death, the independent authority of Bwisha's princes had been eradicated. Those chiefs who had not been replaced by outsiders only retained their position by virtue of their loyalty to the Rwandan monarchy. Rwanda levied heavy taxes on produce and labour. When documented early in the Belgian era, each 'lineage' was said to provide 110 baskets of sorghum, 15 baskets of beans, 2000 leaves of tobacco, perfumes, salt, calabashes, lance shafts, an ivory tusk, animal skins, bracelets, beer, butter and other commodities, as well as 10% of the cattle (Dubuisson 1935). The tax was collected by a 'hill chief', who took a 10% cut, passing the rest on to the 'district chief', who took a 10% cut before passing it to the 'provincial' chief, who took his cut, before dispatching the produce to the centre. The products were carried to the royal court by conscripted porters. These taxes fell most heavily on those subordinate to the ruling lineage. Each lineage also had to supply two man-days of labour in every five to work for the chiefs at various levels of the hierarchy. The threat of Rwanda's elite soldiers (*inkemba*) enforced tax payment (Kashori 1983: 15–23).

Rwandan control was imposed on a political set-up conventionally described as 'nested lineages': the founding lineage that first cleared the land would make land available to other newcomers, who became its political subordinates and who had to pay 'tribute' to their overlords. They in turn could make land that they received available to others, and so on. While this may not capture the specific history in each district, it does represent well the nested sets of dyadic relations that structured access to land, political status and taxation. The heavy taxation by Rwanda accentuated the expropriative nature of these relations. Nominal tribute became a heavy tax, falling disproportionately on those in structurally inferior positions.

The first colonial military post was installed in 1902, when the Congo was the Belgian kings' fiefdom. As the Belgian colonial administration strengthened (after the outrageous exactions of the King's administration were exposed, and power transferred to Belgium), and especially after 1910, when the borders with Rwanda and Uganda were fixed, the Belgians attempted to force Bwisha chiefs to pay taxes to them, not the Rwandan court. Nevertheless, Bwisha princes continued to pay taxes to the Rwandan monarchy until 1914, as to begin with they were not convinced that the Belgians would stay (Matagne 1964; Kashori 1983: 72–7). The Belgian administration soon sought to identify pliable intermediary chiefs of their own through whom they could rule. The Belgians focused their attention on an interpreter, Ndeze, who had worked with them to assist military requisitioning during the First World War (when Belgian- and German-backed forces fought an entrenched battle in the area between 1915 and 1917). Although his claim to rule was tenuous, Belgian support enabled him to be elected as supreme leader over the many principalities. He then consolidated his authority by deposing all Rwandan-backed leaders and replacing them with his own appointees (Misabiro 1980: 19; Bwana Kweli 1985; Munyaruenzi 1980; Bangamwabo 1982). He also gained authority in a similar way over a neighbouring province,

Bwito. For chiefs at every level of the hierarchy, disobedience was sanctioned by suspension of power, either for short periods or for good.

From the 1920s, a powerful coercive combination of this chief, the colonial administration, European entrepreneurs, the army and the police was able to expropriate huge areas of land from cultivators, either for coffee plantations or for a national park. They imposed heavy taxes, and forcibly recruited labour for plantations, road building and infrastructure. Once again, as will become clear, these exactions fell most heavily on political subordinates.

To attract colonial investment and promote the region's economic development, Kivu was privatised. A company called the Comité National de Kivu (CN-Ki) was formed and empowered with the right to collect taxes. It had exclusive rights over forests, mining and all 'vacant ground', which it could sell as it wished, but it was duty bound to re-invest the proceeds in Kivu's infractructure (Mendiaux 1956, Drevet 1977). Legally the rights of local populations to their lands were upheld. However, CNKi was frustrated because first, all the best coffee-growing areas were occupied, secondly, there was no unclaimed land, and thirdly, it was difficult to recruit labour to work the lands that were less populated. With the connivance of pliable chiefs such as Ndeze, and to their huge personal profit, CNKi illegally sold inhabited lands to planters (Mendiaux 1956). By 1930 there were some 240 plantations in Kivu.

Similar 'illegal' methods were used to dispossess inhabitants of what became the Virunga National Park. Parks were established through the corrupt attribution of vacancy – the worst following the forced depopulation of the park area on the pretext of sleeping sickness – and through a public utility law that enabled 'compensation' to be paid to Ndeze. Ndeze's subordinate chiefs could not block the sale, and the population affected was not consulted and received none of the compensation (Nzabandora 1984: 59–62; Gapira 1980: 56–7). Ndeze also profited from shares he acquired in the monopolistic fishing 'cooperative' created on what was then Lake Edward in 1949. Certain local colonial administrators who attempted to contest the methods of the Park authority and the methods of the planters found that they were almost powerless in the face of CNKi and the Park authority (Gapira 1980: 88–91). The latter was answerable to Brussels, not to the colonial state.

Labour as well as land was appropriated. During the First World War, local chiefs had been obliged to send produce, soldiers and porters, leaving a major famine (known locally as Rumanura) in their wake. In the 1920s and 1930s, village chiefs were required to provide 25% of the available male labour force to work on road-building programmes (Northrup 1988: 195). This burden fell most heavily on those in contextually inferior positions. Plantation owners arranged with senior chiefs to force village chiefs to supply labour (Bangamwabo 1982: 49). While it was possible for regular skilled workers to be attached to a plantation and live on its land, local chiefs preferred to keep workers living on 'chiefdom' land, as they maintained authority over them and could tax them. The greater powers, threats and obligations that the chiefs now had meant that they both could and had to extort far higher tributes and corvée (unpaid work for the state) than they previously had. In many instances it was the chiefs, not workers, who received pay. Recruitment was often in the name of chiefs, who directed different subordinates to work each day (cf. Bashizi 1978: 16–19).

The administration and planters attempted to prevent any alternatives to colonial employment, whether by keeping food prices too low to be commercially viable, banning smallholder coffee production or strictly controlling labour mobility. Among men on whom the exactions fell hardest, there were many who fled their natal lands to other regions where they had greater autonomy. Others migrated to Uganda, where work and conditions were reputedly more favourable. The authorities responded, however, by sending 'recapture groups' to find, bring back and punish those who had fled the locality or employment to which they had been restricted. The relatives and wives of those who had fled were forced to work in their place (Bangamwabo 1982: 51).

Half of Bwisha's male population were working on the coffee plantations by 1938 (Northrup 1988: 195), but there were still shortages, prompting forced relocations of population from other regions, from Nande-speaking regions to the north and from Rwanda. During the Second World War, labour conditions worsened, as if this were still possible. Those not working on the plantations were forced to do corvée work for 120 days a year, thus easing plantation recruitment (Anstey 1966: 146–58).

While the settler class had been advantaged during the war, the short-staffed colonial administration had had to cope with a resultant famine and nascent rebellions in 1944–5 (Bezy et al. 1981: 36). Finally, after the war, the administration took steps to strengthen the rights of the workforce, and curb the power of the plantations, chiefs and Park (Drevet 1977: 99). Labour markets were freed and wages rose five-fold. By the mid-1950s more than two-thirds of the male population were employed (Drevet 1977: 99, Bangamwabo 1982: 78).

The DRC achieved independence in 1960, but any gain for the population was short-lived. In the election struggle surrounding independence, Kivu's largest party was the Centre de Regroupement Africaine (CEREA), whose manifesto included opening the park for hunting and farming, and abolishing taxes and corvée. Its vocal membership consisted of those in the newly elected councils, teachers, and those who had been dispossessed during the Belgian regime. It was opposed by a party (ARP) supported by the chiefs and the traditional elite, which sought to 'uphold custom against radicalism', though for want of support it had to merge with the party supported by the white community (PNP). Needless to say, CEREA won overwhelmingly. In Bwisha, Ndeze fled to Belgium, and a newly elected assembly took over from the 'traditional' chiefs.

Yet seven years of political turmoil ensued, including the assassination of the leftist Lumumba, occupation by UN forces, the eventual failure of the leftist Mulele rebellion, and the eventual military success of the CIA-backed Mobutu in the civil war in 1966. Mobutu then consolidated his rule by reinstating many of the 'traditional' chiefs, including Ndeze in Bwisha. Ndeze thus expanded his mandate not only as a traditional chief, but also as the state administrator (until 1973). Rumour of a Batutsi bid for political ascendency in Kivu and their backing for the ill-fated Mulele rebellion of the MNC had aided Ndeze's return to power. Ndeze had already 'cleansed' Bwisha of Batutsi authority once (in the 1920s), and he did so again.

During this period, Kivu's plantation economy collapsed. The plantations remained territorially intact, but of the nine hundred foreign owned plantations in Kivu, only fifty remained in partial operation in 1973. The plantation owners who remained accumulated vast areas of land by purchasing it from those who were leaving. Then foreign assets were nationalised in 1973. In Rutshuru, the family of Ndeze, his loyal subordinates and other members of the state administration acquired the plantations. This, and instances like it thoughout the country, provoked a deeper crisis, and in 1976, a 40% stake in some plantations was ceded back to their original owners to keep them operational. In Bwisha, Mobutu himself was a major personal beneficiary, and the coffee plantations that he had interests in were also granted monopolistic marketing powers.

In short, until the 1950s, an alliance between the colonial administration (plus its army), the traditional chiefs (plus their police), the planters (plus their police) and the park (plus their guards) was able, often illegally and corruptly, to expropriate land from cultivators extort heavy taxes and corvée to build infrastructure, and recruit labour to work in the plantations. From the 1970s, these alliances were strengthened, as Ndeze and many administrators themselves became plantation owners. In the 1950s, the administrations' reform programme had sought to control the monster that it had created by attempting to strengthen the power of the population (and itself) relative to this elite by introducing local democracy and labour laws, but this failed. Wages did improve during the 1950s boom, but restrictions on education and on credit, coupled with the restrictive trading practices of the colonial elite, prevented nationals from acquiring capital in what had become sub-Saharan Africa's second-most industrialised nation. Following Mobutu's ascendency, control passed to the new elite, when the old alliance between capital, state and traditional authority was forged once more.

Plantation profitability and wages slumped. By the mid-1970s many labourers were reluctant to work for wages that had fallen to less than 6% of 1960 levels in real terms. This was especially so given the growing market for, and profitability of food crops, and given emergent opportunities for small-holder coffee production. Employers again found it necessary to coerce unfree labour. This could be achieved in several ways. First, plantation owners could force those who farmed their land to do more unpaid work for them (two days a week). Secondly, they could recruit the labour of the desperate and land destitute. Thirdly, employers were able, given emergent conditions of personal insecurity, to recruit labour by 'giving protection' to employees, squatters and indeed land-holders.

Realising this, employers were not encouraged to reduce levels of violence and in-security. This 'protection racketeering' assisted their recruitment of cheap labour. Indeed, in many cases, landlords and employers were behind the deployment of violence (by hiring soldiers who freelanced from their camps) that became endemic.

Employers who worked in increasingly unprofitable circumstances could thus pass their problems on to their work force, as control over land and security was used to gain control over labour (see Schoepf and Schoepf 1987: 25). Indeed, despite deepening economic crisis, the 1980s saw a huge increase in the demand for large tracts of plantation land by self-financing projects, whether church organisations, the urban entrepreneurial elite, the 'traditional' chiefs or national (often Kinshasa-based) politicians. The control of unfree labour by land-holders was central to the viability of these enterprises.

During this period, the elite managed to expand their land-holdings. At times President Mobutu did make some populist attempts to restrict this and the 'feudal' economy that emerged. In 1973, Mobutu legislated against inherited chief-ships and against traditional authorities having perpetual rights to control land. He legislated in favour of squatters' rights being granted following three years of uncontested occupancy. Yet this altered the rules of the game, and its victors, not the game itself. Indeed, as Schoepf and Schoepf indicated based on their research in south Kivu, these laws actually enabled all 'those with power, wealth and in-fluence...to manipulate the system to appropriate any lands not yet conceded or titled...including lands currently occupied' (1987: 22). The legislation advantaged the state elite over the traditional one in the struggle for spoils. International assistance, in particular in support of ranching (meat-marketing, cattle-health programmes, infrastructural development) exacerbated this by enhancing the profitability of cattle-ranching. By 1991, in the highlands of the Masisi area, west of Bwisha, around 500 families controlled about 60% of the land (Vlassenroot 2002).

In the mid 1980s, a sub-regional committee on land tenure investigated reports of the fraudulent use of the vacancy law and boundary extension. It concluded that:

> Our customary chiefs must henceforth know that feudalism has been abolished, that there is no longer *Bami* ['traditional' royalty] land and cattle. It is wrong that they entrench themselves behind customary jurisdiction, that they dispossess land from their subjects; that they forbid them rights to build permanent homes, and that they deny them all rights of ownership, whether it be land or possessions. They must know that their figurehead on these unconstitutional activities generates interminable land conflicts, which compromise the socio-economic development of their entities, collectivizes individual litigations, and stirs up tribal hatred (Katuala et al. 1986: 89, my translation).

Located Experience of Regional Processes

These processes were generalised throughout the more densely populated regions of Kivu and had profound affects in villages everywhere. In Kagara, the village where I lived in the hills above the town of Rutshuru in the late 1980s, people's exposure to exaction and dispossession was sharply differentiated. This can be seen in respect of personal security and exemption from informal taxation and compulsory labour, as well as in land relations.

First, people obtained protection through different institutions. Many of those who were the descendents of early land-holders, and who thus had more secure rights to land, sought to maintain their rights to both land and their own labour through 'traditional' authorities, notably the village Kapita, his committee, and those he favoured. On the other hand, villagers who had 'state' positions in this bifurcated administration[1] could secure their rights through the state administration that they represented (within the Comité de Base of the Mouvement Populaire pour la Révolution or MRP as it was then called), or through employment in state-supported institutions (e.g. as schoolteachers, Red Cross officials or 'development' representatives). Some other families were able to draw on the backing of their church (whether Catholic, Baptist, Seventh Day Adventist or one of the profusion of new Protestant churches), or the mosque. Churches supported and protected their ministers, and indeed their flocks. To achieve this (and, cynically, to secure a following), the churches fostered regional and national political connections and, with the help of these, operated a sophisticated protection system. Church communities provided legal support in land claims (for example, upholding squatters' rights over traditional rights in national courts) and provided physical protection to those who were being violently harassed. In the Catholic system, for example, one member of the local chapel would follow anyone who had been arrested, while another would be dispatched to the mission to alert the higher authorities and initiate support and release procedures. Lastly, as in the colonial period, plantation owners would ensure protection for their own relatively skilled employees.

People advertised their protection when travelling. Identity cards peered from plastic pockets on the outside of jackets, and metal 'MPR' Party badges on the lapel, bibles in hand and crosses hanging loose all signified protection to any military or police operative that one might encounter. These modes of protection clearly hark back to colonial times, when administrative jobs, social clout or employment would exempt the lucky from army recruitment, tax and forced labour.

The importance of such protection extended to land and labour. Land grabbing was not restricted to the major players. Thus it also became possible for landholders, whether high- or low-ranking chiefs, or representatives of more powerful

---

1. See Mamdani 1996 for further analysis of bifurcation between state and traditional authority throughout the continent.

lineages, to claim that lands that they or their parents had once ceded to strangers had simply been 'let'. They redefined the 'tributes' that the strangers had paid as 'rent', allowing them to claim that the land still belonged to them. Such land grabbing was limited where I lived to the actions of a huge neighbouring plantation that seized a third of the village's land after successfully pursuing what the village felt was a false boundary dispute.

In this particular village, the founding lineage had lost political control to a ritually illegitimate appointee. They were poor and in no position to exert their ancestral rights. Until the 1960s, newcomers soliciting land in the village were usually granted some by this family. From the 1970s, however, a growing market for land had grown up due to land scarcity, reductions in plantation work, declining wages and increased reliance on farming for food and cash, alongside an increase in 'distress sales' by the poor. Wealthier villages consolidated their holdings, disparaging those who sold because of their lack of 'ability' (*ukuntu*), their foolish impulsiveness, and their inability to 'resist meat' (and drink). Land arrangements ceased to be ritually significant.

In a neighbouring village, expropriation occurred differently. A large ancestral landholding family had tried to evict those to whom they had granted land under past social and economic conditions in the ways described above, by redefining their subordinates as tenants and squatters. In this instance, the churches directly supported the tenants' and squatters' case in the state court. They also used its rituals (exorcism) to oppose directly the ancestors (redefined as devils) of past land-holders who were particularly feared.

It is possible to draw too sharp a distinction between this 'grabbing by direct expropriation and land losses through the market. Those in vulnerable positions with respect to mobility and labour were led to sell land. In this respect, continuing control over land has come to depend more on political connections and protection, as well as its income effects, as much as on inheritance and the assertion of rights. A similar story is told by André and Platteau (1998) in pre-genocide Rwanda, where access to land began to depend more on access to off-farm income (urban employment and mortgage facilities) than on inheritance. In the village, all modern land transactions are imaged in relation to the notions of the possessor and the dispossessor, in stark contrast to past relations of the politico-ritual chief and subordinate, which had earlier been the stuff of political and social alliance.

In short, with the collapse of the economy in the 1970s and 1980s, the distinction between those who had invested in protective institutions (and who had documents showing them to be part of a greater community), and those who had not, became increasingly important. My fairly robust assessment, based on key informants, suggested that about a quarter of adult men in the village could avoid direct expropriation. For example, they felt safe in using the roads without being vulnerable to expropriation from the military and police of assorted forces, and they were exempt from forced labour and labour tribute for their land. When it came to constructing a road to the village, these people were strongly in favour, finding common interest and a source of friendship in these issues – a wealthy elite with a 'wider' outlook (Fairhead 1992). On the other hand, a poorer majority, many of whom lacked any documentation whatsoever, felt that the road would bring yet further control and expropriation from the centre, not to mention them being forced to build this vehicle of their own oppression themselves.

Protection for the village elite did not come cheap. For example, the Kapita used to exempt relatives, friends and respected men from compulsory state labour, for which they paid twenty litres of banana wine and a chicken annually. The compulsory labour burden then fell on younger and poorer men instead. Despite the opportunities for 'buy out', however, it was better to have 'real' exemption than to pay others for a piece of theirs, as such payments inevitably increased. Yet proper protection itself required self-exploitation. None of the jobs that guaranteed protection paid a salary: the jobs had to pay for themselves.

Social changes have added to, and shaped, patterns of marginalisation from land and livelihood. Vulnerable people who had hitherto had access to land via customary land claims find that such claims are no longer being honoured by land-holders. This is particularly true of return migrants, separated women, wives in polygynous marriages, widows, the handicapped, orphans and the children of broken marriages. While this is linked to land shortages amongst the land poor, it is accentuated throughout society by that the trend towards land-holding becoming more dependent on purchase than inheritance, as purchased land is largely excluded from these wider forms of social rights and entitlements. As André and Platteau (1998) also note in Rwanda, a particularly important transformation has occured in the number of children who are born of marriages which are not 'legal' because poor men have been unable to provide the bridewealth required of a marriage. This has two effects. First, wives of such households usually adopt a strategy of maintaining more independent economic activities. Secondly, wives and the children of such marriages have very poor claims to land. André and Platteau suggest that in Rwanda, the children of more than two thirds of marriages have precarious tenure. Whether or not the proportions are so high in the Kivu case is unclear. The manner in which rights vary with assorted forms of partial payment has evolved, and it has been the young man's responsibility to pay bridewealth, especially among the majority of the poor since the economic collapse of the 1960s and 1970s.

It is not my intention to document in detail how these modes of exaction and economic decline and the social changes associated with them are shaping land use. Rather, I would like to suggest a few implications that will be suggestive of the field that I have explored elsewhere (Fairhead 1990). First, few people now let land, or indeed offer any debt at all. Anyone who does make such arrangements ensures that they are more formalised, restricting how tenants use the land: no perennial crops and no permanent dwellings are allowed. Land use in the region is thus shaped by the need to assert tenure over the land you wish to claim, by establishing perennial crops, whether coffee, bananas or exotic trees, and building perennial houses, that is, those with metal roofs, or inversely, by refusing these things. This response to tenurial ambiguity is generic to much of East Africa.

Most farmers hold land under a variety of tenure arrangements. For those with limited land, their most secure land must be devoted to perennials that they cannot cultivate elsewhere. These crops tend to reduce erosion and be under the control of men. The more seasonal food crops, those under women's or 'household' control, and which are more erosion-sensitive, tend to be marginalised on lands which farmers hold in a less secure way, often at some distance from home. The tenure system has thus disrupted potentially more sustainable and integrated farming methods. Moreover, the legacy of the history of land possession is that ecologically marginal and highly erosion-prone land has often remained in the possession of chiefs and large landowners. It is these fragile lands which are let to land-poor farmers, who only cultivate seasonal crops there. In this instance, insecure tenure certainly hinders land improvements, although this is not necessarily a general feature of land insecurity in sub-Saharan Africa (cf. Place and Hazell 1993).

A third impact concerns the greater individual autonomy in economic relations between parents and children, and between husbands and wives. Given the economic tensions that exist in many households, many, especially poorer women have pursued a range of land-use strategies to avoid losing control over their produce. This includes cultivating crops that involve less male participation in production, cultivating outside seasonal patterns, and 'storing in the field' rather than in the house to limit bulk supply (and to protect stocks against soldiers and looting). They also tend to sell stocks earlier.

Exit Options and Rebel Movements

From the early colonial period, many young men in structurally poor positions had sought an exit option, whether in migration to the copper mines to the south or to Uganda to the east. In the early period, as already noted, attempts were made to track such dissenters down or to harm their families. Out-migration became popular again in the 1960s and 1970s, when Ugandan wages were three times those in Congo. More than half the men living in the village in the 1980s had worked in Uganda at one time, and many others remained. Yet by the 1980s, opportunities for out-migration to find employment had become much more restricted. This was a period when many Congolese began migrating south, into Zambia, Angola and South Africa, acquiring a dubious reputation throughout the continent.

Other alternatives have been speculative gold or coltan digging, or settling in remote regions in the forest. Migrants to these areas, as strangers without secure networks, become subordinate to the mine owners or the land chiefs of the forest tracts. Thus while the ability of entrepreneurial migrants to 'get by' has been celebrated as part of the DRC's 'informal economy', this has itself been shadowed by an informal polity, such as those that I have described which gate-keep protection and economic opportunity, and which are linked to modes of protection and exaction. So those taking the mining option – in the DRC, at least – do not escape Kivu's predatory economy.

On occasions, options have emerged to link up with rebels. Thus, the rebel movements linked to the 1965 Mulele rebellion continued in South Kivu until the 1980s. It was eventually restricted in its operations to parts of South Kivu controlling gold mining there and, according to credible accounts (Schatzberg 1988), trading gold with their opponents, the army of Mobutu, in exchange for arms. The rebel commander, Laurent Kabila, traded the remainder of the gold out of Burundi and Tanzania. This earlier 'rebellion' found a way to become self-sustaining. For low-ranking soldiers working among the rebels, or as national soldiers in the '*Zone Rouge*' region of the conflict, the conflict did not provide an opportunity for accumulation. For populations living in theatre of rebellion, it was a decade of impoverishment and depopulation.

In short, wider forms of exaction that date back to early colonial times remain the central forces shaping village life. They shape people's differential relations with the different institutions that link the village to the wider political field and their investments in these. They shape people's access to their own labour, their mobility and personal geography (using footpaths or roads). They shape modes of marriage, inheritance, disinheritance and destitution.

Coltan and the Current Conflict

Before considering how the contemporary conflict is being shaped by the strategies of foreign powers, I would like to review how the emergent war economy could be understood as a development of these existing economic and political patterns. As with the remnants of the Mulele rebellion, which fought on between 1967 and 1980 under Laurent Kabila, the first rebellion against Mobutu (1996–98, also led by Kabila) and now the second rebellion against Kabila and then his son's presidency has developed into a self-financing – indeed extremely profitable – endeavour.

The new occupying armies took over existing modes of self-financing, based on practices of exaction and forging links with a new, and not so new, economic elite. Yet these dynamics in Kivu were accentuated by the boom in the mining of coltan from late 1999 to early 2001. Coltan is mined in particular areas throughout Kivu. Different mines were captured by different forces. Some mining areas fell under Rwandan and rebel control. Other zones were controlled by their opponents, the former Rwandan army and their militia. According to some informants to the Pole Institute (2001), it is Congolese Hutu (from Bwisha?) who transport the material across the lines to sell in Rwandan controlled areas. Some mines are controlled by Mai-mai forces, — a militia that began as ethnic-linked protection forces, but which also became freelance in operation. Other mines (e.g. in Lubero) are controlled by Ugandan forces and Ugandan-backed rebels. Militias and armies with their origins in other causes now fight to control the mines. Spoliation now also focuses on coltan mining sites as the object of dispute.

Yet it is not just control of the mines, but also the control of labour which is important. As the UN report summarises: 'With minor exceptions, the objective of military activity is to secure access to mining sites or ensure a supply of captive labour' (UN 2002, paragraph 93).

Many of the Coltan reserves in the region appear to have been developed initially by young men who gained authorisation by land owners and authorities. Yet now most of the work is no longer conducted by them, but by employees, and coerced labour.

As the final report of the UN panel of experts states:

> The bulk of coltan...as much as 60 to 70 per cent, has been mined under the direct surveillance of the Rwandan Patriotic Army (RPA) mining détachés and evacuated by aircraft from airstrips near mining sites directly to Kigali or Cyangugu. No taxes are paid. Rwandan military aircraft, Victor Bout's aircraft and small airline companies are used in the evacuation of the coltan. RPA has maintained control over most of the coltan sites where rich deposits are found, where the percentage of tantalum is high, and where local airstrips are accessible. A variety of forced labour regimes are found at sites that have been managed by RPA mining détachés, some for coltan collection, some for transport, others for domestic services. Many accounts report the widespread use of prisoners imported from Rwanda who work as indentured labour. (UN 2002, paragraph 75)

Other mines remain under the control of manager supervisors, themselves under the surveillance of police monitors. Miners are day labourers without a contract. When the price of coltan fell in 2001, the coltan economy did not cease, but was maintained through the use of conscript and forced labour. One commercial informant to the UN Panel 'explained that, because of the collapsed international coltan market, prices for the mineral in the eastern Democratic Republic of the Congo had dropped dramatically. However...the continuing international interest in coltan from the Democratic Republic of the Congo is due to the very low labour costs for extracting the mineral' (UN 2002, para 109)

In summing up the mode of illegal exploitation, the UN report identifies networks of:

> a small core of political and military elites and business persons and, in the case of the occupied areas, selected rebel leaders and administrators. Some members of the elite networks occupy key positions in their respective Governments or rebel groups. Members of these networks cooperate to generate revenue and, in the case of Rwanda, institutional financial gain. The elite networks ensure the viability of their economic activities through control over the military and other security forces that they use to intimidate, threaten violence or carry out selected acts of violence. The networks monopolize production, commerce and fiscal functions. The elite networks maintain the facade of rebel administrations in the occupied areas to generate public revenues that they then divert into the networks, thereby depleting the public treasury. (UN 2002)

Most journalistic and academic reports have focused on the smaller-scale coltan exploitation which they have had access to. They focus on the entrepreneurial peasant echoing works celebrating the 'entrepreneurial' means that the poor use to 'get by' (cf. de Boeck 1999; Jackson 2001). From this perspective, the poor's engagement with mining has been considered as one more means of 'getting by', thus exposing the continuities in this mode of economic life. Yet in regions where entrepreneurial youths continue to mine, access is not straightforward. In Rwandan-held areas, they tend to be Rwandan-speaking Tutsi youth. As one informant to the Pole Institute put it, 'At the moment it is a high-risk job, especially if you are not a Hutu or a Tutsi. Our young Hunde miners are shot at point-blank range' (Pole 2001). In other regions, miners, intermediaries and major traders all had to pay a 'licence' fee to RCD rebels, which itself was a major investment. What is missing in this focus on resourcefulness is attention to the less 'heroic' continuities that I have foregrounded in this chapter: the entrepreneurial abilities of the elite, invaders and military. Unfortunately the anthropology of resourcefulness in celebration of everyday struggle and humour has played into the claims of corporations such as the Bayer group, which claim that their tantalum originates from 'peasant suppliers', not from rebel groups. Yet as the UN report bluntly noted at this time, 'in fact, no coltan exits from the eastern Democratic Republic of the Congo without benefiting either the rebel group or foreign armies.' Missing from our accounts, then, has been the story of the three million who did not 'get by'.

The trade in coltan is also monopolised. The UN report suggests that only:

> A smaller portion, perhaps 15 to 25 per cent of the total coltan exported, is purchased by comptoirs owned by Rwandans who buy from local négotiants at remote coltan sites or from the agents of local defence groups. More typically these comptoirs, owned by Rwandan army officers or those closely linked to the Government of Rwanda, such as MHI comptoir, Eagle Wings or Rwanda Metals, have obtained their own mining sites and conscript their own workers to exploit the sites under severe conditions.

The view of those not involved is that the boom mostly enriches only the elite, whose experience of the coltan economy mirrors that of plantations:

> On the whole the relationship [of the mines] with the authorities is good. With the local population the relationship is not good. The population is unhappy with the mining conditions. They also criticise the fact that mining takes place on the land of large landowners and only benefits them (Pole Institute 2001).

A prevalent image in much of the literature has been the apparent 'banditry' of militia forces. Thus militia have been known to 'attack their own village'; their own 'parents'; even their own traditional chiefs (Jackson 2001). Yet when the differentiated experiences of exaction at the local level are clarified, a common logic of the settling of scores emerges in which chiefly families are targeted by those who have been in structurally subordinate positions.

International Dimensions to the Conflict

In similar works that sketch out the long history and local manifestations of Congo's looting economy, once dubbed its kleptocracy, one tendency has been to consider it in relation to 'Mobutu' and 'African corruption'. Yet from the outset of Belgian rule, these patterns of governance have reflected international interest in what is now the DRC.

Early Belgian interest in Congo was driven by the pre-First World War rubber boom and the wider 'Scramble for Africa'. While Belgium soon became Congo's main trading partner, the United States became the principal market for its raw materials from the 1940s. Indeed, the country soon gained a Cold War strategic interest for its uranium. By the late 1950s, it had an experimental nuclear reactor, and at independence became a nuclear state. Yet its strategic importance grew further around its cobalt and manganese. As Mazrui and Ajayi note, in the 1970s '[a] major reason why the West was bailing out Mobutu Sese Seko...was the importance of Zaire's cobalt for western technology and industry' (1993:651) This mineral has become strategically central. Indeed, the DRC had the credentials of being the Saudi Arabia of cobalt' (Adedeji 1993, 426). Cobalt is a critical ingredient in the superalloys used in air- and land-based turbine engines, as well as for rechargeable batteries for cell phones and computers. Environmental pressures for zero emission vehicles will massively increase demand for this 'oil of the future'.

Strategic minerals are those that are militarily, politically or economically essential. The most significant strategic minerals are those for which supply is highly concentrated in a limited number of states, from which major military-industrial powers must import. Congo's cobalt and now the tantalum (in coltan) can claim this status. All five major capitalist countries (France, Germany, Japan, UK, USA) are critically[1] dependent on cobalt and Tantalum. The tensile, heat and electrical properties of tantalum make it a crucial ingredient in armour penetration and missile technology, housing radioactive elements, including in nuclear reactors, manufacturing capacitors for third-generation computer technology (e.g. in mobile phones), rocket motors and radiation shielding.

Changing patterns of international resource demand have led to increased import dependence on these minerals. As declared strategic minerals, the US has at times accumulated extensive stockpiles of cobalt and tantalum. This trend towards increasing dependence preoccupies many military and economic strategists the world over. Over the last decade, international security officials have been paying even greater attention to intensified competition over these strategic materials, and this has regained centrality in American Security Planning. Indeed Klare, writing in *Foreign Affairs*, goes further, arguing that there is now a 'new ge-

---

1. That is, when supplies come from few suppliers, over long distances, or from a country of a different ideology.

ography of conflict, a reconfigured cartography in which resource flows rather than political and ideological divisions constitute the major fault lines' (2001: 51). Nowhere is this more appropriate than in southern Africa for its minerals and in western Africa for its oil. At the heart of all this is the DRC.

Strategic resources have now acquired further importance following the attacks on the USA on September 11th 2001. First, Africa's 'non-Islamic oil' has become central to the geopolitics of energy. Secondly, as former Assistant Secretary of State Susan Rice argued in the context of the US House of Representatives' deliberations on Africa and the war on global terrorism:

> We must recognize that regimes lacking legitimacy and failed states are convenient safe havens as well as breeding grounds for terrorists. If we are serious about our anti-terrorism commitment...the US must become more rather than less engaged in the difficult task of peacemaking, peacekeeping and national reconstruction – from the Great Lakes to Sierra Leone, from Liberia to Sudan and Somalia. We must also find effective ways to secure Africa's vast natural resources – its diamonds, cobalt, uranium, oil, timber, coltan, its gold – so they do not provide currency for the world's terrorists. (Rice 2001: 12)

While these aspects preoccupy strategists, they also offer immense profit to those who control their supply. Strategic minerals tend to be price–inelastic: that is, if prices rise, the amount demanded does not fall. Rather, if supply can be assured, the buyer is often willing to pay a very high price. As Hveem (1986) notes, in strategic terms, embargoes are worse than price increases. Under such conditions, there is a huge potential for monopolistic behaviour, and conglomerates controlling strategic elements can make massive profits by forming cartels, through intra-firm trade etc. There have been many times that neither cobalt nor tantalum have had a traded world price: prices tend to be set by producers or negotiated in contractual arrangements. Those who control these minerals can exert huge leverage ('rents') over industries that depend on them, especially if they form cartels. Control has been highly concentrated at the corporate level.

In the 1990s, for example, the reduction in Zaire's (as it then was) cobalt output (from 10,000 tonnes/annum in 1992 to ca. 2–3,000 tonnes) forced the price up from about $6/pound to $25–$33/pound. This made access to the DRC's cobalt reserves worth more to corporations which control the rest of the world's supply (principally American Mineral Fields, which controls much of Canada's reserves). Informed analysts predict that if the DRC's cobalt production picks up again, the price of cobalt may drop from $25/pound to $7/pound (*The Economist*, May 3rd 1997: 62), massively reducing, for example, the value and extraction profitability of American Mineral Field's Canadian reserves. It is not surprising, then, that the principle firm competing for the DRC's cobalt reserves at that time was AMF, which not only controlled much of the Canadian reserves, but could maintain their value by limiting the DRC's supply. Cuba, the other major cobalt producer, was embargoed internationally.

Entrepreneurs will go to great lengths to secure reserves. Those who already have reserves remain undaunted by backing both sides of a conflict, and even brokering peace negotiations, as Anglo-American did in South Africa. On the other hand, non-established firms who are seeking to capture reserves can back one side, perhaps hoping, in the event of victory, to displace competitors. In the DRC, the major established mining corporations were largely francophone, but following the conflict, anglophone ones are taking over. *Africa Confidential* has referred to 'considerable brawling among foreign investors' and notes that 'French and Belgians, Japanese and South Africans, suspect that the advance of the Alliance's troops will mainly benefit North American mining corporations' (25 April 1997, 38[9], 3).

North American, European and Asian corporations have struck deals with both governments and rebels. At the same time, the world's leading mining corporations have supported protagonists in the conflict, profiting both from their interests there and, indeed, from the increased value of their reserves elsewhere when conflict disrupts Congolese production.

Many of the corporations operating in the DRC and its neighbours have strong political connnections. These are hard to research in detail, but some indication of the links involved can be gauged from the 'revolving door' that sees senior figures in government moving in and out of corporations. In recent years, for example, Barrick Gold, which has large interests in the DRC, has counted three former CIA directors and two former North American Presidents in its management (George Bush Snr., Richard Helms, Robert Gates and Brian Molroney). The Bechtel Corporation, which also worked with Laurent Kabila during his first rebellion, has had former US Secretary of State George Schultz alongside Philip Habib and Casper Weinberger working for it, as well as CIA directors William Casey and Richard Helms. Haliburton Oil – which, together with its subsidiary, Brown and Root, has major oil and other interests in the region – had current US Vice-President Richard Cheyney as its CEO until his nomination. Until recently Chevron Oil, which is now involved in a $2bn investment in the DRC, counted Condoleezza Rice as a member of its board, prior towhich she was a Special Assistant to George Bush, and is now US National Security Advisor. Corporate expansion in conflict zones has coincided with an explosion in private security firms, mostly mercenaries. The largest private security transnationals not only work closely with the US government, but are owned by former members. The Vinnell Corporation of Fairfax, Virginia, for example, is owned by BDM International Inc. and controlled by the Carlyle Group, which counts former ex-CIA Vice-Director Frank Carlucci and US Secretary of State James Baker among its major shareholders. Carlucci was Secretary of Defense under Ronald Reagan and George Bush Snr. and, it might be noted, was also former Second Secretary at the US embassy in the DRC, and later became Deputy Director of the CIA. The nature of corporate and political links can perhaps be gauged well in the work of Cohen & Woods, a Washington-based lobbying firm. On the one hand, this has worked for both mining and security firms who are seeking contracts and concessions in Africa, such as MPRI in Angola, while on the other hand it has worked for African leaders seeking US political support, such as the late Laurent Kabila. This is managed by Herman Cohen, former Assistant Secretary of State for Foreign Affairs, and Jim Woods, former Assistant Secretary of State of US Defense.

The firm that is most implicated in exporting coltan from Rwanda is Trinitech International, which itself owns Eagle Wings Resources. Its main office is in Rwanda, and its manager there in the early 1990s was President Kageme's brother-in-law. It collaborates with the Rwandan People's Army in order to receive privileged access to coltan sites and captive labour. It was exporting to the Ulba Metallurgical Plant in Kazakhstan, to its parent company Trinitech International Inc. in the United States, and to Bayer. Its official owners are Robert and Eileen Raun, the former apparently a luminary of the University of Nebraska, one-time Secretary of Agriculture in that state, and a one-time governor of the Kellogg foundation.

Conclusion

Environmental resources are fundamental to poor and indebted modern African economies. This paper has focused less on how patterns of governance have been able to influence the management of environmental resources than the inverse, namely how the transnational dimensions of the management of valuable environmental resources influence patterns of governance. It is this that modern policy must address. As Montague has recently argued for the DRC, 'In order for investment to be used as an effective tool for development, multinationals must understand that massive corporate investments have a negative impact on society in the absence of state stability. Indeed, their financial leverage only exacerbates state instability' (Montague 2002: 115). The present chapter has traced how these transnational engagements shape natural resources management.

Secondly, there have been several periods of economic recession, during which the continued profitability of enterprises rooted in these alliances has been maintained by control over unfree labour, in many cases linked either to 'protection racketeering' or to extending control over land. It is clear that the 'war-lord' nature of the contemporary DRC represents an extension of earlier practices that have long been current in the region. The classic distinctions between 'war' and 'peace' throw this strong continuity out of focus. The analysis here supports Keen's argument that 'war can usefully be seen as a deepening of exploitative processes already existing in "normal" times' (1994: 12)

Thirdly, the conflict in the region is not simply about 'one people' against others. Because of this, a prevalent image in much of the literature on conflict in Congo and elsewhere has been the apparent 'banditry' of militia forces. Yet when the differentiated experiences of exaction at the local level are clarified, the form that this takes become more comprehensible. Understanding these attacks requires a consideration of a century of engagement between transnational corporate and imperial interests and Congolese society.

Bibliography

Adedeji, A. 1993. "Comparative strategies of economic decolonization in Africa" in A. A. Mazrui, (ed.) *Africa since 1935*. UNESCO General History of Africa, Volume 8, pp. 393–434. Berkeley, CA: Heinemann.

André, C. and J.-P. Platteau 1998. "Land Tenure under Unbearable Stress: Rwanda Caught in the Malthusian Trap" *Journal of Economic Behaviour and Organization*, Vol. 34 (1): 1–47.

Anstey, R. 1966. *King Leopold's Legacy*. London: Oxford University Press.

Bangamwabo, R., 1982. *L'impact de la colonisation economique Européenne sur l'agriculture paysanne Bwisha (Territoire de Rutshuru): fin XIXième siecle-1960. Travail de fin d'études*, Bukavu: UNAZA ISP.

Bashizi, C. 1978. "Processus de domination socio-economique et marché du travail au Bushi (1920–1940" in *Enquêtes et documents d'histoire africaine* 3, 1–29.

Bezy, F. et al. 1981. *Accumulation et sous-développement au Zaire, 1960–1980*. Louvain-La-Neuve: Presses Universitaire de Louvain.

Bwana-Kweli, N.Y.F. 1985. *Gisigari et Rugari: deux Chefferies du Bwisha précolonial. Travail de fin d'études*, Bukavu: UNAZA ISP

de Boeck, F. 1999. "Domesticating Diamonds and Dollars: Identity, Expenditure and Sharing in Southwestern Zaire (1984–1997)" in B. Meyer and P. Geschiere (eds), *Globalization and Identity: Dialectics of Flow and Closure*, Oxford: Blackwell.

Drevet, J.F. 1977. *Les plantations européennes dans le Kivu d'altitude*. Thèse de doctorat 3ème cycle en géographie. Paris: Université de Paris X.

Dubuisson, M. 1935. "Note sur le tribut dans la zone de Rutshuru" in *Bulletin Juridique Indigènes et du Droit Coutumier Congolais*. III (3), 61–63 and III (4) 84–89.

Fairhead, J. 1990. *Fields of Struggle: Towards a Social History of Farming Knowledge and Practice in a Bwisha Community, Kivu, Zaire*. PhD Thesis, University of London (SOAS).

Fairhead, J. 1992. "Paths of Authority: Roads, the State and the Market in Eastern Zaire" in *European Journal of Development Research* 4, 2, 17–35.

Fetter, B. 1988. "Changing War Aims: Central Africa's Role 1940–41, as seen from Leopoldville" in *African Affairs* 87, 348, 377–92.

Gapira, W. M. Z., 1980. *Les incidences socio-economiques et politiques de la creation du Parc National Albert dans le Territoire de Rutshuru (1925–1960). Travail de fin d'études*, Bukavu: UNAZA ISP

Hveem, H, 1986. "Minerals as a Factor in Strategic Policy and Action" in A. Westing (ed.) *Global Resources and International Conflict: Environmental Factors in Strategic Policy and Action*. Pp. 55–84. Oxford: Oxford University Press.

Jackson, Stephen, 2001. "'Our Riches are being Looted!': War Economies and Rumour in the Kivus, D.R. Congo" in *Politique Africaine*, 84, 117–36.

Kashori, A. 1983. *Le rôle socio-politique des missionaires Pères Blancs dans le Territoire de Rutshuru (1911–1960). Travail de fin d'études,* Bukavu: UNAZA ISP

Katuala, K. K. and Mwamba Tshibasu 1986. *Les grands conflicts foncières du Nord-Kivu: philosophie, action preventive et rectificative et rapport de la Commission Foncière Sous Régionale*. Goma: MPR.

Keen, D. 1994 *The benefits of famine: a political economy of famine and relief in south western Sudan 1983–1989*. Princeton: Princeton University Press

Klare, M. 2001. "The New Geography of Conflict" in *Foreign Affairs*, June 2001.

Mamdani, M. 1996, *Citizen and subject: contemporary Africa and the legacy of late colonialism*. London: James Currey.

Matagne, A. 1964. "Le Mwami Musinga cherchait, il y a cinquante ans, à s'introduire au Kivu" in *Revue Belgo-Congolaise Illustrée* 2, 21–7.

Mazrui and Ajayi, J.F. A. 1993. "Trends in Philosophy and Science in Africa" in A. A. Mazrui (ed.) *Africa since 1935*. UNESCO General History of Africa, Volume 8, pp. 633–677. Berkeley, CA: Heinemann.

Mendiaux, E. 1956. "Le Comite National du Kivu" in *Zaire: Revue Congolaise,* Octobre 1956, 803–13 and Novembre 1956, 927–64.

Misabiro, N. 1980. *Essai d'histoire politique du Bwisha sous Ndeze 1920–1980. Travail de fin d'études,* Bukavu: UNAZA ISP

Montague, D. 2002. "Stolen Goods: Coltan and Conflict in the Democratic Republic of Congo" in *SAIS Review* 22, 1 (winter/spring 2002), 103–18.

Munyaruenzi, B. 1980. *Contribution à l'histoire de l'exploration et de la colonisation dans la Zone de Rutshuru (1901–1960). Travail de fin d'études,* Bukavu: UNAZA ISP

Northrup, D. 1988. *Beyond the Bend in the River: African Labour in Eastern Zaire 1865–1940.* Ohio: Ohio University Press.

Nzabandora, N. M. 1984. "L'action et les pratiques magico-religieuses dans la philosophie des Banyabwisha de Rutshuru au Kivu (Est du Zaire)" in *Cahiers de CERUKI* N. S. 17, 51–78.

Place, F. and P. Hazell 1993. "Productivity Effects of Land Tenure Systems in Sub-Saharan Africa" in *Journal of Agricultural Economics*, 75(1): 10–19.

Pole Institute 2001. "The Coltan Phenomeno" http://www.pole-institute.org/documents/polinst_coltan.rtf (accessed 29 March 2002).

Rice, S. 2001. "Submission to 'Africa and the war on global terrorism'". Hearing before US House of Representatives, Committee on Social Relations (Subcommittee on Africa), 107th Congress, 1st Session (No. 107–46), Nov. 15th 2001.

Schatzberg, M. G. 1988. *The Dialectics of Oppression in Zaire.* Bloomington and Indianapolis: Indiana University Press.

Schoepf, B. and C. Schoepf 1987. "Food Crisis and Agrarian Change in Eastern Highlands of Zaire" in *Urban Anthropology,* 16, 1, 5–37.

UN 2001. "UN Report of the Panel of Experts on the Illegal Exploitation of Natural Resources and Other Forms of Wealth of the Democratic Republic of the Congo" (April 12, 2001) http://www.globalpolicy.org/security/issues/kongidx.htm

UN Security Council, 2002. "Final Report of the Panel of Experts on the Illegal Exploitation of Natural Resources and Other Forms of Wealth of DR Congo" Date: 16 Oct 2002 ref S/2002/1146, (http://www.reliefweb.int/w/rwb.nsf/vID/706B89B947E5993DC1256C590052B353? OpenDocument)

Vlassenroot, Koen 2002. *The Making of a New Order: Dynamics of Conflicts and Dialectics of War in South Kivu (DR Congo).* Ghent: PhD thesis, Ghent University.

Vunabandi, M., 1979. *La dynamique de forces sociales au Bwisha.* Memoire de Licence en Sociologie, UNAZA, Lubumbashi.

About the Authors

Sonja Avontuur is an anthropologist who received her MA from Utrecht University, for which she worked with the Center of Environmental Studies at Leiden University, researching time-labour investment among the Mafa in the Mandara mountains of North Cameroon. After graduation she received a grant from the VSB fund for post-graduate work in the Kapsiki area together with Walter van Beek. She now lives in Nigeria, working for a Dutch development corporation.

Simon Batterbury is Lecturer in the School of Anthropology, Geography and Environmental Studies at the University of Melbourne, Australia. He previously taught geography and development studies at Arizona, the London School of Economics and the University of Brunel, and in 2002 he was visiting professor at Roskilde University, Denmark. He has worked on the political ecology of dryland agriculture and rural development in West Africa for a decade.

Torben Birch-Thomsen is Associate Professor at the Institute of Geography, University of Copenhagen, from which he also holds a PhD. His field of research is the environmental and socio-economic effects of land-use intensification (in particular in relation to the introduction of new technologies) in farming systems, and more generally the relationship between changing livelihood strategies and natural resource management. He has research experience of disciplinary as well as interdisciplinary fieldwork in Tanzania, Zambia, South Africa and Swaziland.

Christian Boehm completed his Ph.D. at the Institute of Anthropology, University of Copenhagen in 2004. He carried out both field research and applied consultancy work in Lesotho between 1998 and 2004. He has written on various topics related to natural resource management in Lesotho and is currently working on issues of gender and social reproduction in relation to agrarian change in southern Africa.

James Fairhead is Professor at the Department of Social Anthropology, University of Sussex. His fieldwork in the Democratic Republic of Congo and the Republic of Guinea focused on farming and food systems, and on colonial and post-colonial sciences, policy and administration. Two books (*Misreading the African Landscape* and *Reframing Deforestation*, both co-authored with Melissa Leach) confront analytical traditions in African environmental sciences to expose their political, social and economic commitments. His latest book compares environmental knowledge and policy in West Africa and the Caribbean.

Quentin Gausset is Associate Professor at the Institute of Anthropology in the University of Copenhagen. He defended his PhD on the negotiation of identity in Central Cameroon at the Free University of Brussels. Since then he has worked on AIDS prevention in Zambia, and on the socio-cultural aspects of natural resource management in various interdisciplinary projects in Burkina Faso, Tanzania, southern Africa and Malaysia.

Kristine Juul is a Lecturer at the Institute of Geography and Development Studies at Roskilde University Center, Denmark, from which she also holds a Ph.D. Her field of research is mainly on natural resource management, land tenure issues and micro-politics in rural Sahel (Senegal).

Leif Manger is a Professor at the Department of Social Anthropology, University of Bergen. His main research has been related to the Sudan and includes studies into household adaptations in oasis environments, mountain environments and savannah plains. He has also published works on topics such as trade, communal labour and socio-cultural processes of Arabisation and Islamisation. He is currently finishing a monograph on the migration history of people from Hadramaut in Yemen to areas around the Indian Ocean region, and is also involved in research on East Africa and Palestine.

Michael Mortimore is a geographer who taught and researched at Ahmadu Bello and Bayero Universities in northern Nigeria, before becoming a full-time researcher on African dryland development and environmental management, associated with the Overseas Development Institute, London, Cambridge University, and finally with Drylands Research, a small independent research organisation based in the UK. His experiences in the field have led him consistently to challenge some of the pessimistic scenarios that have tended to dominate debates on the African drylands.

Walter van Beek is an anthropologist with a joint appointment in the African Studies Centre at Leiden and the Department of Cultural Anthropology at Utrecht University. He has specialized on West Africa, mainly Cameroon and Mali, in particular on the Kapsiki/Higi of northern Nigeria and northern Cameroon, and the Dogon of Mali, his main thematic interests being cultural ecology, religion and tourism. He recently published a book entitled *The Dogon: Africa's People of the Cliffs*. His present project is a book on the transformation of Kapsiki traditional religion.

D. Andrew Wardell has worked as an advisor on forestry and natural resource management issues for two decades in East and West Africa and Southeast Asia. He is currently completing a Ph.D., 'Towards an Environmental History of Tropical Dry Forests in West Africa', at the Institute of Geography, University of Copenhagen. His research interests focus on the history and politics of social and environmental change associated with colonial and post-colonial conservationism in northern Ghana and Burkina Faso.

Michael A. Whyte is Associate Professor at the Institute of Anthropology, University of Copenhagen. He has carried out long-term field research in eastern Uganda and western Kenya on issues including kinship, food security, HIV/AIDS and agricultural and economic change. He collaborates with Danish and Ugandan colleagues on the long-term Tororo Community Health project.